The Responsibility to Protect and International Law

The Responsibility to Protect and International Law

Edited by

Alex J. Bellamy
Sara E. Davies
Luke Glanville

MARTINUS NIJHOFF PUBLISHERS

LEIDEN • BOSTON
2011

Cover illustration: The UN Photo by Mark Garten is reprinted on the cover with permission, and shows The International Court of Justice (The Hague, The Netherlands) commemorating its 60th anniversary.

Also published in Volumes 1 and 2 (2009–2010) of Brill's journal *Global Responsibility to Protect.*

This book is printed on acid-free paper.

Library of Congress Cataloging-in-Publication Data

The responsibility to protect and international law / edited by Alex J. Bellamy, Sara E. Davies, Luke Glanville.
p. cm.
Includes index.
ISBN 978-90-04-18869-3 (pbk. : alk. paper) 1. International obligations. 2. Government liability (International law) 3. Intervention (International law) 4. Sovereignty. I. Bellamy, Alex J., 1975- II. Davies, Sara Ellen III. Glanville, Luke.
KZ4080.R47 2011
342.08'8--dc22

2010040545

ISBN 978 90 04 18869 3

Contents

Introduction

Alex J. Bellamy, Sara E. Davies and Luke Glanville

The Responsibility to Protect (RtoP) was adopted in 2005 by heads of state and government in paragraphs 138-140 of the World Summit Outcomes Document.[1] It was subsequently reaffirmed by UN Security Council Resolutions 1674 (28 April 2006) and 1894 (11 November 2009). As agreed by governments, the RtoP rests on three equally important and non-sequential pillars: (1) the primary responsibility of the state to protect its own populations from genocide, war crimes, ethnic cleansing and crimes against humanity and their incitement; (2) the international community's responsibility to assist the state to fulfill its RtoP; (3) the international responsibility to take timely and decisive action, in accordance with the UN Charter, in cases where the host state has manifestly failed to protect its population from the four crimes.

Few would disagree with the proposition that the RtoP has rapidly become a prominent feature in international debates about preventing genocide and mass atrocities and protecting the intended victims. Five years on from its adoption, RtoP boasts a Global Centre and network of regional affiliates dedicated to advocacy and research, a global coalition of non-governmental organisations, a dedicated academic journal and book series, a research fund sponsored by the Australian government, and has spawned a range of offshoots including the 'IR2P' (individual responsibility to protect) and 'W2I' (will to intervene), focusing respectively on engaging individuals as agents of change and generating the political will to intervene to put an end to genocide and mass atrocities.[2] More importantly, RtoP has made its way onto the international diplomatic agenda. By appointing Edward Luck as his Special Advisor and publishing a report on implementing the RtoP, UN Secretary-General

[1] A/60/L.1, 20 September 2005.

[2] The Global Centre for the Responsibility to Protect was established in 2008 by a group of prominent NGOs and activists (see www.globalr2p.org). Its associates are: Asia-Pacific Centre for the Responsibility to Protect (www.r2pasiapacific.org), Fundación para las Relaciones

Ban Ki-moon has confronted the UN membership with the challenge of translating its 2005 commitment from 'words to deeds'.[3] This challenge was taken up by the General Assembly in 2009, when it agreed to give further consideration to the Secretary-General's proposals.[4] On the other hand, RtoP has become part of the diplomatic language of humanitarian emergencies, used by governments, international institutions, NGOs and independent commissions to justify behaviour, cajole compliance and demand international action. Indeed, those using the principle in the past few years have included some of its chief critics from the past: Egypt used RtoP to call for an international force to protect the people of Gaza; Russia referred to RtoP in order to justify its 2008 intervention in Georgia to prevent 'genocide' in South Ossetia; and India reminded the government of Sri Lanka that it had a 'responsibility to protect' all populations in its care.[5]

For all this apparent progress, however, disagreement and uncertainty abounds. Much as they did before 2005, many critics argue either that the

---

Internacionales y el Diálogo Exterior (www.fride.org), Kofi Annan International Peacekeeping Training Centre (www.kaiptc.org) and the Norwegian Institute of International Affairs (www.nupi.no). The International Coalition for the Responsibility to Protect evolved out of the World Federalist Movement-Institute for Global Policy 'Responsibility to Protect-Civil Society' initiative which was initially established in 2003 with funding from the Canadian government to consult and promote the principle. The coalition aims to replicate the huge NGO coalition established to advocate for the international convention banning land mines (www.responsibilitytoprotect.org). The journal, *Global Responsibility to Protect*, published its first edition in 2009 and Routledge's RtoP book series is scheduled to publish its first books in 2010. For information on IR2P and W2I see www.iR2P.org and http://migs.concordia.ca/W2I/W2I_Project.html respectively. Ramesh Thakur also highlights the range of RtoP related activities. See Ramesh Thakur, 'The Responsibility to Protect: Yesterday, Today, Tomorrow', presentation at the Basillie School of International Affairs, Waterloo, 11 November 2009.

[3] Ban Ki-moon, *Implementing the Responsibility to Protect*, report of the Secretary-General, A/63/677, 12 January 2009. The challenge of translating RtoP from words to deeds was first outlined by the Secretary-General in his 2008 speech in Berlin. See, Ban Ki-moon, 'On Responsible Sovereignty: International Cooperation for a Changed World', Berlin, SG/SM11701, 15 July 2008.

[4] General Assembly Resolution 63/308, 7 October 2009.

[5] Respectively, Statement by Maged Adbul Aziz, Permanent Representative of Egypt to the UN, before the tenth emergency special session (resumed) on illegal Israeli actions in occupied East Jerusalem and the rest of the Occupied Palestinian Territory, New York, 15 July 2009; Interview by Minister of Foreign Affaires of the Russian Federation Sergey Lavrov to BBC, Moscow, August 9, 2008 (available at: http://globalr2p.org/pdf/related/GeorgiaRussia.pdf) and 'India to Sri Lanka: Killing of Tamil Civilians Must Stop', *Sindh Today*, 22 April 2009. On the opposition of these governments to RtoP in 2005 and before see Alex J. Bellamy,'Whither the Responsibility to Protect? Humanitarian Intervention and the 2005 World Summit', *Ethics and International Affairs*, 20 (2) 2006.

RtoP is a dangerous and imperialist doctrine that threatens to undermine the national sovereignty and political autonomy of the weak or that it is little other than rhetorical posturing that promises little tangible improvement in the protection of vulnerable people.[6] To further complicate matters, profound disagreements have emerged about the function, meaning and proper use of RtoP. The term has been inconsistently used, including by France (in relation to Myanmar) and Russia (in relation to Georgia) to justify the actual or potential use of coercive force in situations where there was no apparent manifest failure to protect populations from genocide and mass atrocities, whilst China has repeatedly argued that the UN Security Council should only become engaged in matters that pose threats to *international* peace and security and that RtoP must not be used, even in diplomacy, to coerce governments to alter their behaviour.[7]

Given this, it is not surprising that it is widely understood that the relationship between the RtoP principle and international law requires further clarification.[8] Before the emergence of RtoP, questions about the legal quality of international measures to prevent genocide and mass atrocities and protect the intended victims, and the existence or not of legal duties owed to people in foreign countries, tended to be framed around an enduring struggle between sovereignty and human rights. In this account, sovereignty referred to the rights that states enjoyed to territorial integrity, political independence, and non-intervention. Where sovereign states were either unwilling or unable to protect the fundamental freedoms of their citizens, it was held that sovereignty and human rights come into conflict. This tension is evident in the UN Charter. Whilst calling for cooperation to reaffirm faith in fundamental human rights, the Charter (Article 2[4]) outlaws war as an instrument of policy with only two exceptions (each state's inherent right to self-defense [Article 51] and collective measures authorised by the UN Security Council [Chapter VII]) and affirms the principle of non-interference (Article 2[7])

[6] For instance, Philip Cunliffe, *Critical Perspectives on the Responsibility to Protect* (London: Routledge, 2010).

[7] Nick Wheeler and Frazer Egerton suggest that this means that the meaning and scope of RtoP remains contested, in contrast to Edward Luck who argues that it is important to distinguish between what RtoP is (as agreed by states) and what individual activists would like it to be. See Nicholas J. Wheeler and Frazer Egerton, 'The Responsibility to Protect: "Precious Commitment" or a "Promise Unfulfilled"?', *Global Responsibility to Protect*, 1/1: 114-132 (2009).

[8] A point recognised by Edward Luck, among others. See Edward C. Luck, 'The United Nations and the Responsibility to Protect', *Stanley Foundation Policy Analysis Brief*, August 2008.

by prohibiting the UN from interfering 'in matters essentially within the domestic jurisdiction of states.' These legal rights, it was often argued, constituted a powerful barrier to timely and decisive international responses to genocide and mass atrocities, and it proved very difficult to build sufficient consensus in the UN Security Council to persuade it to authorise such action against a full-functioning state guilty of perpetrating genocide or mass atrocities. For example, in a March 2005 Security Council debate on whether to refer alleged crimes in Darfur to the International Criminal Court (ICC), the US representative explained that country's abstention by arguing that the Court 'strikes at the essence of the nature of sovereignty.'[9]

States that acted without the authority of the Security Council sometimes paid a high price. For example, in 1979, when Vietnam invaded Cambodia and ousted the murderous Khmer Rouge regime, responsible for the death of some two million Cambodians, it was condemned for violating Cambodian sovereignty. China's representative at the UN described Vietnam's act as a 'great mockery of and insult to the United Nations and its member states' and sponsored a resolution condemning Vietnam's 'aggression.' The US agreed.[10] France argued that 'the notion that because a regime is detestable foreign intervention is justified and forcible overthrow is legitimate is extremely dangerous. That could ultimately jeopardise the very maintenance of law and order.'[11]

However, there are grounds for doubting the extent to which international law actually acted as a barrier to timely and decisive responses to genocide and mass atrocities. Simon Chesterman demonstrated that sovereignty has not in fact inhibited unilateral or collective intervention to uphold human rights in other countries. In response to arguments that intervention could be promoted by relaxing the prohibition on the use of force, Chesterman argued that: 'implicit in many of the arguments for a right of humanitarian intervention is the suggestion that the present normative order is preventing interventions that should take place. This is simply not true. Interventions do not take place because states do not want them to take place'.[12] Ultimately, he argued, it was not primarily concerns about sovereignty that prevented timely

[9] S/PV.5158, 31 March 2005, p. 12.

[10] Cited in Nicholas J. Wheeler, *Saving Strangers: Humanitarian Intervention in International Society* (Oxford: Oxford University Press, 2000), pp. 90-91.

[11] Cited in Chesterman, *Just War or Just Peace?, Humanitarian Intervention and International Law* (Oxford: Oxford University Press, 2001), p. 80.

[12] Ibid., 231.

intervention in Rwanda, but rather the basic political fact that no state wanted to risk its own troops to save strangers from genocide.

What, though, of Vietnam's invasion of Cambodia? Was it not the case that Vietnam paid a heavy political and economic price because it was seen as violating Cambodia's sovereignty? This position certainly has merit but needs to be viewed alongside two other considerations. First, Vietnam was not principally motivated by humanitarian concerns and nor did it justify its invasion as a humanitarian intervention. Second, and perhaps more importantly, we need to take the arguments leveled against Vietnam with a pinch of Cold War salt. Whilst not denying the fact that many states, particularly some members of the Non-Aligned Movement, opposed Vietnam on principled grounds, political considerations played an important part in shaping the way that international society reacted to the intervention.[13] In the same year as Vietnam's invasion of Cambodia, Tanzania—a highly regarded state with a well-respected President, Julius Nyerere—invaded Uganda and deposed Idi Amin with barely a ripple of condemnation.[14]

However we interpret these past cases, it is clear that international law did not facilitate a consensus on collective action to prevent and end genocide and mass atrocities beyond the idea that the Security Council has the discretion to act whenever it sees fit. More often than not, the Council exercised its discretion to not act. This is where the RtoP, a principle which seeks to change the relationship between sovereignty, the responsibilities of states to their own people, and the wider duties of the international community come into play and why understanding the relationship between RtoP and international law is so important. To date, however, there is very little consensus about the nature of this relationship or its normative quality.

On the one hand, a number of academics and policy advisers have argued that RtoP represents a new legal norm. For some, this new legal norm provides a basis for legitimising coercive interference in the domestic affairs of states which are unable or unwilling to protect their populations from genocide or mass atrocities. For example, Alicia Bannon argued that 'the [2005 World] Summit agreement strengthens the legal justification for limited forms of unilateral and regional action –including military action – if the United Nations fails to act to protect populations from genocide and other atrocities'.[15]

[13] Wheeler, *Saving Strangers*, pp., 78-110.

[14] On this see Grant Evans and Kelvin Rowley, *Red Brotherhood at War: Vietnam, Cambodia and Laos since 1975*, 2nd ed. (London: Verso, 1990).

[15] Alicia L. Bannon, 'The Responsibility to Protect: The UN World Summit and the Question of Unilateralism', *The Yale Law Journal*, 115 (2006), p. 1158.

The following year, Stephen John Stedman, a senior advisor to former UN Secretary-General Kofi Annan, argued that Annan's reform agenda for the UN had included, 'a new norm, the responsibility to protect, to legalize humanitarian intervention' and then claimed that the Summit had succeeded in establishing 'a new norm to legalize humanitarian intervention'.[16]

For others, like former UN Human Rights Commissioner, Louise Arbour, when combined with the 1948 Genocide Convention and the recent ruling of the International Court of Justice (ICJ) in *Bosnia vs. Serbia*, RtoP creates something approximating a new legal duty to prevent genocide.[17] It is well known that 1948 Genocide Convention not only prohibits genocide but establishes a duty to prevent and punish it (Article 1). This duty to prevent genocide is widely understood to be a principle of customary international law.[18] However, it was never clear whether this general duty amounted to a legal obligation to intervene to halt specific genocides. Although some legal scholars have argued that Article 1 imposes a duty on the UN and its member states to act (including through military intervention) wherever a genocide takes place,[19] the majority view seemed to support former US Secretary of State Colin Powell's assertion that the Convention's language did not impose such a wide-ranging obligation. Jerry Fowler, for example, argued that 'the language of the [Genocide] Convention does not provide any indication that such an extensive obligation was contemplated. Indeed it would be quite bizarre to think that the drafters intended in 1948 to make intervention in the internal affairs of other states obligatory.'[20] However, important new light was shed on this issue by the ICJ's 2007 ruling in the *Bosnia and Herzegovina v. Serbia and Montenegro* case.

The Court found that Serbia was not guilty of genocide but had violated its Article 1 obligation to prevent and punish the crime of genocide. The ICJ found that, whilst states are not obliged to succeed in their efforts to prevent genocide, they 'must employ all means which are reasonably available to them

[16] Stephen John Stedman, 'UN Transformation in an Era of Soft Balancing', *International Affairs*, 83/5 (2007), pp. 933 and 938.

[17] Louise Arbour, 'The Responsibility to Protect as a Duty of Care in International Law and Practice', *Review of International Studies*, 34: 445-58 (2008).

[18] William Schabas, *Genocide in International Law: The Crime of Crimes* (Cambridge: Cambridge University Press, 2000), 500.

[19] Stephen J. Toope, 'Does International Law Impose a Duty upon the UN to Prevent Genocide?', *McGill Law Journal*, 46/1: 187-94 (2000).

[20] Jerry Fowler, 'A New Chapter of Irony: The Legal Definition of Genocide and the Implications of Powell's Determination,' in Samuel Totten and Eric Markusen, eds., *Genocide in Darfur: Investigating the Atrocities in the Sudan* (London: Routledge, 2006), 131.

to do so'.[21] Of course, it remains to be seen what measures may be thought to be 'reasonably available' to states in given situations. It is unlikely that each individual state now has a responsibility to intervene militarily to end genocide, and it should be remembered that measures to end genocide must be consistent with international law, which prohibits the use of force except in self-defence or with the express authorisation of the UN Security Council.[22] However, Louise Arbour argued that the ruling—especially when taken in conjunction with the RtoP principle—imposes specific responsibilities on the members of the UN Security Council, and the permanent members especially.[23] The UN Security Council has the legal authority to authorise armed intervention whenever it identifies a threat to international peace and security. Moreover, as the world's leading military powers, permanent members of the Security Council have the military capacity to intervene to halt genocide. Thus armed with both the collective authority to intervene and—between them—the capacity to do so, it could be argued that armed intervention to halt genocide falls well within the scope of 'reasonably available' measures for permanent members of the Security Council.

This is not to say, of course, that armed intervention will be the most appropriate course of action in every case. And it should be noted that this line of argument depends on a very liberal interpretation of what the law requires, which goes well beyond what most lawyers – including those in this volume – are prepared to admit. Furthermore, whilst the RtoP principle enjoys the unanimous support of the UN General Assembly, it does not resolve difficult questions about the most appropriate and effective response to specific cases of genocide and mass atrocities. Moreover, even with these caveats the idea that there might be a right or duty to intervene is controversial.

Others challenge the very idea that RtoP is legally progressive or even that it is normatively positive. Indeed, most legal commentators agree that RtoP is not yet an international legal norm for various reasons, including that it is too vaguely worded, lacks clarity and has not been appropriately legislated.[24] In addition, Ekkehard Strauss has argued that the General Assembly resolution that gave effect to the global consensus on RtoP in 2005 is a non-binding

---

[21] In Marko Milanovic, 'State Responsibility for Genocide: A Follow-Up,' *European Journal of International Law* 18/4 (2007), p. 686.

[22] Mark Gibney, 'Genocide and State Responsibility,' *Human Rights Law Review* 7/4 (2007), p. 767.

[23] Arbour, 'The Responsibility to Protect'.

[24] Especially Carsten Stahn, 'Responsibility to Protect: Political Rhetoric or Emerging Legal Norm?', *American Journal of International Law,* 101/1 (2007), p. 102.

recommendation for Member States rather than a statement of law. Whilst acknowledging that General Assembly resolutions may provide evidence of customary international law when accompanied by general practice and *opinio juris*, he points out that such resolutions cannot create *new* law by themselves.[25] More troubling, though, is the fact that at least one prominent international lawyer has argued that it is 'dangerous' to conceive RtoP in terms of a legal norm because that would involve redefining sovereignty, enabling self-interested coercive intervention, and expanding the scope for potential (warranted and sometimes unwarranted) interference in the domestic affairs of states.[26]

This latter critique chimes well with long standing concerns about the RtoP agenda. Opponents—including many Third World states—maintain that international order and the preservation of core values such as the right to self-determination requires something approximating an absolute ban on the use of force outside the two parameters set out by the UN Charter—Security Council authorisation (Chapter VII) and self-defence (Article 51)—and that the Security Council should interpret its remit narrowly.[27] The starting point for this position is the assumption that international society comprises a plurality of diverse communities each with different ideas about the best way to live. According to this view, international society is based on rules—the UN Charter's rules on the use of force first among them—that permit these communities to coexist relatively peacefully.[28] In a world characterised by radical disagreements about how societies should govern themselves, proponents of this view hold that a right and duty of humanitarian intervention would create disorder, as states would wage wars to protect and violently export their own cultural preferences. What is more, as a legal norm RtoP would open the door to potential abuse. Historically, states have shown a distinct predilection towards 'abusing' humanitarian justifications to legitimise interference up to and including armed invasion that was anything but humanitarian. Most notoriously, Hitler insisted that the 1939 invasion of Czechoslovakia was inspired by a desire to protect Czechoslovak citizens of German ethnicity

[25] See chapter in this volume.

[26] See Jose E. Alvarez, 'The Schizophrenias of R2P', paper presented at The Hague, 30 June 2007.

[27] For a good exposition of this position, linking it to the views of several Third World governments see Mohammed Ayoob, 'Third World Perspectives on Humanitarian Intervention and International Administration,' *Global Governance* 10/1: 99-118 (2004).

[28] A position set out and defended at length by Robert H. Jackson, *The Global Covenant: Human Conduct in a World of States* (Oxford: Oxford University Press, 2002).

whose 'life and liberty' were threatened by their own government.[29] It was precisely because of the fear that states would exploit any loophole in the ban on the use of force that the delegates who wrote the UN Charter issued a comprehensive ban with only the two limited exceptions: force used in self-defense and under the authority of the Security Council.[30] In addition to the problem of abuse, many post-colonial states continue to oppose humanitarian intervention because they consider it a dangerous affront to another core principle, self-determination. They worry that a duty to intervene would grant a license for the great powers to interfere in their domestic affairs, undermining their right to self-government.[31]

Although these are powerful arguments which should temper enthusiasm for the development of new legal norms that relate to mass atrocities and the use of force, it is important to avoid the belief that talk of legal duties to prevent or respond to genocide and mass atrocities is an agenda that is exclusively, or even primarily, concerned with imposing Western values on the rest of the world. Most importantly, it is important to not fall into the trap of mistakenly assuming that the post-colonial world speaks as one on this issue. There are good grounds for thinking that there is genuine consensus in some parts of the global south that RtoP, even when it countenances armed intervention (when properly authorised), is a legitimate response to genocide and mass atrocities. Nine years before NATO intervened in Kosovo without the authority of the Security Council, a group of West African states (ECOWAS) did likewise in Liberia. And four years before the adoption of the RtoP principle by world leaders, members of the African Union gave that regional institution a right to intervene in response to serious humanitarian emergencies.[32]

As might be expected, the UN Secretary-General, his advisors and other UN staff have tended to take a middle-road that downplays the transformative potential of RtoP for international law. The approach most commonly adopted by the UN is to emphasise that the RtoP is based on well established principles within existing international law. It is worth thinking about this in three primary senses. First, the crimes to which the concept relates (genocide, war crimes, ethnic cleansing and crimes against humanity) are crimes that have

---

[29] Ian Brownlie, 'Humanitarian Intervention,' in John N. Moore, ed., *Law and Civil War in the Modern World* (Baltimore: Johns Hopkins University Press, 1974), 217-221.

[30] An argument put forth in detail by Chesterman, *Just War or Just Peace?*

[31] A position set out by Ayoob, 'Third World Perspectives'.

[32] See Paul D. Williams, 'From Non-Interference to Non-Indifference: The Origins and Development of the African Union's Security Culture,' *African Affairs* 106/423: 253-79 (2007).

already been agreed by states and enumerated in international humanitarian and human rights law. Second, under customary international law, states already have obligations to prevent and punish genocide, war crimes and crimes against humanity; assist others to fulfill their obligations under International Humanitarian Law; and promote compliance with the law. Third, the mechanisms through which the RtoP can be implemented are consistent with existing international law. Paragraphs 138 and 139 of the World Summit Outcome Document identify four principal ways in which RtoP can be implemented, each of which is consistent with existing international law: (a) the primary responsibility rests with the State itself. This is the cornerstone of sovereignty; (b) the international community may provide assistance, such as capacity-building, mediation and diplomacy. Such assistance may only be provided at the request and with the express consent of the state concerned and is consistent with the state's sovereign right to make bilateral and multilateral agreements; (c) the UN Security Council might take measures in a manner consistent with Chapters VI, VII and VIII of the UN Charter, the General Assembly might make recommendations on the basis of Article 11 of the Charter, and other Organs of the UN might act in accordance with the Charter; (d) paragraph 139 of the World Summit Outcome Document explicitly envisages a role for regional arrangements. Such roles must, of course, be consistent with the charters, constitutions or guiding principles of the regional arrangement concerned and with the UN Charter. Any other mechanisms that may be called upon in relation to the implementation of the RtoP (such as, for instance, the International Criminal Court) are guided by their own constitutions and statutes which are voluntarily accepted by participating states and their scope and jurisdiction are limited by these agreements and general principles of international law.

Although it did not start out this way, the RtoP agreed in 2005 is consistent with the principle of non-interference enumerated in the UN Charter (Article 2(7)). Article 2(7) states that: 'Nothing contained in the present Charter shall authorize the United Nations to intervene in matters which are essentially within the domestic jurisdiction of any state or shall require the Members to submit such matters to settlement under the present Charter; but this principle shall not prejudice the application of enforcement measures under Chapter VII'. Where states have voluntarily entered into specific international legal obligations, matters relating to those obligations cease to be 'essentially within the domestic jurisdiction of any state'. For example, the UN Human Rights Council (formerly Commission) is authorised through the mechanism set out in Article 68 of the UN Charter. Through their voluntary membership of the UN, states accept that the Economic and Social Council (ECOSOC) has the right to make such provisions for the promotion of human rights. As such, the Human Rights Council's work cannot be considered a breach of Article 2(7) because the matter has ceased to be 'essentially within the domestic jurisdiction' of the state owing to its membership of the UN and accession to the Charter. The same applies to regional bodies to which states voluntarily accede. Of course, such bodies must act only in strict accordance with the provisions of the charters, statutes, treaties or guidelines to which states have voluntarily acceded. Article 2(7) also affirms that the principle of non-interference 'shall not prejudice' the application of enforcement measures by the UN Security Council acting under Chapter VII of the Charter.

All of this serves to reinforce the Secretary-General's argument that 'the responsibility to protect does not alter, indeed it reinforces, the legal obligations of Member States to refrain from the use of force except in conformity with the Charter'.[33] This position was endorsed by the UN membership during a 2009 General Assembly debate on RtoP. Several member states insisted that *the RtoP must be implemented and exercised in a manner consistent with international law and the UN Charter*. Significantly, the Non-Aligned Movement in particular stressed that the RtoP must not be used to legitimise unilateral coercive interference in the domestic affairs of states and many others agreed that the principle was embedded in existing international law.[34]

The purpose of this book is to interrogate all of these claims in more detail. It is interested, in particular, in three key issues. First, understanding the legal content of RtoP in terms of the legal claims implied by the principle and how they sit within the contemporary framework of international laws. Second, unpacking the question of whether RtoP has legal effects, particularly the question of whether it creates new legal duties or responsibilities. Third, understanding the various ways in which the implementation of RtoP might impact upon international law and how the law might be utilised to aid implementation, especially in areas such as the prevention of genocide and mass atrocities and international criminal prosecution. In pursuing these avenues of inquiry, the book draws upon a variety of theoretical traditions and advances a range of different arguments. A summary of the key common points that

---

[33] Ban Ki-moon, *Implementing the Responsibility to Protect,* A/63/677, 12 January 2009, para 3.

[34] Statement by Maged A. Abdelaziz, Permanent Representative of Egypt, on Behalf of the Non-Aligned Movement on Agenda Items 44 and 107: 'Integrated and coordinated implementation of and follow-up to the outcomes of the major United Nations conferences and summits in the economic, social and related fields; follow-up to the outcome of the Millennium Summit: report of the Secretary-General', New York, 23 July 2009.

emerge are outlined in the brief conclusion. Because we think that each of the chapters rewards a careful reading in that they all contribute new understandings to the debates outlined above, we will not try to summarise their argument here but instead urge the reader to engage with them all. Although several of the chapters touch of each of the three themes identified here, we have organised the chapters sequentially so that the book first examines the legal content of RtoP in some detail, then turns to the question of legal duties and finally consider the implementation issues.

Sovereignty, Choice, and the Responsibility to Protect

Edward C. Luck

Abstract
It is commonly asserted that the chief obstacle to advancing acceptance of the responsibility to protect (RtoP) is the reluctance of developing countries to compromise their sovereignty. This paper argues, instead, that both developing and some of the more powerful developed countries have concerns about the implications of RtoP for their sovereignty. The former are more likely to be concerned about territorial sovereignty and the latter about decision-making sovereignty. Both sets of concerns were openly expressed during the debates leading up to the consensus at the 2005 World Summit on RtoP. That consensus was facilitated by the fact that the wording of the relevant provisions of its Outcome Document took both types of reservations about sovereignty into account. The paper argues that the recognition that countries of the North and the South tend to be more united than divided by their determination to preserve their sovereignty should facilitate efforts to achieve consensus on how to operationalise and implement the responsibility to protect.

Keywords
sovereignty, United Nations Charter, UN World Summit 2005, North-South debate, UN General Assembly, UN Security Council, Westphalian sovereignty, Non-Aligned Movement, RtoP Lite

Introduction

It has become a common refrain to assert that the responsibility to protect populations from genocide, war crimes, ethnic cleansing, and crimes against humanity presents a challenge to traditional conceptions of state sovereignty.[1] This, it is said, is the chief reason that some smaller and developing countries

[1] It is not the place of this essay either to define the components of RtoP or to chronicle its development. These tasks are accomplished, however, in two recent RtoP volumes: Gareth Evans, *The Responsibility to Protect: Ending Mass Atrocity Crimes Once and For All* (Washington, D.C.: Brookings Institution Press, 2008) and Alex J. Bellamy, *A Responsibility to Protect: The Global Effort to End Mass Atrocities* (Cambridge: Polity, forthcoming 2008).

have had reservations about embracing the concept. Their reservations, in turn, are widely seen as the primary obstacles to gaining global acceptance of a robust RtoP regime. Further, it is asserted that more developed states, less concerned about their sovereignty because they are more capable of defending themselves militarily or are part of a strong regional bloc, like the European Union, are more likely to accept the responsibility to protect without crippling reservations. This paper contends, on the contrary, that some major powers of the North have acute sovereignty concerns about RtoP as well, though of a different sort. Smaller and weaker states, particularly those that have suffered colonialism, are more prone to interpret sovereignty in territorial terms. Some powerful states, including most pointedly the United States, tend to see sovereignty in terms of freedom of policy choice and hence are reluctant to accept any interpretation of RtoP that implies an automaticity of response.

Rather than seeing sovereignty as the dividing line in a North-South debate over RtoP, this article argues that both sources of sovereignty-induced ambivalence – that affecting the North and that affecting the South – were largely addressed in the formulation of RtoP contained in the Outcome Document from the 2005 World Summit. Otherwise, there could not have been a consensus outcome. Though RtoP has yet to achieve status as a norm in terms of being the product of a legally binding convention, there is no open dissent to the pledge in paragraph 138 of the Outcome Document that the assembled heads of state and government accept the responsibility to prevent the four crimes and their incitement and "will act in accordance with it". The General Assembly subsequently endorsed the Outcome Document unanimously. The areas of continuing divergence relate to how to operationalise and implement those agreed provisions. In moving forward on that front, the UN Secretary-General and UN Member States need to bear in mind both sets of sovereignty concerns if they are to avoid an unnecessary and caricatured North-South debate over a principle that is well grounded in existing international law and that has broad geographical and political appeal. Sovereignty remains an issue, of course, but one that should guide the approach to RtoP doctrine and practice, not one that should divide the membership and doom the concept to the world of wishful thinking.

Types and Sources of Sovereignty

Steve Krasner identifies four distinct ways in which the term sovereignty is commonly used, as follows:

- domestic sovereignty, referring to the organization of public authority within a state and to the level of effective control exercised by those holding authority;
- interdependence sovereignty, referring to the ability of public authorities to control transborder movements;
- international legal sovereignty, referring to the mutual recognition of states or other entities; and
- Westphalian sovereignty, referring to the exclusion of external actors from domestic authority configurations.[2]

Sovereignty, he underscores, involves both authority and control, with the mix varying among the four types.[3] In his view, Westphalian sovereignty and international legal sovereignty are all about authority, whether to exclude external actors or to make international agreements with them. Interdependence sovereignty, he argues, relates to the control of movements across borders, something that is especially challenging in an era of the internet, persistent migration, and globalization. Domestic sovereignty, in his scheme, requires both authority and control.

These two characteristics – authority and control – are, in turn, deeply intertwined with notions of and perceptions of legitimacy. Domestically and internationally, legitimacy, though a subjective concept, is a cornerstone of power, what Ian Hurd calls one of the 'three currencies of power'.[4] However, it does not necessarily follow that domestic and international conceptions of legitimacy always coincide. They have distinct sources, embedded either in local or in global values, cultures, traditions, and legal, political, and constitutional structures. These will overlap in some respects and diverge in others. The degree of convergence is likely to be higher if the global norms were produced through extensive negotiating and bargaining processes among the representatives of diverse states in multilateral and global fora and if they have been sustained through practice. In such cases, global norms will reflect, more or less, the common elements of local values from different regions and cultures. Over time, global norms should be integrated into local laws, customs, and practices. When the process is flawed, conditions change, or the process of integration and absorption is incomplete, so that local and global values clash, then the latter are likely to give way if, in fact, the state is perceived by

---

[2] Stephen D. Krasner, *Sovereignty: Organized Hypocrisy* (Princeton, N.J.: Princeton University Press, 1999), p. 9.

[3] Ibid., p. 10 and passim.

[4] Ian Hurd, 'Legitimacy and Authority in International Politics', *International Organization*, vol. 53, no. 2 (Spring 1999), pp. 379-408.

its people to be legitimate and representative. As this author has detailed elsewhere, this helps to explain, for instance, the rocky relationship between the United States and international institutions.[5] The same could be said for other societies that organize their political and economic affairs in quite different ways, but that manage to sustain broad public support without coercion.

But what does the notion of domestic sovereignty tell us about the responsibility to protect and attitudes toward it in different countries and parts of the world? It helps to explain why limiting RtoP to the four crimes and violations listed in the Outcome Document from the 2005 World Summit – genocide, war crimes, ethnic cleansing, and crimes against humanity – was critical to gaining consensus support for it.[6] Three of the four – all except ethnic cleansing – had been included five years earlier in the Constitutive Act of the African Union (Article 4(h)). It declared "the right of the Union to intervene in a Member State pursuant to a decision of the Assembly in respect of grave circumstances, namely: war crimes, genocide and crimes against humanity". As in the UN's subsequent Outcome Document, this right was reserved for the Union, to be decided on a high-level inter-governmental basis, of course, not for individual states or ad hoc groupings of them. These three crimes, moreover, are well established in international law and no state would claim the right or authority under the cloak of domestic sovereignty to commit such acts. There is no caucus for genocide or the other three crimes and violations either in the United Nations or in any regional or sub-regional body, whether populated by developing or developed countries.

As is often asserted, RtoP in some respects is a relatively new and novel concept. Yet it should also be recognised that it has deep roots not only in human rights, humanitarian, and refugee law, but also in the very notion of sovereignty.[7] Even Thomas Hobbes's seventeenth century masterpiece, *Leviathan* – often portrayed as the ultimate ode to absolute unadulterated

[5] See Edward C. Luck, 'The United States, International Organization, and the Quest for Legitimacy', in Stewart Patrick and Shepard Forman, eds., *Multilateralism and US Foreign Policy* (Boulder, CO: Lynne Rienner for the Center on International Cooperation, 2001), pp. 47-74 and *Mixed Messages: American Politics and International Organization, 1919-1999* (Washington, D.C.: Brookings Institution Press for the Century Foundation, 1999).

[6] Jean Ping, President of the General Assembly during the period when the language of the Outcome Document was negotiated, cites the suggestion of the "Ambassador of Pakistan" to "link" RtoP to these specific crimes as the breakthrough step in the negotiation. H.E. Mr. Jean Ping, Chairman of the African Union Commission, Keynote Address, Roundtable, High-Level Meeting of Experts on "The Responsibility to Protect in Africa", October 23, 2008, Addis Ababa, Ethiopia. Available through the International Peace Institute (IPI) or the African Union.

[7] One of the key contributions to the intellectual development of RtoP in this regard is the idea of "sovereignty as responsibility" developed in Francis M. Deng, Sadikiel Kimaro, Terrence

sovereignty – recognized that the sovereign power had an obligation to protect the people under its rule. Sovereignty was, and remains, a two-way street through which loyalty is offered by the population in return for order and protection. In a recent article in *Policy Review*, Peter Berkowitz put it well:

> Hobbes's political theory shows why sovereignty, though absolute and indivisible in its proper sphere, is in the end limited by the power that brings it into being and maintains it, namely, each individual's natural and inalienable right to self-preservation. And this limitation illuminates both the good reasons that states have for respecting the claims of national sovereignty, and the conditions under which rulers surrender the right to govern their people and other nations become free to intervene.
>
> In Hobbes's political theory, the individual's natural and inalienable right to preserve himself by all means necessary both justifies the erection of a sovereign power and sets firm limits on it. Only an agreed-upon sovereign with absolute and indivisible powers, argues Hobbes, can protect subjects from each other and from threats. But in the end, the subject's obligation to obey runs no further than the sovereign's capacity to protect.[8]

Thus, RtoP seeks to reinforce one of the essential elements of statehood and sovereignty: the protection of people from organised violence. It does not, in fact, challenge the sovereign authority of states to do something that any of them would admit to wanting to do in the first place. The principle of state responsibility, what the Secretary-General calls the bedrock of RtoP, is both politically and legally legitimate and consistent with the core claims of sovereignty. RtoP has been championed, as well, by civil society the world over. Questions concerning domestic sovereignty would only come into play if a state were to claim the right to commit such crimes against its people, a claim that would readily be seen as illegitimate domestically and internationally. Domestic sovereignty, therefore, need not pose a barrier, legally or politically, for RtoP.

Lyons, Donald Rothschild, and I. William Zartman, *Sovereignty as Responsibility: Conflict Management in Africa* (Washington, D.C.: The Brookings Institution, 1996). For broader discussions of the diverse intellectual traditions that added to this foundation, see S. Neil MacFarlane and Yuen Foong Khong, *Human Security and the UN: A Critical History* (Bloomington, IN: Indiana University Press, 2006), and Edward C. Luck, 'The Responsible Sovereign and the Responsibility to Protect' in Joachim W. Müller and Karl P. Sauvant, eds., *Annual Review of United Nations Affairs 2006/2007*, vol. 1 (Oxford: Oxford University Press, 2008). For a useful bibliography, see *The Responsibility to Protect: Research, Bibliography, Background*, Supplementary Volume to the Report of the International Commission on Intervention and State Sovereignty (Ottawa, Canada: International Development Research Centre, December 2001), pp. 225-336.

[8] Peter Berkowitz, "Leviathan Then and Now", *Policy Review*, Iss. 151 (October/November 2008), p. 18.

Interdependence sovereignty, with its emphasis on control not authority, has relatively little to do with global norms or perceptions of legitimacy. The realities of the global marketplace and of the uncaring side of globalisation may affect a weak state's capacity for fully implementing its responsibility to protect, for example by undermining government capacity, by exacerbating ethnic divisions, or by reducing the government's ability to exercise control over its territory and to overcome any armed groups intent on intimidating segments of its population by committing RtoP crimes. But it seems unlikely that the state would oppose the adoption of global RtoP principles simply because it was unhappy with the terms of trade or its inability to resist foreign cultural influences. Indeed, under Secretary-General Ban Ki-moon's approach to RtoP, supporting the state, including through military assistance, in such circumstances would be part of the second (assistance and capacity building) pillar of his strategy for operationalising the concept.[9]

On the other hand, if RtoP advocates were to neglect its African roots or to highlight only its more coercive, militarist, and interventionist dimensions, then those developing (or developed) countries most concerned about interdependence sovereignty might be tempted to see this as part of a larger and darker effort to overwhelm traditional cultures and local values. But such a presentation of RtoP would be a serious distortion of the responsibility to protect as it was agreed at the 2005 Summit and described in the Outcome Document (paragraphs 138-140). Properly understood then, RtoP, as accepted by the world's heads of state and government, would not impinge on interdependence sovereignty and might even bolster it when the state lacks capacity or is under siege by armed groups ready to ignore their own protection responsibilities.

Krasner's third type of sovereignty, international legal sovereignty, should also not pose a significant obstacle to the full realisation of RtoP. In his lexicon, international legal sovereignty relates rather strictly to the matter of state recognition.[10] Recognition and non-recognition, of course, have often been used as political tools, as a mean of signaling acceptance or rejection of a particular government or its policies. As a rule, such decisions are taken unilaterally, as recognition is a matter of one state recognising another. Lesser steps, such as withdrawing one's diplomatic representatives from a foreign capital or asking those of another country to leave yours, serve similar signaling purposes. From time to time, the Security Council and-or the General

[9] Speech by Secretary-General Ban Ki-moon, Berlin, U.N. Document SG/SM/11701, 15 July 2008.

[10] Krasner, op. cit., pp. 14-20.

Assembly have urged UN Member States to take such diplomatic steps as a form of sanctions against a particular regime. Withdrawal of recognition or reduction of diplomatic representation could be ways of expressing the unhappiness of UN members over a state's failure to protect its population from RtoP crimes, but this remains an under-utilized tool.

Membership in the United Nations or other international organisations is not the equivalent of recognition, but it can hold high symbolic value, especially to states and governments seeking greater international legitimacy. Here the UN has some discretion. Under Article 6 of the UN Charter, "a Member of the United Nations which has persistently violated the Principles contained in the present Charter may be expelled from the Organization by the General Assembly upon the recommendation of the Security Council". Likewise, admission is decided by the Assembly upon the recommendation of the Council (Article 4(2)). According to Article 5, "a Member of the United Nations against which preventive or enforcement action has been taken by the Security Council may be suspended from exercise of the rights and privileges of membership by the General Assembly upon the recommendation of the Security Council. The exercise of these rights and privileges may be restored by the Security Council". Again, these tools could be employed in cases of RtoP crimes and the violation of the pledge undertaken in paragraph 138 of the Outcome Document, but so far they have not been invoked to this end.[11] None of this, however, should pose conceptual or political barriers either to the acceptance of RtoP as a principle or to its implementation. Indeed, the possibility of utilising diplomatic sanctions in cases of RtoP crimes should reassure those concerned that military intervention is the only conceivable response to such violations. Weak states may feel vulnerable to the use of such measures by more powerful ones, of course, but they are unlikely to claim that states do not have a sovereign right to choose whom to recognise and at what diplomatic level representation will be set.

The relationship between RtoP and Krasner's fourth category – the notion of Westphalian sovereignty – on the other hand, is far more complex and consequential. It is here, in the related concepts of territorial and decision-making sovereignty posed in this paper, that questions arise for both developed and developing countries about how the implementation of the responsibility to protect could in some ways condition their sovereignty,

[11] Though the International Criminal Court (ICC) is not a UN body, the possibility of referral to the ICC of individuals accused of RtoP crimes can be a most helpful tool for discouraging or deterring the commission or incitement of such crimes.

depending on how it is carried out. Much of the rest of this essay is devoted to shedding light on the policy implications of these dilemmas and sensitivities.

Sovereignty Concerns, North and South

As Krasner notes, the Westphalian model of sovereignty 'is based on two principles: territoriality and the exclusion of external actors from domestic authority structures'.[12] The well-established norms of territorial integrity and non-intervention in internal affairs are usually associated with the Westphalian conception of sovereignty. They are embodied, as well, in two of the UN's founding principles. Article 2(4) declares that "all Members shall refrain in their international relations from the threat or use of force against the territorial integrity or political independence of any state, or in any other manner inconsistent with the Purposes of the United Nations". According to Article 2(7), "nothing contained in the present Charter shall authorize the United Nations to intervene in matters which are essentially within the domestic jurisdiction of any state or shall require the Members to submit such matters to settlement under the present Charter; but this principle shall not prejudice the application of enforcement measures under Chapter VII". Neither of these principles suggests that a state is free to do as it pleases within its borders or that sovereignty is absolute. The Charter's provisions on human rights and on the Council's authority to investigate "any situation which might lead to international friction or give rise to a dispute" (Article 34) underscore that there is a legitimate international interest in abuses of populations within states of an RtoP magnitude.

Nevertheless, the concern among many states that RtoP principles might be misused by powerful states or groups of states to justify coercive interventions undertaken for other reasons is eminently understandable. This is particularly so on the part of those who have been subject to colonialism, which was itself often justified by appeals to moral and humane principles. These concerns featured prominently in the debates leading up to the 2005 World Summit. Indeed, judging by the tone expressed by many developing countries at that point, there was little reason to be optimistic about the prospects for achieving the Summit's endorsement of RtoP. In April 2005, for instance, the Permanent Representative of Egypt to the UN, Ambassador Maged Abdelaziz, stated that 'the "Responsibility to Protect" conflicts directly with such well established

[12] Krasner, op. cit., p. 20.

principles enshrined in the Charter particularly those related to the use of force, sovereignty, territorial integrity and non interference in the internal affairs of states. . . . It would allow the strong to judge the weak'.[13] Two months later, the Foreign Ministers of the countries in the Non-Aligned Movement (NAM) likewise noted the 'similarities between the new expression "responsibility to protect" and "humanitarian intervention"' and requested the NAM Co-ordinating Bureau to consider RtoP's 'implications on the basis of the principles of non-interference and non-intervention as well as the respect for territorial integrity and national sovereignty'.[14]

In the intensive negotiations leading to the inclusion of the RtoP section in the Outcome Document, these concerns were addressed in several ways in the evolving text. As noted above, then-President of the General Assembly Jean Ping has stressed the importance of the decision to limit the scope of RtoP to the four specific crimes and violations. Paragraph 139 underscores the centrality of United Nations processes and principles in making any decision to respond to situations in which "national authorities are manifestly failing to protect their populations" from the four crimes and violations. Rather than emphasising military intervention, the whole panoply of "diplomatic, humanitarian and other peaceful means, in accordance with Chapters VI and VIII of the Charter" are included in the RtoP toolkit alongside possible Chapter VII enforcement measures. The international community, moreover, is to "help," "assist," "support," and "encourage" states in meeting their RtoP obligations. The value of preventive measures is also stressed, as the international community is to help build state capacity and to assist "those which are under stress before crises and conflicts break out". The General Assembly, moreover, is "to continue consideration" of RtoP "bearing in mind the principles of the Charter and international law". Clearly, these provisions in the text made a real difference, for the RtoP section was included in the consensus document when other important and controversial issues, such as disarmament and non-proliferation, were dropped due to persistent differences of view.

The developing countries, however, were not the only ones to express some angst over the implications of RtoP for state sovereignty. Here, the second

[13] Statement by Ambassador Maged Abdelaziz, Informational Thematic Consultations on Cluster III: Freedom to Live in Dignity in the Report of the Secretary-General entitled *On Larger Freedom: Towards Development, Security and Human Rights for All*, April 19, 2005.

[14] Statement by the Chairman of the Coordinating Bureau of the Non-Aligned Movement, Ambassador Radzi Rahman, on behalf of the Non-Aligned Movement at the Informal Meeting of the Plenary of the General Assembly Concerning the Draft Outcome Document, June 21, 2005, http://www.un.int/Malaysia/NAM/nam210605.html.

dimension of Westphalian sovereignty, that related to 'the exclusion of external actors from domestic authority structures', to use Krasner's words, came into play. The handful of states with major force projection capabilities were decidedly unenthusiastic – as were many other Member States as well – about allowing multilateral organisations to decide how, where, and when their forces would be deployed. The United States, with by far the largest military capacity and the longest history of dissenting from global decision-making processes, was most vocal and candid on this score, but its reservations were, in this case at least, widely shared among the ranks of relatively affluent and militarily competent countries. Where some feared the allegedly interventionist tendencies of the big powers, the latter have long tended to resist the calls to intervene in RtoP-type situations unless their strategic interests were also at stake.

John Bolton, then the US Permanent Representative to the UN, was typically blunt and to the point. With historical accuracy,[15] he noted in a letter to the other Member States of August 30, 2005, the eve of the Summit, that "the Charter has never been interpreted as creating a legal obligation for Security Council members to support enforcement action'.[16] He cautioned against formulations that would appear to equate the responsibilities of the state and the international community for RtoP, as they are 'not of the same character'. In his view, the obligation and responsibilities posited under RtoP are 'not of a legal character' and 'we do not accept that either the United Nations as a whole, or the Security Council, or individual states, have an obligation to intervene under international law. We also believe that what the United Nations does in a particular situation should depend on the specific circumstances'. In other words, the US was not about to concede what it saw as its sovereign right of choice.[17]

China and the Russian Federation tended simply to stress, as most states did, the requirement that any enforcement action be decided by the Security

[15] See, for instance, Edward C. Luck, 'A Council for All Seasons: The Creation of the Security Council and Its Relevance Today' in Vaughan Lowe, Adam Roberts, Jennifer Welsh, and Dominik Zaum, eds., *The UN Security Council and War: The Evolution of Thought and Practice Since 1945* (Oxford: Oxford University Press, 2008), pp. 62-85.

[16] Letter from Ambassador John R. Bolton to UN Member States, August 30, 2005, http://www.reformtheun.org/index.php/issues/100?theme=alt4.

[17] Ambassador Bolton's views on RtoP have been echoed by writings produced by some of America's more prominent conservative think tanks. See, for instance, Steven Groves, 'The U.S. Should Reject the U.N. "Responsibility to Protect' Doctrine"', Executive Summary Backgrounder No. 2103 (Washington, D.C.: The Heritage Foundation, May 1, 2008) and Christopher Preble, 'Missing the Point in the Bolton Debate', appeared on cato.org (The Cato Institute), May 12, 2005, http://www.cato.org/pub_display.php?pub_id=3764.

Council and through well-established Charter rules.[18] This, of course, would preserve the right of any of the five permanent members of the Council to veto any enforcement action of which they did not approve. On this, of course, states concerned about either decision-making or territorial sovereignty could agree.

As in the case of territorial sovereignty, the RtoP text in the Outcome Document accommodated these concerns as well. Paragraph 138, as noted above, underscores the centrality of state responsibility, with the international community playing a supporting role in assistance and prevention. Chapter VII responses to manifest state failure are to be decided "on a case-by-case basis", according to paragraph 139. Cooperation with regional organisations is to be "as appropriate". Again, the reference to Charter rules and principles reinforces the centrality of the Security Council and the veto power over forceful action.

RtoP Lite?

All of these caveats have led some RtoP advocates to term the outcome "RtoP lite". Yet what more could have been expected from a gathering of the leaders of the world's sovereign states? Have any of the human rights and humanitarian conventions of the past sixty years had any more robust enforcement mechanisms or any greater assurance of automaticity of response? In the nation-state era, there will be limits to both the practicality and the wisdom of formally breaching the proper boundaries of sovereignty. When not abused, sovereignty has permitted both some sense of order in international and domestic affairs and the growth of the very norms and institutions, like RtoP, that at times seem to challenge its legitimacy and redefine its limits.

The responsibility to protect has both operational and aspirational significance, informing current practices and policies on the one hand and affirming higher standards to be pursued over time on the other. Both tracks need to be pursued vigorously, for they are mutually reinforcing. RtoP has proven to be a politically powerful idea, whose time appears to have come. As such, its greatest contributions over time may lie less in setting rules and guidelines for inter-governmental mechanisms to follow and more in influencing the

[18] On this, Ambassador Bolton dissented. In his letter, he argued that 'we should not preclude the possibility of action absent authorization by the Security Council. There may be cases that involve humanitarian catastrophes [sic] but for which there is also a legitimate basis for states to act in self-defense. The text should not foreclose this possibility'. Interestingly, this claim would compromise US veto power in return for wider freedom to act outside of UN strictures.

conceptions of interest, doctrine and strategy within national capitals, and hence voting patterns in international bodies. If influential states do not reconsider their national interests and values because of the growing prominence of RtoP in public and political circles, then posting rules for the Security Council and other inter-governmental bodies to follow would make little difference. If national values and perspectives change because of RtoP, however, the rules and guidelines would hardly be needed. The first step toward achieving unity of purpose and real consensus in the UN, according to the argument in this paper, is to cast aside the easy characterisation that some states are hooked on narrow conceptions of sovereignty, while others have evolved beyond such constraints. One of the things that unites states in their approach to RtoP, not surprisingly, is that they are all concerned about preserving their national sovereignty, just in different ways. After all, they are all states and that is what states do.

A Bird in the Hand is Worth Two in the Bush – On the Assumed Legal Nature of the Responsibility to Protect

Ekkehard Strauss[1]

Abstract

Based on the jurisprudence of the International Court of Justice that resolutions of the General Assembly can only create legal provisions in exceptional circumstances, the review of the negotiation history of the Summit Outcome Document and the recent practice of the General Assembly, the Security Council and the Human Rights Council related to the implementation of the agreement on the responsibility to protect leads to the conclusion that no new collective legal obligation has been created. Instead, the responsibility offers an opportunity to improve the implementation of existing legal obligations to protect populations from genocide, war crimes, crimes against humanity and ethnic cleansing. If used for the development of a continuum of civil and military action to prevent and halt only these exceptional crimes, the necessary practice and opinio juris might be created over time, to establish the responsibility to protect as a norm of international customary law.

Keywords

Responsibility to Protect, World Summit negotiations, Security Council, General Assembly, Human Rights Council, Secretary-General, prevention of genocide, customary international law, opinio juris

Introduction

'Based on the evidence we have seen from observations on the ground, we have every reason to believe that acts of genocide have occurred in Rwanda'.[2]

People around the world remember the careful stammer of world leaders to avoid using the term 'genocide' to the events that unfolded in Rwanda and had been reported on front pages of leading newspapers since the beginning of April 1994.[3] Since the prevention of genocide has been an obligation under

[1] Opinions presented in this article are not necessarly those of the United Nations.

[2] Christine Shelly, spokesperson of the US State Department, on 10 June 1994.

[3] See e.gt. Samantha Power, 'Bystanders to Genocide', *The Atlantic*, September 2001, available at http://www.theatlantic.com/doc/200109/power-genocide/6

public international law, heads of state and government were afraid that they would have to commit to action if they agreed that the killings in Rwanda constituted, in fact, genocide.

With a view to this experience, it is surprising how much space the discussion about the legal character of the responsibility to protect has taken up within the deliberations on the implementation of the agreement contained in paragraph 138 and 139 of the 2005 Summit Outcome Document.[4] While the responsibility to protect builds on existing legal obligations related to genocide, war crimes, ethnic cleansing and crimes against humanity,[5] it will be argued in the following that the agreement on the responsibility to protect did not create additional legal obligations. This conclusion will be based on a review of the negotiation history of the Summit Outcome Document and the recent practice of principal organs of the United Nations in implementing the responsibility to protect.[6] The legal content of paragraph 138 and 139 will be reviewed in the light of the recent jurisprudence of the International Court of Justice and the International Tribunals, in particular on the obligation to prevent genocide. Finally, the possible added value of the responsibility to protect for the future efforts of the United Nations in preventing or halting genocide, war crimes, ethnic cleansing and crimes against humanity will be considered in the light of the experience of past failures to respond effectively to these crimes.

Two Birds in the Bush? – The Assumed Legal Nature of the Agreement on the Responsibility to Protect in the Summit Outcome Document

The Legal Effect of General Assembly Resolutions

According to article 38 of the Statute of the International Court of Justice, the sources of international law are limited to international treaties, custom and

[4] In November 2004, the High-level Panel on Threats, Challenges and Change 'endorse[d] the emerging norm that there is a collective international responsibility to protect, exercisable by the Security Council authorizing military intervention as a last resort, in the event of genocide and other large scale killing, ethnic cleansing or serious violations of international humanitarian law which sovereign Governments have proven powerless or unwilling to prevent', *A more secure world: our shared responsibility*. Report of the High-level Panel on Threats, Challenges and Change, A/59/565, 17 November 2004, para. 203.

[5] On the key elements of the responsibility to protect see e.g. Sabine von Schorlemer, 'The Responsibility to Protect as an Element of Peace. Recommendations for its Operationalization', Development and Peace Foundation, *Policy Paper 28* (2007) pp. 5-7.

[6] The information on the Summit negotiations is based on the author's own account and conversations with former and present members of delegations. Notes on those conversations are on file with the author.

general principles of law. The Summit Outcome Document was adopted by the General Assembly by resolution, which is a non-binding recommendation for member states. However, resolutions can make an important contribution to the development of international treaties by promoting main principles for future agreements. Thus, resolutions of the General Assembly often function as a starting point, frame or concept for discussion on establishing or creating international law.[7]

In some instances, resolutions of the General Assembly constitute evidence of customary international law or contribute to its formation. Customary international law requires a general practice of states accompanied by opinio juris. However, resolutions of the General Assembly do not create new rules of customary international law as such. Some authors claim that the necessary state practice is manifest when states vote for a resolution.[8] According to the International Court of Justice, resolutions can provide evidence for the existence of a certain rule or of emergence of opinio juris.[9] In very rare cases, states might have had the clear intention to lay down a legal provision in a resolution of the General Assembly. However, those exceptional circumstances could only be considered if those states with particular interests in the issue agreed to the rule in question.[10]

The Negotiation History of the Summit Outcome Document

In order to identify any intention of member states to create a new legal obligation, it is required to review the negotiations of the agreement on the responsibility to protect in the Summit Outcome Document.

After the Government had sponsored the International Commission on Intervention and State Sovereignty (ICISS) which had presented its report, entitled 'The Responsibility to Protect', to the Secretary-General at the end of 2001,[11] Canada proposed to include the responsibility to protect in the Summit Outcome Document within its ongoing effort to implement the recommendations of the ICISS. The 2005 World Summit offered the opportunity

[7] On the legal nature and legal effect of resolutions of the General Assembly see Hailbronner/ Klein, Art. 10 in: Bruno Simma, *The Charter of the United Nations*, 2nd ed. (Oxford University Press, 2002) paras. 43-54.

[8] See e.g. Obed Y. Asamoah, *The Legal Significance of the Declarations of the General Assembly of the United Nations* (The Hague, 1966), pp. 46-57.

[9] Legality of the Threat or Use of Nuclear Weapons, Advisory Opinion, ICJ Reports 1996, p. 254.

[10] Hailbronner/ Klein, supra, para. 57.

[11] ICISS, *The Responsibility to Protect* (Ottawa, 2002).

to reconsider the proposals of the ICISS on how to bridge the gap between legality and legitimacy in situations of gross and systematic violations of human rights.[12]

Initially, the Canadian delegation chose to link the responsibility to protect with considerations on human security. This line of argument raised immediate concerns with some member states, including supporters of the responsibility to protect. Japan argued that, notwithstanding considerable overlap of the approach to human security with the responsibility to protect, the latter paved the way for armed intervention, while the former prioritized prevention.[13] The concept of human security has been defined as the protection of 'the vital core of all human lives in ways that enhance human freedoms and fulfilment'.[14] It encompasses human rights, good governance and access to economic opportunity, education and health care.[15] Human security seeks to complement state security, enhance human rights and strengthen human development, it also seeks to protect people against a broad range of threats to individuals and communities and, further, to empower them to act on their own behalf.[16]

The draft Outcome Document of 3 June 2005 submitted by the President of the General Assembly, Jean Ping, included the responsibility to protect in a section on human rights and rule of law together with human security and the strengthening of the Office of the High Commissioner for Human Rights (OHCHR).[17]

The main substantive concern regarding an agreement on the responsibility to protect was related to the principle of sovereignty and non-intervention. Another concern that was raised with some frequency was unilateral action under the auspices of the responsibility to protect. However, the African

---

[12] Details of the methodology and the procedure of the Commission are summarized in ICISS, *The Responsibility to Protect. Research, Bibliography, Background*, (Ottawa, 2002), pp. 341-344.

[13] See Asia-Pcific Center for the Responsibility to Protect, *Japan and the Republic of Korea on the Responsibility to Protect* (Brisbane, 2008), p. 7.

[14] Human Security Center, *Human Security Report 2005. War and Peace in the 21st Century*, (University of British Colombia, 2005).

[15] United Nations Development Programme, *Human Development Report 1994. New Dimensions of Human Security* (Oxford University Press, 1994).

[16] Neil MacFarlane/ Yuen Foong Khong, *Human Security and the UN: A Critical History* (Indiana University Press, 2006).

[17] Draft Outcome Document by the President of the General Assembly of 3 June 2005, available at http://www.responsibilitytoprotect.org/index.php/united_nations/

countries broadly supported the idea, pointing at a similar provision in the Charter of the African Union.[18]

At the beginning of the negotiation process, the draft paragraphs on the responsibility to protect were not very prominent in the negotiations. Security Council expansion was the first priority for member states and other initiatives were considered mainly in the broader context of cooperation on the main issues. The structure of the negotiations by main clusters, i.e. human rights, peace and security and development, forced the heads of delegation to focus on the most important questions related to peace and security, institutional reform and the guiding principles of the document, leaving their experts with little guidance for the discussion on the responsibility to protect. The responsibility to protect was perceived as an interest mainly of Canada, the European Union and Japan. Initially, the US Government did not consider it a priority.[19] Thus, member states assumed that a rejection could pay to get concessions in other areas of the document. It was expected that, ultimately, Russia would succeed in convincing the supporters to take the provisions out of the text.

In their comments on the amended draft Document of 22 July 2005,[20] member states repeated their previous positions and it became clear that a consensus was going to be difficult to extract. However, outgoing Secretary-General Kofi Annan considered an agreement on the responsibility to protect to be a core area of the Summit Outcome Document. With a view to the experience in Rwanda and Srebrenica, he felt that the credibility of the United Nations and the principles of the Charter required clear guidance to the member states on how to engage in similar situations in the future.[21] At the end of his tenure, he wanted to witness the transition from principle to operational action. With a view to the importance of a successful Summit for his legacy the Secretariat extended its mediation efforts between member states on the responsibility to protect. In a marathon of meetings with permanent representatives the members of a small mediation team recalled

[18] See on the general political dynamics of the World Summit Alex Bellamy, 'Whither the Responsibility to Protect? Humanitarian Intervention and the 2005 World Summit', *Ethics and International Affairs*, Vol. 20 (2006) p. 151 et seq.

[19] Strong support came from the Task Force on the United Nations, *American Interests and UN Reform*, United States Institute for Peace (Washington D.C., 2005) p. 27 et seq.

[20] Revised draft outcome document of the high-level plenary meeting of the General Assembly of September 2005 submitted by the President of the General Assembly, A/59/HPLM/CRP.1/Rev.1, 22 July 2005.

[21] See e.g. Press Release SG/SM/10000, SC/8444, 12 July 2005.

the situations in Rwanda and Srebrenica and urged delegates to put forward the joint interest of all member states, and not to repeat previous failures.[22]

On 5 August, Jean Ping presented another revised draft Outcome Document. With regard to the responsibility to protect, the document limited the scope of protection to genocide, war crimes, ethnic cleansing and crimes against humanity. The member states agreed that this responsibility entailed the prevention of such crimes, including their incitement. They acknowledged that the international community, through the United Nations, also had the 'obligation' - changed from 'responsibility' - to use diplomatic, humanitarian and other peaceful means to help protect populations from these crimes if national authorities were unwilling or unable to protect their populations.[23]

On 17 August, the recently appointed Permanent Representative of the United States to the United Nations, Ambassador John Bolton, sent to his colleagues a list of amendments and changes to the draft document negotiated for almost one year. The United States had indicated earlier that it would accept most of the human rights and collective security agenda of the draft Document, but many delegations had expected some development in the US position after a harsh rejection of the draft by the US delegation in the General Assembly two weeks earlier.[24] Initially, many Western countries appreciated the US initiative as they perceived the negotiations as giving in too much on development without getting back enough on the responsibility to protect. However, only Algeria, Cuba, Egypt, Iran and Venezuela supported the idea of new negotiations publicly.

The draft paragraph on the responsibility to protect was completely altered by the amendments and the clause urging the five permanent members of the Security Council not to veto action aimed at halting or preventing genocide or ethnic cleansing was deleted. The United States requested, inter alia, to drop the reference to incitement and change the wording back to 'responsibility' when describing the role of the international community. Ambassador Bolton further explained the position of the United States on the section on

---

[22] See for details on the involvement of the Secretariat in the negotiations of the Summit Outcome document James Traub, *The Best Intentions. Kofi Annan and the UN in the Era of American World Power*, (New York, 2006), p. 359 et seq., 373 et seq.

[23] Revised draft outcome document of the high-level plenary meeting of the General Assembly of September 2005 submitted by the President of the General Assembly, A/59/HPLM/CRP.1/Rev.2, 5 August 2005.

[24] Julian Borger, 'Road map for US relations with rest of world. Hundreds of deletions and insertions on just about every global issue could undermine the UN summit agreement', *The Guardian*, 27 August 2005.

responsibility to protect in the revised draft Document in a letter dated 30 August 2005 and proposed the following wording:

> 118. We underscore that national authorities have a responsibility to protect their populations and, in cases involving genocide, ethnic cleansing crimes against humanity and other large-scale atrocities in which national authorities are unwilling or unable to protect their citizens. Then the international community should be prepared to use diplomatic, humanitarian, and other methods to protect civilian populations. And if such methods appear insufficient the Security Council may out of necessity decide to take action under the Charter, including enforcement action, if so required.[25]

The last-minute demands by the United States changed the dynamics of the negotiations significantly as other member states felt the United States' call for revisions allowed them to insist on their previous positions.[26] Russia, for example, expressed its general objections to any attempt to give the authority to the United Nations to intervene in cases of genocide. China also voiced concern regarding the responsibility to protect.

In order to save the Summit, Jean Ping appointed a core group of thirty member states to work through Ambassador Bolton's list concentrating on the main issues.[27] This group was later replaced by only 12 member states. On 2 September, the core group reported that the sub-group on the responsibility to protect had two readings of the draft text, and despite efforts to reach agreement, fundamental differences remained. The group did succeed in identifying the most critical points of divergence and discussions had been more focused with delegations being represented at the level of Ambassadors. However, when no progress was made with a harvest document drafted by the United Kingdom and 150 brackets remained to the draft Document, the Secretariat and Jean Ping started to work on a compromise text 24 hours before the heads of state arrived.

It is difficult to establish the details of the drama that unfolded subsequently in Conference Room 4 in the basement of the United Nations until the early hours of the day of the Summit as many witnesses cautiously try to align their records with their current interpretation of the Outcome Document. However, considering the varying accounts of participants in the light of the differences between the text of the final Outcome Document, the revised draft of 5 August

---

[25] US comments on the revised draft outcome document, A/59/HPLM/CRP.1/Rev.2, submitted on 17 August 2005 at 11.06 a.m.

[26] On the background to Ambassador Bolton's initiative see Brian Urquhart, 'One Angry Man', *New York Review of Books*, 6 March 2008, p. 14.

[27] Maggie Farley, 'U.S. Demands Spur Crisis Talks at U.N.', *Los Angeles Times*, 27 August 2005.

and the statements of the heads of state and government at the Summit, some important elements of the discussions can be reconstructed.

Russia, India and Jamaica argued against including the paragraph on responsibility to protect in the Outcome Document. They claimed that the Charter established all necessary standards to address situations of mass atrocities. Furthermore, the responsibility to protect was already part of the international standards on the protection of civilians and the positive obligations deriving from the right to life. Other countries questioned who could determine legally that a Member State was 'unwilling and unable' to protect their populations. With a view to the same wording in the Rome Statute on the International Criminal Court and the recent referral of the situation in Darfur to the Court,[28] many members of the Group of 77 were concerned that, based on a similar assessment, measures of regime change could be taken against the will of the government concerned. It was argued that for lack of common ground the paragraph should leave any definition until later and only describe the 'contours' of the responsibility. At the same time, the member states could not agree on a particular mechanism for future discussions.

Consequently, the Draft Negotiated Outcome distributed on 12 September 2005 took all these concerns into consideration and arrived at the following wording in the Summit Outcome document:

> 138. Each individual State has the responsibility to protect its populations from genocide, war crimes, ethnic cleansing and crimes against humanity. This responsibility entails the prevention of such crimes, including their incitement, through appropriate and necessary means. We accept that responsibility and will act in accordance with it. The international community should, as appropriate, encourage and help States to exercise this responsibility and support the United Nations in establishing an early warning capability.
>
> 139. The international community, through the United Nations, also has the responsibility to use appropriate diplomatic, humanitarian and other peaceful means, in accordance with Chapters VI and VIII of the Charter, to help to protect populations from genocide, war crimes, ethnic cleansing and crimes against humanity. In this context, we are prepared to take collective action, in a timely and decisive manner, through the Security Council, in accordance with the Charter, including Chapter VII, on a case-by-case basis and in cooperation with relevant regional organizations as appropriate, should peaceful means be inadequate and national authorities are manifestly failing to protect their populations from genocide, war crimes, ethnic cleansing and crimes against humanity. We stress the need for the General Assembly to continue consideration of the responsibility to protect populations from genocide, war crimes, ethnic cleansing

---

[28] S/RES/1593 (2005), 31 March 2005.

> and crimes against humanity and its implications, bearing in mind the principles of the Charter and international law. We also intend to commit ourselves, as necessary and appropriate, to helping States build capacity to protect their populations from genocide, war crimes, ethnic cleansing and crimes against humanity and to assisting those which are under stress before crises and conflicts break out.
>
> 140. We fully support the mission of the Special Adviser of the Secretary-General on the Prevention of Genocide.[29]

The length of the sentences and the many sub-clauses reveal the effort of including the diverse positions in a compromise text. The two paragraphs separate the responsibility of individual states and the responsibility of the international community. The latter requires that national authorities of a member state are 'manifestly failing' to meet their responsibility. Compared with the previous criteria of states being 'unwilling and unable', this wording indicated the intention to base any assessment on evidence rather than a judgment on motives. Furthermore, the responsibility to protect is not qualified further as either an emerging norm of international law or another obligation. The responsibility to prevent in paragraph 138 is mainly expressed as an appeal. Paragraph 139 shows the agreement on the application of non-military means, while the member states could only agree on the application of non-consensual means on a case-by-case basis. The paragraph concludes with the general caveat of the need for the General Assembly to further consider the responsibility to protect without the specific timetable 'at its 60th Session'. The appeal to the permanent members of the Security Council regarding the exercise of their veto was not included.[30]

It can therefore be concluded that the negotiations of the provisions of the Summit Outcome Document related to the responsibility to protect cannot provide evidence for the exceptional intention of member states to lay down a legal provision in a resolution of the General Assembly.

The Practice of the General Assembly and the Security Council Since the World Summit

Following the above, the practice of the General Assembly and the Security Council since the adoption of the Summit Outcome Document should be

---

[29] A/RES/60/1, 24 October 2005.

[30] See for a more comprehensive analysis of the Summit Outcome document Carsten Stahn, 'Responsibility to Protect: Political Rhetoric or Emerging Legal Norm?', *AJIL*, Vol. 101, No. 1, pp. 99-120.

reviewed for any general practice related to the application of the responsibility to protect that could lead to the conclusion that, in fact, a legal norm has been established. Even though the formation of human rights or humanitarian obligations through customary law will always be challenged by the violation of the rule in question, at least, state practice should evidence general recognition of a legal obligation.[31]

Even though the Summit Outcome Document was adopted without a vote, the subsequent statements of heads of state and government indicated the divisions prevailing on the responsibility to protect. Prime Minister Paul Martin of Canada referred to the responsibility to protect as a 'powerful norm of international behaviour' and he was 'proud that R2P has Canadian lineage, that it is now a principle for all the world'. He argued that the responsibility to protect stood for clear, multilaterally agreed criteria on what the international community should do when civilians are at risk. Iceland and Italy referred to the responsibility to protect as concept and principle respectively while Mauritius called it a 'norm of collective action' and Norway a 'duty to help'. Indonesia underlined the need for a consensus on the responsibility to protect and Switzerland called on member states to make every effort to define together the criteria for its implementation. Fierce criticism came from President Hugo Chavez Frias of Venezuela, who called on member states not to allow a handful of countries to try to reinterpret the principles of international law and to give way to doctrines like pre-emptive war and the 'so called responsibility to protect'. President Robert G. Mugabe of Zimbabwe warned that the responsibility to protect needed careful scrutiny in order to test the motives of its proponents.[32]

While the Summit Outcome document 'stressed the need for the General Assembly to continue consideration of the responsibility to protect', member states did not discuss the issue in substance during subsequent sessions. Only in July 2008 did the Secretary-General use the occasion of a conference in Berlin to announce that, later in the year, he intended to report to the General Assembly on his proposed approach and the challenges posed by the Summit Outcome document.[33]

At the beginning of each session, the General Assembly devotes a period of two weeks to a general debate, which is often attended by heads of state and government or foreign ministers. The subjects raised in these statements are

[31] North Sea Continental Shelf, ICJ Reports 1969, p. 43.

[32] All statements are available at http://www.un.org/webcast/summit2005/statements.html

[33] Press Release SG/SM/11701, 15 July 2008.

often indicative of the priority interests of delegations during the following session. During the General Debate of the 61st Session, in September 2006, only 13 Member States, in their majority members of the European Union, referred to the responsibility to protect when reviewing the status of implementation of the Summit Outcome.[34] During the General Debate of the 62nd Session, at the end of September 2007, eight Member States mentioned the responsibility to protect in their statements.[35]

In December 2007, the Fifth Committee of the General Assembly considered agenda item 128 on the Proposed programme budget for the biennium 2008-2009. In his report on Estimates in respect of special political missions, good offices and other political initiatives authorised by the General Assembly and/ or the Security Council,[36] the Secretary-General informed the General Assembly about his decision to appoint a Special Adviser for the Responsibility to Protect at the Assistant Secretary-General level in order 'to operationalize the concept and to develop the doctrine of the responsibility to protect'. The Secretary-General argued that such a position would complement the work of the Special Adviser on the Prevention of Genocide and should work closely with the latter to advance and consolidate the 2005 World Summit consensus and provide advice and recommendations in this regard. With a view to ensure effective coordination between the two Special Advisers, the Secretary-General requested additional staff for the Office of the Special Adviser on the Prevention of Genocide.[37] Instead, the Fifth Committee adopted a resolution on the proposed programme budget for the biennium 2008-2009 in which it implicitly turned down the appointment of a Special Adviser on the Responsibility to Protect within the Office of the Special Adviser on the Prevention of Genocide.[38] In March 2008, the Fifth Committee again discussed the appointment by the Secretary-General of a Special Adviser on the Responsibility to Protect. All delegations taking the floor in the discussion expressed concern at the appointment procedure that did not involve the General Assembly as such notwithstanding previous discussions on the issue in December. In addition, Cuba, Egypt, Morocco, Nicaragua, Pakistan and Sudan stated that the General Assembly did not sufficiently discuss the agreement on the responsibility

[34] Statements during the General Debate of the 61st Session can be reviewed at http://www.un.org/webcast/ga/61/index.shtml

[35] Statements during the General Debate of the 62nd Session can be reviewed at http://www.un.org/webcast/ga/62

[36] A/62/512/Add.1, 30 October 2007, para. 31.

[37] Ibid., para. 38.

[38] See Press Release GA/AB/3835, 22 December 2007; A/RES/62/238, 20 February 2008, p. 4.

to protect in the Summit Outcome Document and member states lacked consensus on its content and definition.[39] On 22 May 2008, a thematic debate on human security provided a rare example in which member states referred to the responsibility to protect in substantive statements.[40] During the General Debate at the opening of the 63rd session of the General Assembly, 17 member states referred to the responsibility to protect in their statements.[41]

A preliminary review of the practice of the General Assembly regarding the responsibility to protect does not reveal much progress from the positions held by member states during the negotiations of the Summit Outcome Document. At the beginning of 2009, the Secretary-General suggested that the General Assembly debate his proposals for the implementation of the responsibility to protect that he described in his report on the concept, and that the Assembly consider a periodic review of its activities.[42]

It can be concluded that, since the 2005 World Summit, the number of member states referring to the responsibility to protect in their statements in the general debate did not increase significantly. Those member states publicly supporting the operationalization of the responsibility to protect belong almost exclusively to the European Union and its associated states. When they were put to the test, they could not ensure that the Secretary-General's initiative regarding a Special Adviser be approved by the General Assembly. The only country situations referred to during the General Debate of the 61st and 62nd session in the context of the responsibility to protect have been Darfur, Myanmar, Zimbabwe and Eastern DRC, but without suggesting any concrete steps that could be applied. It also remains unclear whether the recommendations provided in the report of the Secretary-General entail a regular report leading to a periodic discussion by the General Assembly on the implementation of the agreement on the responsibility to protect.

Within the Security Council, member states made public statements related to the responsibility to protect almost exclusively in the context of the protection of civilians in armed conflict. Since the adoption of the Summit Outcome Document in September 2005, the Security Council held six open debates on the protection of civilians in armed conflict.[43]

---

[39] See Press Release GA/AB/3837, 4 May 2008.

[40] See for details Press Release GA/10711, 23 May 2008.

[41] All statements can be found at http://www.un.org/ga/63/generaldebate/

[42] *Implementing the responsibility to protect.* Report of the Secretary-General, A/63/677, 12 January 2009, para. 71.

[43] See for a detailed analysis Ekkehard Strauss, *The Emperor's New Clothes? – The United Nations and the implementation of the responsibility to protect* (Baden-Baden, 2009), pp. 48-56.

Prior to the public debate on 9 December 2005, the United Kingdom had circulated a draft resolution on the Protection of Civilians in Armed Conflict, which referred to the responsibility to protect in the preamble and the operational part of the text as follows[44]:

> PP 4. Recalling the 2005 World Summit Outcome Document, including its provisions regarding the responsibility to protect populations from genocide, war crimes, ethnic cleansing and crimes against humanity, and in this regard the responsibly of individual Member States as well as the international community acting through the United Nations, including the Security Council…
>
> OP 6. Recalls the 2005 World Summit Outcome Document, and underlines the importance of its provisions regarding the responsibility to protect populations from genocide, war crimes, ethnic cleansing and crimes against humanity, including in this regard the responsibility of individual Member States as well as the international community acting through the United Nations, including the Security Council…

Negotiations on the resolution began in late November 2005, but member states were unable to reach agreement on several aspects of the text, including the responsibility to protect. China and Russia, supported by three non-permanent members, promoted a cautious approach and considered the reference in the text premature. The responsibility to protect, they argued, should first be addressed by the General Assembly in more detail before it was included in a Security Council resolution. They were concerned that rapid interventions in exercise of the responsibility to protect could occur.[45] In early March 2006, the negotiation process was moving forward a little, when China changed its position and indicated that it could accept a reference to the responsibility to protect in the text, if the exact same language of the Summit Outcome Document was used. In addition, four of the new non-permanent members of the Council, who replaced the previous opponents, were in favour of a resolution endorsing the concept. Thus, the Russian position became increasingly isolated.[46] Many Council members expressed frustration over the difficulties of agreeing on language for something that had been endorsed by the heads of states and governments only recently. Finally, the United Kingdom distributed a revised text of a draft resolution and on 28 April 2006, the

---

[44] Draft of 21 November 2005 at 10.07 a.m., available at http://www.responsibilitytoprotect.org/index.php/united-nations/

[45] Security Council Report, Update Report No. 4, Protection of Civilians in Armed Conflict, 13 January 2006, p. 1.

[46] Security Council Report, Update Report No. 1, Protection of Civilians in Armed Conflict, 8 March 2006, p. 1.

Security Council passed resolution 1674 (2006), including the following operative paragraph on the responsibility to protect:

> Reaffirms the provisions of paragraphs 138 and 139 of the 2005 World Summit Outcome Document regarding the responsibility to protect populations from genocide, war crimes, ethnic cleansing and crimes against humanity...[47]

During subsequent debates, statements followed the same pattern seen during the negotiations of resolution 1674. Russia joined China with the latter refining its position further by warning that it was not appropriate to expand, wilfully interpret or even abuse the responsibility to protect, while many other member states had expressed their concern and misgivings. Instead, all sides should abide by the agreed elements of the Summit Outcome Document, i.e. its limitations to the four listed crimes. The United States repeated a reluctant statement with hardly any changes in the wording related to the responsibility to protect underlining that in situations where a government was unable or unwilling to protect its civilians, the international community had a complementary role to play.[48] During the public debate on 22 June 2007 the representative of Mexico provided an appropriate summary of the status of discussions in the Security Council, when he stated that:

> [d]espite the consensus reached in 2005, we cannot deny that an atmosphere of mistrust prevails over that subject. While some States see in the new principle the mere continuance of interventionist policies aimed at destabilizing political regimes, others promote its application in a selective manner, limiting its scope to cases significant for their foreign policy interests. For this reason, it is essential that States commit to reaching new agreements that give true content to such an important principle in an objective and impartial manner.[49]

In resolution 1706 (2006) concerning the situation in Sudan, the Council indirectly referred to the responsibility to protect when it quoted from the wording of resolution 1674 (2006) in a paragraph of the preamble rather than directly reaffirming the Summit Outcome Document:

> Reaffirming its previous resolutions 1325 (2000) on women, peace and security, 1502 (2003) on the protection of humanitarian and United Nations personnel, 1612 (2005) on children in armed conflict, and 1674 (2006) on the protection of civilians in armed conflict, which reaffirms inter alia the provisions of paragraphs 138 and 139 of the 2005 United Nations World Summit outcome document [...][50]

---

47 S/RES/1674 (2006), 28 April 2006, p. 2.

48 See e.g. S/PV.5319, p. 8; S/PV.5703, p. 9; S/PV.5898, p. 12.

49 See for a detailed record S/PV.5703.

50 S/RES/1706 (2006), 31 August 2006, p. 1.

When taking the floor after the vote on the resolution, the representatives of Argentina, Ghana and Tanzania pointed at the responsibility of the international community to protect the civilian population in Darfur.[51]

In resolution 1814 (2008) concerning the situation in Somalia, the Security-Council:

> Reaffirms its previous resolutions 1325 (2000) on women, peace and security, and 1674 (2006) and 1738 (2006) on the protection of civilians in armed conflict and stresses the responsibility of all parties and armed groups in Somalia to take appropriate steps to protect the civilian population in the country, consistent with international humanitarian, human rights and refugee law, in particular by avoiding any indiscriminate attacks on populated areas [.][52]

When presenting the Report of the Secretary-General to the Security Council, the Special Representative of the Secretary-General in Somalia, Ahmedou Ould-Abdallah, made reference to the responsibility to protect and its adoption at the World Summit and argued that the international community had a clearly mandated responsibility to become involved in a country where there are widespread violations of human rights and humanitarian law.[53] Notwithstanding these references to the responsibility to protect during the briefing, the resolution repeated wording used as well for other country situations, where the responsibility to protect had not been invoked during the debate.[54]

The agreement in the Summit Outcome Document on the responsibility to protect did not succeed in creating a momentum for a consensus on addressing more systematically situations of genocide, war crimes and crimes against humanity. On the contrary, the close connection established with the protection of civilians became a liability for the operationalization of the responsibility to protect for several reasons.

First, the concept of the protection of civilians is both broader and narrower than the responsibility to protect. It is broader as far as it includes all violations of human rights and humanitarian law of a large number of the civilian population affected by armed conflict, while the responsibility to protect is limited to particular categories of crime. It is narrower as it limits the attention to violations occurring in armed conflict, while genocide and crimes against humanity could as well be committed outside such situations.

Second, the protection of civilians is linked to the broader idea of rights-based humanitarian action as a new approach to address human suffering.

[51] See for a detailed record S/PV.5519.

[52] S/RES/1814 (2008), 15 May 2008, p. 5.

[53] See S/PV.5858.

[54] See e.g. S/RES/1856 (2008), p. 2; S/RES/1834 (2008), p. 1.

Therefore, the humanitarian principles of humanity, neutrality and independence apply to the concept and result in a difficult challenge on the ground to 'securing the protection of civilians that is demanded in law from all those responsible for enforcing these laws'.[55] It is already a challenge for humanitarian agencies to encourage states and individuals to meet their humanitarian responsibilities while applying humanitarian principles. The responsibility to protect is based on the consensus that the international community must not remain neutral in situations, where genocide, war crimes and crimes against humanity might occur. Both approaches seem to be incompatible.

Third, neither statements of the Under-Secretary-Generals for Humanitarian Affairs, the reports of the Secretary-General, nor the statements of member states indicate a clear conceptual understanding of the relationship between the protection of civilians and the responsibility to protect. Instead, member states differ significantly in their understanding of the content of the Summit Outcome Document and the role of the Security Council in operationalizing the agreement.[56] Therefore, there is a risk that some members of the Council will explore this link in favour of limiting the discussions on responsibility to protect to the context of the protection of civilians and, in particular, to the responsibilities to prevent and to rebuild rather than the question of non-consensual military action. The Secretariat risks perpetuating this tendency through assisting the Council in its discussions without clearly distinguishing the responsibility to protect from the concept of protection of civilians in armed conflict.

While little is known about the reasons for the Security Council to consider the responsibility to protect in one particular country-related resolution but not another, when read in conjunction with the statements during the discussions on the protection of civilians and other thematic discussions, some conclusions can be drawn.[57]

The lack of unity has prevented the Council so far from applying the responsibility to protect on a specific country situation. At the same time, those member states trying to further the agreement in the Summit Outcome Document consider its application on a specific country situation important

---

[55] Hugo Slim and Luis Enrique Eguren, *Humanitarian Protection, A Guidance Booklet*, p. 19.

[56] In addition, there is a difference in understanding between France and the United Kingdom, i.e. the main supporters of the responsibility to protect. While the latter's approach is based on an interpretation of the Summit Outcome Document, the former appears to reintroduce the 'devoir d'ingerence'. See e.g. Press Release SC/9454, 24 September 2008.

[57] See for details on references to the responsibility to protect during thematic discussions of the Security Council Ekkehard Strauss, *The Emperor's New Clothes*, pp. 54-56.

for any progress on operationalization. Therefore, it did not come as a surprise that the United Kingdom has tried to introduce references to the responsibility to protect in resolutions under its lead. However, at the same time, these resolutions did not reflect more than the minimum consensus within the Council: the consideration of the responsibility to protect in the context of the protection of civilians and only within the limits of the exact wording of the Summit Outcome Document. In this regard, the wording of resolutions 1674, 1706 and 1814 shows a regressive tendency within the Council to include references to the responsibility to protect. Resolutions 1706 and 1814 referred to resolution 1674 only in the context of the protection of civilians rather than as a self-standing and cross-cutting consideration on the whole situation in Darfur and Somalia. Only resolution 1706 contains an explicit reference to the Summit Outcome Document. This analysis is supported by an example of draft resolutions where wording related to the responsibility to protect was deleted upon request of some Council members.[58] In December 2008, the Security Council Ad-hoc Working Group on conflict prevention and resolution held a meeting on the responsibility to protect with a view to contribute to the ongoing debate, which could initiate the beginning of a dialogue on the role of the Council in contributing to the implementation of the agreement in the World Summit Outcome.[59]

In December 2006, the Human Rights Council decided to dispatch a High-Level Mission to assess the human rights situation in Darfur and the needs of the Sudan in this regard.[60] Even though the responsibility to protect was not invoked during the discussion,[61] the High-Level Mission determined that international humanitarian and human rights law was the most appropriate framework for addressing the central issue of the effective protection of civilians in Darfur and decided 'to employ an analysis drawn from the responsibility to protect'.[62] The Mission argued that Sudan joined in the adoption of the

[58] The draft e.g. of resolution 1769 (2007), dated 30 July 2007, contained a reference to the World Summit Outcome document following the title of resolution 1674 (2006) listed in para. 4 of the preamble, see S/RES/1769 (2007), 31 July 2007, p. 1.

[59] See for details Security Council Ad Hoc Working Group On Conflict Prevention And Resolution In Africa, Meeting on "Responsibility to Protect", Chairman Summary, available at http://www.globalr2p/pdf/related/ChairmanSummaryArria.pdf

[60] See for details *Report on the Fourth Special Session of the Human Rights Council*, A/HRC/S-4/5, 22 January 2007.

[61] See United Nations Press Release, 'Human Rights Council opens special session on Darfur', 12 December 2006; 'Special session of Human Rights Council on Darfur continues General Debate', 12 December 2006.

[62] *Report of the High-Level Mission on the situation of human rights in Darfur pursuant to Human Rights Council decision S-4/101*, A/HRC/4/80, 9 March 2007, p. 2.

World Summit Outcome, explicitly accepting the responsibility to protect. In addition, Sudan ratified numerous human rights treaties and signed political agreements that, according to the Mission, together with national legislation and policies, 'underpin this responsibility'.[63]

When reviewing Sudan's action regarding the responsibility to protect, the Mission noted the pattern of large-scale attacks in Darfur and observed that they were characterized by a coordination of operations between Sudanese armed forces and government-supported militia and by grave violations of human rights and humanitarian law. With regard to the well-known pattern of rape of women around Internally Displaced persons (IDP) camps, the Mission concluded that little has been done to diminish the threat or investigate cases reported. Furthermore, the Mission reported large-scale arbitrary arrests of Darfurians and torture, inhuman and degrading treatment by National Security and Military Intelligence.[64] With regard to the violations of economic, social and cultural rights, the Mission found that the widespread displacement and the massive destruction of villages, property and lands has limited further access to food and water, which was further hampered by the obstruction of humanitarian access and a general shrinking of humanitarian space.[65]

The Mission reviewed the international community's responsibility to protect, starting with the activities of the Security Council, including the International Commission of Inquiry on Darfur and the passing of key resolutions. The list included action by other United Nations bodies and agencies such as the Human Rights Council, OHCHR, treaty-bodies and humanitarian organizations as well as action by the African Union. The Mission concluded that as important as these steps may have been, they have not proven adequate in ensuring effective protection on the ground and gross violations of human rights and humanitarian law continued across the region.[66]

Based on an assessment of the most pressing needs in Darfur and previous recommendations by different human rights mechanisms that remained unimplemented, the Mission concluded that the Government of Sudan has manifestly failed to protect the populations of Darfur from large-scale international crimes and has itself orchestrated and participated in these crimes. As such, the obligation of the international community to exercise its responsibility to protect had become evident and urgent.[67]

[63] Ibid., para. 19.
[64] Ibid., para. 38.
[65] Ibid., para. 54.
[66] Ibid., para. 67.
[67] Ibid., para. 76.

When the High-Level Mission presented its Report, controversy erupted about the legitimacy of its findings and the cooperation by the Government of Sudan, since the Mission had not been able to enter Sudan. The application of the responsibility to protect was not discussed in any detail.[68] Finally, the members of the Council agreed to 'take note' of the report of the High-Level Mission which allowed the controversy about its findings and recommendations to prevail without preventing the adoption of a decision. The Human Rights Council decided to convene a group of seven mandate holders to work with the Government of Sudan on the implementation of the different resolutions and recommendations by human rights mechanisms on the situation in Darfur.[69]

The Expert Group agreed to identify the obstacles to the implementation of previous resolutions and to prioritize recommendations and define reachable steps that are tangible for the victims in the short and medium term.[70] Based on the documentation examined, the Group identified four priority areas, i.e. human rights protection, humanitarian access, accountability and justice, and monitoring of implementation of recommendations. For each priority area, the experts selected a number of recommendations, identified steps that could be considered indicators for their implementation and assessed the length of time, between three and twelve month, needed for their implementation. The respective matrix was shared with the Government of Sudan, which agreed with a substantial number of recommendations although it remained unclear sometimes what specific steps it would undertake for their implementation.[71]

---

[68] The representatives of the UK and Canada referred to the responsibility to protect in their statements as an argument for the need for the Council to agree on concrete measures on Darfur, see United Nations Press Release, 'Human Rights Council discusses report of High-Level Mission on Situation of Human Rights in Darfur', 16 March 2007.

[69] Resolution 4/8, Follow-up to decision S-4/101 of 13 December adopted by the Human Rights Council at its fourth special session entitled "Situation of human rights in Darfur", 30 March 2007, see *Report to the General Assembly on the Fourth Session of the Human Rights Council*, A/HRC/4/123, 12 June 2007, p. 18.

[70] *Report on the situation of human rights in Darfur prepared by the group of experts mandated by Human Rights Council resolution 4/8 presided by the Special Rapporteur on the situation of human rights in the Sudan and composed of the Special Representative of the Secretary-General for children and armed conflict, the Special Rapporteur on extrajudicial, summary or arbitrary executions, the Special Representative of the Secretary-General on the situation of human rights defenders, the Representative of the Secretary-General on the human rights of internally displaced persons, the Special Rapporteur on the question of torture and the Special Rapporteur on violence against women, its causes and consequences*, A/HRC/5/6, 8 June 2007, para. 7.

[71] Ibid., para. 11.

In its interim report, the Expert Group noted certain discrepancies between information provided by the Government of Sudan and other sources. The Group concluded that it was not in a position to report that clear impact on the ground had been identified so far and deplored that certain short-term recommendations were not addressed by the Government of Sudan at all.[72] In its final report, the Expert Group highlighted that the process of cooperative engagement with the Government of Sudan worked well in procedural terms, but few recommendations had been fully implemented or have had any tangible impact on the ground. Several recommendations that had been prioritized as short-term and could have been implemented within three months, as they did not require lengthy administrative processes or additional resources, had not been implemented. The Group recommended that the Human Rights Council continued the process of review in accordance with the time frames and indicators for assessing implementation as developed by the Group.[73]

In its consideration of the report, the Human Rights Council adopted without a vote a resolution acknowledging the efforts of the Government of Sudan to implement the recommendations and expressing concern that the implementation of many recommendations has not been fully completed.[74] The text of the resolution was a political compromise that has to be read in conjunction with the resolution extending the mandate of the Special Rapporteur on the situation of human rights in Sudan, in which the Special Rapporteur was requested, inter alia, to ensure effective follow-up and to foster the implementation of the remaining short-term and medium-term recommendations identified in the first report of the Group of Experts.[75] While the European Union did not succeed in extending the mandate of the Group of Experts, the African Group 'respected the specific desires of countries to get support and, thus was encouraging the extension of the mandate'.[76]

---

[72] *Interim report on the situation of human rights in Darfur prepared by the group of experts mandated by the Human Rights Council*, A/HRC/6/7, 22 September 2007.

[73] *Final report on the situation of human rights in Darfur prepared by the group of experts mandated by Human Rights Council resolution 4/8 presided by the Special Rapporteur on the situation of human rights in the Sudan and composed of the Special Representative of the Secretary-General for children and armed conflict, the Special Rapporteur on extrajudicial, summary or arbitrary executions, the Special Representative of the Secretary-General on the situation of human rights defenders, the Representative of the Secretary-General on the human rights of internally displaced persons, the Special Rapporteur on the question of torture and the Special Rapporteur on violence against women, its causes and consequences*, U.N.-Doc. A/HRC/6/19 of 28 November 2007.

[74] A/HRC/6/L.51, 13 December 2007.

[75] A/HRC/6/L.50, 13 December 2007.

[76] Sameh Shoukry (Egypt), as reflected in United Nations Press Release, 'Human Rights Council extends mandates of Experts on the Internally Displaced Persons, Sudan and the Freedom of Religion and Belief', 14 December 2007.

Using the indicators and timelines developed by the Group of Experts, the Special Rapporteur provided a comprehensive assessment of the Government's activities to implement short-term and medium-term recommendations and their impact reported from the ground to the ninth session of the Human Rights Council.[77] During the interactive dialogue with the Special Rapporteur, Sudan, Egypt on behalf of the African Group, Algeria and Cuba expressed their opposition to an extension of the mandate.[78] After intense negotiations between the European Union and the African Group, the Human Rights Council extended the mandate of the Special Rapporteur for six month after passages quoting from the report of the Special Rapporteur had been deleted from the text.[79] The Special Rapporteur was requested to further ensure the follow-up on the implementation of the remaining recommendations of the Group of Experts.

The attempt of the High-Level Mission to apply the responsibility to protect to the human rights situation in Darfur constitutes a very important example for the opportunities related to this approach. Even though its methodology was not set out in detail, it appears that an assessment of the situation could be made based on reports submitted to or by other United Nations entities, such as the Independent Inquiry Mission to Darfur and the regular reports by United Nations Missions and experts. In its follow-up, the Expert Group set an important precedent for the definition and application of measures of short-term, medium-term and long-term prevention in situations of ongoing large-scale violence, their timelines and possible indicators. Many of the recommendations could be adapted easily to other situations of imminent or ongoing large-scale violence with the alleged involvement of the Government.

At the same time, the Human Rights Council proved to be too weak as a body to carry through the full implementation of its recommendations. In addition to unity it lacked any effective sanctions it could have applied. Therefore, for the responsibility to protect to be applicable, other United Nations organs, in particular the Security Council and the Secretary-General need to support the implementation of such recommendations by integrating them into their own work. The continuum of measures within the responsibility

[77] *Report prepared by the Special Rapporteur on the situation of human rights in the Sudan on the status of implementation of the recommendations compiled by the Group of Experts mandated by the Human Rights Council in resolution 4/8 to the Government of the Sudan pursuant to Human Rights Council resolution 6/34*, A/HRC/9/13/Add.1, 2 September 2008.

[78] United Nations Press Release, 'Special Rapporteur on Situation of Human Rights in Sudan presents report to Human Rights Council', 16 September 2008.

[79] See for details A/HRC/9/L.2/Rev.1, 24 September 2008.

to protect requires a joint approach without sharp edges in order to avoid situations falling only within a particular mandate.

Plucking the Bird - the Possible Legal Content of the Responsibility to Protect

In the following, the agreement on the responsibility to protect in the Summit Outcome Document will be reviewed for its possible legal content deriving from references to existing legal obligations.

The Possible Scenario for the Application of the Responsibility to Protect

For this review, it should be recalled that the responsibility to protect was developed as a response to the lack of Security Council action regarding the situation in Kosovo that generated a more general debate about the gap between legality and legitimacy.[80] In other words, it sought to resolve the question of how to react to gross and systematic violations of human rights, if States continued to claim that humanitarian intervention was violating their sovereignty. Secretary-General Kofi Annan summarised the challenges for the United Nations as follows:

> The inability of the international community in Kosovo to reconcile these two equally compelling interests - universal legitimacy and effectiveness in defence of human rights - has revealed the core challenge to the SC and the UN as a whole in the next century: to forge unity behind the principle that massive and systematic violations of human rights - wherever they may take place - should not be allowed to stand.[81]

On the basis of the history of the responsibility to protect and the institutional practice of principal organs of the United Nations to date, it can be concluded that the responsibility to protect would apply to exceptional situations where there has been serious violations of human rights and humanitarian law, and such violations were either imminent or already ongoing. Some members of the ICISS argued that Iraq was a possible case for the application of the responsibility to protect in the late 1980s and early 1990s, but that the situation

[80] Independent International Commission on Kosovo, *Kosovo Report* (Oxford, 2000).

[81] Kofi Annan, Two Concepts of Sovereignty, Address to the 54th Session of the General Assembly, reprinted in: United Nations (ed.), *The Question of Intervention: Statements by the Secretary-General of the United Nations Kofi Annan*, (New York, 1999), p. 39 et seq.

in Iraq at the time of the US-led invasion in 2003 did not meet the responsibility to protect threshold. Gareth Evans considered the situations in Burundi and Macedonia excellent examples for how the preventive dimension of the responsibility to protect would have worked, while he cautioned to characterise other cases of human rights violations or conflict in this context.[82] Later he added Darfur, Kenya, Sri Lanka and Zimbabwe as situations where the responsibility to protect had prima facie application.[83] He illustrated the exceptional character of these situations by arguing that the International Crisis Group identified about 70 different country situations where deadly conflict took place or was about to take place, including violations of human rights and humanitarian law, but only ten to twelve would qualify for the application of the responsibility to protect.[84]

The approach of the responsibility to protect sought to generate a consensus on the most effective response in cases of large-scale killing, ethnic cleansing and crimes against humanity. In order to create this consensus, the responsibility to protect could not be extended across the range of human rights violations and internal conflicts just because they might deteriorate into international crimes in the long-term. However, the criteria and indicators for the exceptional character of such a situation and the application would remain vague and open to political determinations. Situations at risk of conflict and human rights violations would already be known to the international community, but member states might not agree on an exceptional risk, in particular in the case of genocide, war crimes, ethnic cleansing and crimes against humanity. As the cases from the past suggest, most likely the United Nations will be involved already to some extent through, for example, a country team, a humanitarian presence, technical cooperation projects, or the mandates of human rights treaty bodies and special mechanisms of the Human Rights Council. The situation might as well be considered already within the agenda of the Security Council or the General Assembly.

[82] Gareth Evans, 'From Humanitarian Intervention to the Responsibility to Protect', Keynote Address to Symposium on Humanitarian Intervention, University of Wisconsin, Madison, 31 March 2006, available at http://www.crisisgroup.org/home/index.cfm?id= 4521&l=1.

[83] Gareth Evans, *The Responsibility to Protect, Ending Mass Atrocity Crimes Once and For All*, (Washington D.C., 2008), pp. 71-78.

[84] See Gareth Evans, 'Responsibility to Protect in 2007: Five Thoughts for Policy Makers', Presentation to Panel Discussion on The Responsibility to Protect: Ensuring Effective Protection of Populations under Threat of Genocide and Crimes Against Humanity, United Nations, New York, 13 April 2007.

Existing Legal Obligations to Prevent and Punish Genocide, War Crimes, Crimes Against Humanity, and Ethnic Cleansing

Responsibility means being 'legally or morally obliged to take care of something or to carry out a duty' or being 'liable to be blamed for loss or failure'.[85] In international law, responsibility is the corollary of obligation. The ICISS developed the responsibility to protect as a guiding principle for the international community that rested on a wide range of legal obligations and political responsibilities.[86] Furthermore, as discussed above, the negotiation history of the Summit Outcome Document revealed that 'responsibility' was meant not to include a particular legal obligation, but to rest on existing international law. The relevant legal obligations to prevent and punish genocide, war crimes, crimes against humanity and ethnic cleansing have been reviewed already in detail elsewhere.[87] However, in the following, the main legal obligations that may apply to enacting or obliging states and the international community to uphold the responsibility to protect will be considered.

The International Court of Justice has identified an extensive body of customary international law applicable in international armed conflicts which is codified in The Hague Regulations and the four Geneva Conventions, and in the main provisions of the Additional Protocol I to the Conventions.[88] While the extent of customary international law applicable in non-international armed conflicts is less certain, a minimum includes the provisions of common Article 3 to the four Geneva Conventions – the obligation to treat humanely all persons taking no active part in hostilities. Further provisions derive from the Additional Protocol II to the Conventions. According to the Study on Customary International Humanitarian Law by the International Committee of the Red Cross, many of the customary rules applicable in international armed conflict are also applicable in non-international armed conflict.[89] On the one hand, war crimes include serious violations of human rights and humanitarian law such as wilful killing, torture or inhuman treatment, rape,

---

[85] *The Oxford English Dictionary*, (Oxford University Press 2008).

[86] ICISS Report, p. XI.

[87] See e.g. Ekkehard Strauss, *The Emperor's New Clothes*, pp. 28-32.

[88] Advisory Opinion on the legality of the Threat or Use of Nuclear Weapons, ICJ Reports (1996) 226, at p. 257; Protocol Additional to the Geneva Conventions of 12 August 1949, and Relating to the protection of Victims of Non-International Armed Conflicts.

[89] Jean-Marie Henckaerts/ Louise Doswald-Beck, *Customary International Humanitarian Law*, (Cambridge, 2005), pp. 457- 475. See for details Larry Maybee/ Benarji Chakka, *Custom as Source of International Humanitarian Law*, (ICRC New Delhi, 2006).

forced prostitution or forced pregnancy, subjecting detainees to mutilation, or medical or scientific experiments and enlisting and using child soldiers. On the other hand, some crimes merely refer to violations of the conduct of war or the proportionality of means employed for military purposes, such as launching attacks which cause excessive loss of life or injury in relation to the anticipated military advantage, employing weapons, projectiles and material and methods of warfare which are of a nature to cause superfluous injury or unnecessary suffering. With a view to the particular application envisioned for the responsibility to protect, it would be important to identify those war crimes falling outside of the scope of relevant obligations.

Today, crimes against humanity are deemed to be part of international jus cogens and, thus, constitute non-derogable rules of international law.[90] So far, states have not drafted a specialised international convention as a source for obligations to prevent and punish crimes against humanity. However, this category of crimes has been included in the statutes of the ICTY, the ICTR and the Special Court for Sierra Leone[91] and their status has been considered extensively by these courts. Similar to the obligations related to the protection from genocide and war crimes, states must ensure that their organs and officials do not commit crimes against humanity. To this end, states must not condone or tolerate any policy of widespread or systematic attacks against the civilian population by their organs or officials and prevent the commission of crimes against humanity by others within their jurisdiction. Beyond their organs and officials, states must not instruct, direct nor exercise overall control over groups or individuals to commit crimes against humanity. In addition, states must not aid or assist other states to commit crimes against humanity through, for example, supplying weapons in the knowledge that they are being used for this purpose.[92]

The term ethnic cleansing has no immediate legal significance. However, different practices constituting the act of ethnic cleansing, such as the destruction of houses, crops or wells, widespread sexual violence or killings, can be qualified as grave breaches of the Geneva Conventions, war crimes, crimes against humanity and, in certain circumstances, even genocide. The

---

[90] Lauri Hannikainen, *Peremptory Norms (jus cogens) in International Law* (Helsinki, 1988), pp. 596-600.

[91] See article 2 of the Statute of the Special Court for Sierra Leone, *Report of the Secretary-General on the establishment of a Special Court for Sierra Leone*, Enclosure, S/2000/914, 4 October 2000, p. 21 et seq.

[92] See for details Haenkerts/ Beck, supra, customary rule of international humanitarian law no. 140.

breaches of international humanitarian law closely aligned to the practice of ethnic cleansing are deportation and forcible transfer.[93] The term ethnic cleansing among the listed crimes allows a more factual than legal assessment of events on the ground that should be explored more systematically for its capacity to provide an entry point for the application of the responsibility to protect.[94]

The particular importance of the crime of genocide for possible United Nations action in situations of massive and serious violations of human rights or humanitarian law derives from the Advisory Opinion of the International Criminal Court on Reservations to the Convention on the Prevention and Punishment of the Crime of Genocide of 1951 in which the Court held that the provisions of the Convention express pre-existing customary international law and obligations erga omnes.[95] Furthermore, the Court held that the norm prohibiting genocide constitutes jus cogens and, thus, was binding upon all States regardless of their ratification or signature or the Convention.[96] In its judgment in the case of Bosnia and Herzegovina v. Serbia and Montenegro the International Court of Justice identified specific obligations of States to prevent and punish genocide.[97] The Court held that while one of the most effective ways to prevent criminal behaviour was to criminalise and punish it effectively, the obligation to prevent genocide was of a free standing nature. The obligation had a scope beyond the duty to punish and beyond the right to call on the competent organs of the United Nations to take appropriate action. The Court found that states themselves were also under the obligation not to commit genocide. The obligation to prevent was not a duty of result, but of conduct. It involved positive obligations.[98] The Court distinguished between the criminal act, which is committed by individuals entailing individual accountability, and the obligation of the state under international law to

[93] See article 7, para. 1, of the Rome Statute of the International Criminal Court.

[94] Evans, *The Responsibility to Protect*, pp. 12-13.

[95] Advisory Opinion on Reservations to the Genocide Convention, ICJ Reports 1951, p. 23 et seq.

[96] The Court confirmed its earlier statements of 1951 and 1996 in the judgement of 6 February 2006 in the case of Armed Activities on the Territory of the Congo (New Application 2002) (Democratic Republic of the Congo vs. Rwanda), General List No. 126, para. 64.

[97] Case Concerning the Application of the Convention on the Prevention and Punishment of the Crime of Genocide (Bosnia and Herzegovina v. Serbia and Montenegro), Judgement of 26 February 2007, General List No. 91.

[98] Case Concerning the Application of the Convention on the Prevention and Punishment of the Crime of Genocide (Bosnia and Herzegovina v. Serbia and Montenegro), Provisional Measures Order, ICJ Reports 1993, 22, para. 45.

prevent and punish.[99] Failure to meet the latter obligation is not a criminal act, but a breach of an international obligation. On this basis, the ICJ switched from a criminal standard of proof 'beyond reasonable doubt' to 'proof at a high-level of certainty', when considering the violation of this obligation.[100] A state could only be held responsible for breaching its obligation to prevent if the wrongful act, genocide, was actually committed, even though the duty itself began at a time when the State knew, or should have known, that there was a serious risk of genocide occurring.

The obligation to prevent genocide as an obligation erga omnes raises the question of a general obligation of states to prevent the commission of acts contrary to certain norms of general international law. The obligation to prevent genocide could ultimately form the basis of providing guidance on the existence and scope of a duty or responsibility to protect.[101] Following the jurisprudence on genocide, the practice of human rights treaty bodies and the experience of national protection mechanisms, it would be possible to establish a list of underlying legal obligations and corresponding action that had to be implemented in order to meet the obligation to prevent or halt genocide.[102]

Possible Collective Obligation to Protect Populations from Genocide, War Crimes, Crimes Against Humanity and Ethnic Cleansing

Many commentators have argued that paragraph 138 in the Summit Outcome Document created an additional obligation for the international community to protect civilian populations from the listed crimes. They consider the responsibility to protect a new international norm separate from existing legal obligations that, ultimately, rested upon the obligation to prevent and punish genocide.[103] According to this line of argument, the responsibility to protect

99 See Mark Gibney, 'Genocide and State Responsibility', *Human Rights Law Journal*, Volume 7 (2007), No. 4, p. 760 et seq.

100 Judgement of 26 February 2007, para. 210.

101 Andrea Gattini, 'Breach of the Obligation to Prevent and Reparation Thereof in the ICJ's Genocide Judgement', *European Journal of International Law*, Volume 18 (2007), No. 4, p. 695 et seq.

102 See for details Ekkehard Strauss, *Prävention von Menschenrechtsverletzungen als Aufgabe internationaler Organisationen. Rechtsgrundlagen und inhaltliche Ansätze* (Berlin, 2001), pp. 315-326.

103 See on the following in particular Louise Arbour, 'The Responsibility to Protect as a duty of care in international law and practice', Trinity College Dublin, 23 November 2007.

discarded the notion of a right to intervene by configuring a permanent duty to protect individuals against abusive behaviour. The onus of protection fell by default on the international community and encompassed a continuum of prevention, reaction and commitment to rebuild. This norm was engaged from the earliest stages of a situation of concern. The most serious implication of this norm was that all States were now burdened with the responsibility to take action and could no longer claim a discretionary right to intervene.

However, apart from the lack of any evidence in the negotiation history of an intent to be legally bound by the agreement on the responsibility to protect, the different nature of international human rights and humanitarian law has to be taken into consideration, when interpreting the Summit Outcome Document. Arguably, while only the former intends to establish rights and duties in the relationship between individuals and the state, the latter intends to introduce standards of state behaviour that could lead to individual criminal responsibility in cases of 'grave breaches'.[104]

The concept of a collective obligation of the international community set out in paragraph 138 of the Summit Outcome receives some support from the International Law Commission (ILC) Draft Articles on State Responsibility, which determine that where the responsible state commits a serious breach of a peremptory norm of international law, other states have an obligation to cooperate to bring an end to that serious breach through lawful means.[105] The cooperation might be organised through an international organization, such as the United Nations, or through collective cooperation outside the United Nations. Furthermore, states must not recognise as lawful any situation created by the serious breach in question, neither formally nor through any act from which recognition would be implicit. However, the ILC itself recognises that this aspect of its Draft Articles may go further than current customary law.[106]

Therefore, if the responsibility to protect established a collective legal obligation of the international community, failure to implement would entail some legal sanctions. One could argue that inaction of the Security Council in

[104] See for details Rene Provost, *International Law and Human Rights Law* (Cambridge, 2003).

[105] ILC Draft Articles 40 and 41, A/CN.4/L.600, 11 August 2000. See for the drafting history and main content James Crawford, *The International Law Commission's Articles on State Responsibility: Introduction, Text and Commentaries*, (Cambridge University Press, 2002).

[106] Commentary to Draft Article 2, para. (3), *Yearbook of the International Law Commission*, 2001, vol. II, Part Two.

the face of genocide, war crimes, crimes against humanity and ethnic cleansing could trigger some kind of right or even duty of member states to protest, but it is difficult to imagine how non-compliance of a political body could practically be challenged. The wording of the Summit Outcome Document is hardly precise enough to allow holding member states accountable for their inaction in the Security Council. Instead, the requirement of manifest failure may be used as a means to challenge the legality and timing of collective action by the international community.[107] The establishment of a duty of the Security Council to intervene in fulfilment of a responsibility to protect the population in a state would require an agreement on objective criteria for the establishment of manifest failure and the requirement of collective action in order to make it more difficult for member states not to act. However, member states did not include in the Summit Outcome Document the criteria for collective military action that was developed by the ICISS to focus international decision making and make it more predictable.[108]

The United Nations Charter provides for the requirements and limits of collective action against a member state in articles 39 and 40. The practice of the Security Council on these provisions has led to controversy about the lawfulness of the use of armed force for the prevention or discontinuation of massive violations of human rights in a member state.[109] There is still no consensus among member states recognizing such interventions as a general exception to the prohibition laid down in article 2 (4) of the Charter. Thus, the risk for a split between legality and legitimacy will remain in cases where the Security Council refuses to stop violations of human rights and humanitarian law on the basis of article 39 and 42 of the Charter. A practice of the Security Council to consider internal conflict a threat to international peace and security has been established since the conflict in Palestine in 1948 and Congo in 1961.[110] Since the end of the Cold War, it seems to be widely accepted that extreme violence within a state can give rise to Chapter VII enforcement action. The Security Council has established a consistent practice with regard to Angola, Burundi, Liberia, Rwanda, Sierra Leone, Somalia, and Timor Leste in this regard. Therefore, the Security Council could build its application of the responsibility to protect on its practice that a threat to the

---

[107] Stahn, Responsibility to Protect, p. 106.

[108] Ingo Winkelmann, "Responsibility to Protect": Die Verantwortung der Internationalen Gemeinschaft zur Gewährung von Schutz, in: Pierre-Marie Dupuy et al. (eds.), *Völkerrecht als Wertordnung*, (Kehl, 2006), pp. 449, 458.

[109] Randelzhofer, Article 2 (4), in: Simma, *The Charter of the United Nations*, para. 53.

[110] S/RES/54, 15 July 1948; S/RES/161B, 21 February 1961.

peace can be considered in cases of mass atrocities, if it was in some way linked to a present or impending armed conflict or other destabilization of the security situation of a country or region.[111]

The Bird in the Hand: The Added Value of the Responsibility to Protect

While it is well understood that international law is considered the strongest form of international obligations among states, the history of failure to prevent genocide, war crimes and crimes against humanity during the last sixty years, notwithstanding applicable peremptory norms of international customary law to prevent and punish such crimes, suggests that not much would be added by an additional norm as such. Instead, the responsibility to protect should build the framework for targeted action as a viable political option for the United Nations in order to protect victims of exceptionally grave violations of human rights and humanitarian law. Thus, the responsibility to protect would provide the framework for preventing and halting crimes that fall under the jurisdiction of the International Criminal Court. In this understanding, the responsibility to protect would make existing legal obligations more effective and overcome the fundamental deficit in their application as established in numerous reports: lack of resources and lack of political will.[112] Under the leadership of the Secretary-General, these two gaps have to be addressed.

According to article 99 of the Charter, the Secretary-General is entitled to take political initiative in the maintenance of international peace and security. This provision is considered to form the legal basis for every political activity of the Secretary-General, which he performs on his own initiative.[113] The right to initiative of the Secretary-General covers 'any matter', while the right of member states is limited to 'any dispute or situation'. Article 99 of the Charter provides the legal basis for leadership of the Secretary-General on the operationalization of the responsibility to protect within the Secretariat, agencies and funds. The provision has been interpreted earlier as requiring the Secretary-General to collect and evaluate a broad range of information. With regard to the prevention of genocide, war crimes and crimes against humanity, the

---

[111] Frowein/ Krisch, Article 39, in: Simma, supra, para. 21.

[112] See e.g. *Report of the Independent Inquiry into the actions of the United Nations during the 1994 genocide in Rwanda*, S/1999/1257, 16 December 1999, p. 3.

[113] Fiedler, Article 99, in: Simma, supra, para. 5.

Security Council requested the Secretary-General to bring to its attention cases of serious violations of international law, including human rights and humanitarian law and on potential conflicts arising from ethnic or religious conflicts.[114] It has been concluded earlier that, on this basis, the Secretary-General is entitled to develop the necessary methodologies and resources in order to fulfill this task.

It can be assumed that increased political commitment of member states would result in providing the United Nations with the required resources.[115] However, the discussion in the Security Council, whether genocide was taking place in Darfur or Rwanda, which replaced the discussion about timely and decisive action, indicated that member states no longer share a common legal or ethic consensus on the basis of which they could rally behind collective action to halt or prevent mass atrocities under all circumstances. Discussions among member states in the General Assembly and in the Human Rights Council reflect a general trend of gradual withdrawal from international standards on human rights, democracy and the rule of law offering exceptional security or economic circumstances as justification. It has become increasingly difficult to agree on joint action in support of human rights and justice in extreme cases, overriding national souvereignty.[116] According to their own accounts, the Permanent Representatives of Slovenia and Bangaldesh respectively referred to universal values when leading negotiations on the responsibility to protect on behalf of the President of the General Assembly during the preparations of the World Summit 2005. A common consensus within the United Nations on the legal nature of the responsibility to protect would require first an agreement on a minimum of values, positions and measures.[117]

In order to fill the commitment gap, the United Nations require an ethically determined vision for its role in cases of genocide, war crimes and crimes against humanity, and concrete concepts for its implementation. The development of such concepts requires a clear separation from national interests and must be result oriented. The Secretary-General could promote such an ethic

[114] S/RES/1366 (2001), 30 August 2001.

[115] After the Second World War, $ 1,448 million had been invested in the reconstruction of Germany through the Marshall Plan between 1948 and 1951. It is estimated that the US-led war in Iraq costs $ 12 billion per month.

[116] See for a detailed analysis from the perspective of the European Union Richard Gowan/ Franziska Brantner, *A Global Force for Human Rights? An Audit of European Power at the UN*, European Council on Foreign Relations, 2008.

[117] See for the following Hans Küng, *Projekt Weltethos* (München 1990).

by calling on Member States to be more transparent on the implementation of their obligations to prevent genocide, war crimes and crimes against humanity at the national level in concrete situations as well as applying these standards consequently within his own responsibility.

Political commitment to act has depended often on the availability of acceptable options for action. In this regard, it is important to develop a list of measures that could be proposed to different organs of the United Nations with a view to defining the continuum of steps which lays at the heart of the responsibility to protect. An example for such a continuum can be found in the reports of the Expert Group on Darfur, created by the Human Rights Council.[118] In this regard, it is important to include steps on the implementation of the responsibility to rebuild, when presenting the continuum. The consideration of military intervention as 'ultimate measure' often leads to leaving the continuum incomplete. Over time, preventive measures can move from the short-term to the mid- and long-term based on causal links established through experience in country situations rather than abstract considerations on the relationship between security, development and human rights.[119]

The implementation of the responsibility to protect populations from genocide, war crimes and crimes against humanity will require cooperation of different mandates, institutions and organs within the United Nations. In summary, activities within four broad areas seem to be required: (1) consultations with Member States to establish the ethic vision of the role of the United Nations in situations of mass atrocities, (2) consultations with departments, agencies and funds to develop the repertoire of measures short of military intervention, (3) monitoring the approximately ten country situations which might qualify for the application of the responsibility to protect with a view to establish capacities and needs, and (4) consultations with DPKO and Member States on ways to establish military capacities for operations in situations of imminent or ongoing genocide, war crimes and crimes against humanity, limited to the physical protection of groups at risk.

---

[118] *Final report on the situation of human rights in Darfur prepared by the group of experts mandated by the Human Rights Council in its resolution 4/8,* supra.

[119] The example of hate-speech is a case in point. After the ICTR had established the causal link between the activities of Radio Milles Collines and the subsequent genocide, governments accepted hate-speech as an early-warning indicator for genocide. See Nahamana, Barayagwiz and Ngeze, Case No. ICTR-99-52-T.

The availability of practical tools will support unity among member states to apply the responsibility to protect on a case-by-case basis. Ultimately, this practice, based on a common ethic vision supporting the agreement that such action was required to meet existing legal obligations, might lead to a new norm of international customary law.

The Responsibility to Protect and the Use of Force: Building Legality?

*Jutta Brunnée and Stephen J. Toope**

Abstract

The rapid rise of the responsibility to protect provides us with a unique opportunity to consider the impact of a decade or so of determined norm entrepreneurship. The responsibility to protect has not yet become a binding norm of international law, and in this article we examine what factors are holding back or promoting this development. We draw on an 'interactional' account of international law, which focuses on three inter-locking elements. First, legal norms are social norms and as such they are connected to social practice – they must be grounded in shared understandings. Second, what distinguishes law from other types of social ordering is not so much form or pedigree, as adherence to specific criteria of legality. When norm creation meets these criteria and, third, is matched with norm application that also satisfies the legality requirements, international law will have legitimacy and generate a sense of commitment among those to whom it is addressed. After highlighting key steps in the norm building process so far, from the 2001 report of the International Commission on Intervention and State Sovereignty to the General Assembly debate in 2009, we offer a brief sketch of our theoretical framework, and employ it to examine the trajectory of the responsibility to protect norm, concluding with an assessment of its current and potential status as binding law. Although the responsibility to protect, including its potential for the collectively authorized use of force, is increasingly supported by globally shared understandings, the norm falls short on several of the legality criteria. Furthermore, given the inconsistent practice on protective use of force, no practice of legality can be said to have evolved. Proponents of the norm face a lot of hard work ahead.

Keywords

responsibility to protect, use of force, international law, legal norms, Lon Fuller, constructivism

---

* Metcalf Chair in Environmental Law, Faculty of Law, University of Toronto; and President and Vice-Chancellor, University of British Columbia, respectively. This paper draws upon Jutta Brunnée, 'International Law and Collective Concerns: Reflections on the Responsibility to Protect', in Tafsir Malick Ndiaye and Rüdiger Wolfrum (eds.), *Law of the Sea, Environmental Law and Settlement of Disputes* (Leiden: Martinus Nijhoff, 2007) and Jutta Brunnée and Stephen J. Toope, *Legitimacy and Legality in International Law: An Interactional Account* (Cambridge: Cambridge University Press, 2010).

Introduction

In July 2009, the United Nations General Assembly held two and a half days of plenary debate on the report that Secretary General Ban-Ki Moon had submitted on 'Implementing the Responsibility to Protect.'[1] The interventions of 94 speakers, representing a remarkable 180 member states and groups of states, as well as two observers,[2] suggest that support for the responsibility to protect is growing around the world. Only a small number of states continue directly to challenge the emerging norm; most are looking to refine it, especially as it relates to the use of force.

Our focus in this article is on this latter, most controversial, dimension of the responsibility to protect. As outlined in the *2005 World Summit Outcome* document [*Summit Outcome*], the responsibility to protect encompasses the possibility of collective military action through the Security Council. Such action would be taken on a 'case by case basis,' and only as a last resort, 'should peaceful means be inadequate and national authorities manifestly fail to protect their populations' from 'genocide, war crimes, ethnic cleansing and crimes against humanity.'[3] However, many states remain concerned about the parameters for military action, asking who would determine whether a situation involves one of the specified international crimes; calling for criteria to guide decisions on whether and when the use of force is appropriate; and suggesting that permanent members of the Security Council not use their veto power in cases involving the responsibility to protect.

The relatively rapid rise of the responsibility to protect provides us with a unique opportunity to consider the impact of a decade or so of determined norm entrepreneurship. Most observers today conclude that the responsibility to protect has not yet become a binding norm of international law.[4]

---

[1] *Implementing the Responsibility to Protect*, Report by the Secretary-General, UN Doc. A/63/677, 12 January 2009; http://daccessdds.un.org/doc/UNDOC/GEN/N09/206/10/PDF/N0920610.pdf?OpenElement.

[2] See Global Centre for the Responsibility to Protect, *Implementing the Responsibility to Protect- The 2009 General Assembly Debate: An Assessment*, August 2009, p. 1; at http://www.responsibilitytoprotect.org/index.php/component/content/article/35-r2pcs-topics/2522-report-by-the-global-centre-for-r2p-the-2009-general-assembly-debate-an-assessment-.

[3] UN General Assembly, *2005 World Summit Outcome*, UN Doc. A/RES/60/1 (24 October 2005), para.138-139; at www.un.org/summit2005/documents.html.

[4] See e.g. Max W. Matthews, 'Tracking the Emergence of a New International Norm: The Responsibility to Protect and the Crisis in Darfur', *B.C. Int'l Comp. L. Rev.* 31: 137-152 (2008); Carsten Stahn, 'Responsibility to Protect: Political Rhetoric or Emerging Legal Norm?' *American Journal of International Law* 101: 99-120 (2007).

We share this assessment, but we believe it is important to take a closer look at what it would take for the responsibility to protect to become legally binding, and what factors are holding back or promoting this development. In our view, a standard assessment of whether or not the norm has become binding as customary or treaty law is not sufficiently nuanced to reveal the salient dynamics.

In this article, we offer a more finely grained perspective on how international law is created and maintained. We draw on what we call an 'interactional' account of international law, which focuses on three inter-locking elements.[5] First, legal norms are social norms and as such they are connected to social practice – they must be grounded in shared understandings. Second, what distinguishes law from other types of social ordering is not so much form or pedigree, as adherence to specific criteria of legality: generality, promulgation, non-retroactivity, clarity, non-contradiction, not asking the impossible, constancy, and congruence between rules and official action. When norm creation meets these criteria and, third, is matched with norm application that also satisfies the legality requirements, international law will have legitimacy and generate a sense of commitment among those to whom it is addressed.

We first highlight key steps in the norm building process so far, beginning with the 2001 report of the International Commission on Intervention and State Sovereignty (ICISS) and leading to the debate in the General Assembly in 2009. Next we offer a brief sketch of our theoretical framework, employing it to examine the trajectory of the responsibility to protect norm. We consider the evolution of shared normative understandings, especially concerning the protective use of force through the Security Council. We then assess the collective action aspects of the emerging norm against the requirements of legality. We conclude that the norm as it is currently articulated fares poorly on several of the abovementioned criteria, notably on generality, clarity, consistency, constancy, and congruence between norm and practice. The continuing debates about appropriate parameters for recourse to force can, we suggest, be read as debates about strengthening the legality of the responsibility to protect, and hence about whether to build it into a legal norm or not. By implication, they are also debates about the extent to which political decision-making in the Security Council should yield to considerations of legality.

[5] Brunnée and Toope, *Legitimacy and Legality in International Law*. (The book offers a novel account of how international legal obligation is created and maintained, drawing together the work of legal theorist, Lon Fuller, and insights of constructivist International Relations scholars.)

The Norm Building Process

The surprisingly rapid evolution of the concept of responsibility to protect over the last fifteen years or so was driven in large part by extraordinarily grave human rights crises in certain countries, as well as by the failure of the world community to intervene to prevent further atrocities from being perpetrated upon civilian populations. The Rwandan genocide encapsulates this failure,[6] but it is not a unique case, as the horrors of Cambodia, Zaire/Congo, Liberia, Sierra Leone and, most recently, Darfur attest. These crises prompted the African Union to provide, in its Constitutive Act of 2000, for a right of the Union to intervene in a member state in the case of 'grave circumstances, namely: war crimes, genocide and crimes against humanity.'[7] However, the immediate impetus for concerted global efforts to elaborate the concept of responsibility to protect was arguably provided by the NATO intervention in Kosovo in 1999. Kosovo raised again the fundamental questions whether or not a norm of humanitarian intervention existed and, if so, who could invoke it, only the Security Council or individual states?[8] In justifying the intervention, most of the NATO states (with the exception of Belgium) side-stepped these thorny issues and refused to posit a general norm of humanitarian intervention. Instead, the NATO partners argued a 'moral duty' or a 'necessity' to act.[9]

Shortly after Kosovo, Canada, one of the participants in the NATO intervention, promoted the creation of an independent International Commission on Intervention and State Sovereignty.[10] In its articulation of the responsibility to protect,[11] the ICISS sought to transcend the intractable debates

---

[6] See, e.g., Michael Barnett, *Eyewitness to a Genocide: the United Nations and Rwanda* (Ithaca, NY: Cornell University Press, 2002).

[7] African Union, *Constitutive Act* (2000), Article 4 (h); at http://www.africa-union.org/root/au/AboutAu/Constitutive_Act_en.htm

[8] Independent International Commission on Kosovo, *The Kosovo Report - Conflict, International Response, Lessons Learned* (2000).

[9] See e.g. Javier Solana, Secretary-General of NATO, Press Statement, NATO Press Release (1999) 040, 23 March 1999, at www.nato.int/docu/pr/1999/p99-040e.htm. Or see *Declaration by the [UK] Parliamentary Under Secretary of State*, reprinted in *British Yearbook of International Law* 69: 593 (1998) (claiming that "in the exceptional circumstances of Kosovo it was considered that the use of force would be justified on the ground of overwhelming humanitarian necessity, without Security Council authorization").

[10] International Commission on Intervention and State Sovereignty (ICISS), *The Responsibility to Protect,* December 2001; at www.dfait-maeci.gc.ca/iciss-ciise/report-en.asp.

[11] Of course, the idea of a responsibility to protect can be traced further back. See e.g. Olivier Corten and Pierre Klein, *Droit d'ingérence ou obligation de réaction? Les possibilités d'action visant*

surrounding a 'right' to humanitarian intervention.[12] The responsibility to protect was not about rights at all, but about duties. The primary duty holder was the sovereign state, which should offer security and protection to its own citizens. The report emphasized the overriding importance of a wide spectrum of proactive measures and assistance to local governments in discharging their responsibility to protect, as well as the importance of non-military forms of pressure.[13] But it also offered a set of carefully crafted threshold criteria for recourse to collective military action where there was 'serious and irreparable harm occurring to human beings, or imminently likely to occur.' The triggering events identified by ICISS were 'large scale loss of life ... with genocidal intent or not, which [was] the product either of deliberate state action, or state neglect, or inability to act, or a failed state situation,' or 'large scale ethnic cleansing.'[14] In cases where a state failed in its protective obligation, or where it was the perpetrator of massive human rights violations, collective military action could be authorized internationally to protect victims within a sovereign state.[15] To guide decisions on military action, the ICISS outlined a 'just cause threshold,' a set of 'precautionary principles,' and criteria for 'right authority.'[16] While the Commission identified the Security Council as the most appropriate body for decisions on military intervention for human protection purposes, it warned that individual states might feel compelled to act in the face of inaction by the Council.[17] To avoid Council paralysis, the ICISS report recommended that permanent members agree to a 'code of conduct' for the use of the veto in relation to actions needed to stop or avert a significant humanitarian crisis.[18]

The ICISS report was released shortly after the attacks of 11 September 2001. The sensitivity of its recommendations was further increased by the

---

à assurer le respect des droits de la personne face au principe de non-intervention (Brussels: Bruylant, 1992); and Francis M. Deng, et al, *Sovereignty as Responsibility: Conflict Management in Africa* (Washington, D.C.: Brookings Institution Press, 1996).

[12] See e.g. J. L. Holzgrefe and Robert O. Keohane (eds.), *Humanitarian Intervention: Ethical, Legal and Political Dilemmas* (Cambridge: Cambridge University Press, 2003).

[13] ICISS, *The Responsibility to Protect*, pp. 19-31.

[14] Ibid., pp. XII and 32.

[15] ICISS envisaged that this authorization should be sought first through the Security Council, and in case of an inability or refusal to act, through a revitalization of the "Uniting for Peace" resolution of the General Assembly or through a reference to a regional organization. See ibid., pp. XII-XIII, and 47-51.

[16] Ibid., at XII. For a detailed discussion, see Jutta Brunnée and Stephen J. Toope, 'Slouching Towards New Just Wars: International Law and the Use of Force after September 11', *NILR* LI: 363-392 (2004).

[17] ICISS, *The Responsibility to Protect*, pp. XII and 47-55; XIII.

[18] Ibid., pp. XIII and 51.

intervention in Iraq, led by the United States and Britain without authorization by the Security Council.[19] By November 2003, the worry over the 'lack of agreement amongst Member States on the proper role of the United Nations in providing collective security' prompted then UN Secretary General, Kofi Annan, to convene the High-level Panel on Threats, Challenges and Change.[20] The panel's report was published in December 2004.[21] With respect to the use of force for the protection of people, the report drew extensively on the ICISS recommendations. The panel endorsed 'the emerging norm that there is a collective international responsibility to protect, exercisable by the Security Council authorizing military intervention as a last resort.'[22] The High-level Panel's invocation of triggering events for collective military action was similar to that of ICISS: 'genocide and other large scale killing, ethnic cleansing or serious violation of international humanitarian law.'[23] In addition, the panel emphasized that guidelines on the use of force, whether to address external threats to states' security or grave humanitarian crises within states, could 'maximize the possibility of achieving Security Council consensus,' and 'minimize the possibility of individual Member States bypassing the Security Council.'[24] The criteria, which the panel suggested should be 'embodied in declaratory resolutions of the Security Council and the General Assembly,' were: seriousness of threat, proper purpose, last resort, proportional means, and balance of consequences.[25]

In his response to the High-level Panel report, the Secretary-General highlighted the question whether states have the right, or even obligation, to use force protectively to rescue citizens from genocide or comparable crimes against humanity.[26] This move from a list of grave human rights violations to the concept of international crime as the trigger for action represented a crucial shift in emphasis. Another shift was equally important. Whereas both

---

[19] See Jutta Brunnée and Stephen J. Toope, 'The Use of Force: International Law After Iraq', *International & Comparative Law Quarterly* 53: 785-806 (2004).

[20] *In Larger Freedom: Towards development, security and human rights for all*, Report by the Secretary-General, UN Doc. A/59.2005, 21 March 2005, para. 76; at www.un.org/largerfreedom/contents.htm.

[21] *A More Secure World: Our Shared Responsibility*, Report of the High-level Panel on Threats, Challenges and Change, UN Doc. A/59/565 (29 November 2004); at http://www.un.org/secureworld.

[22] Ibid., para. 203.

[23] Ibid.

[24] Ibid., para. 206.

[25] Ibid., paras. 207-208. Of course, these criteria harken back to traditional just war theory. See Brunnée and Toope, 'Slouching Towards New "Just Wars"'.

[26] *In Larger Freedom*, paras. 122 and 125.

ICISS and the High-level Panel had left open the possibility of unilateral action where the Security Council could not act in the face of crisis, the Secretary-General's response stressed that the task was 'not to find alternatives to the Security Council as a source of authority but to make it work better.'[27] To this end, the Secretary-General endorsed ICISS' and the High-level Panel's calls for criteria for intervention, emphasizing that the formulation and application of such criteria was essential to achieve legitimacy amongst states and global public opinion for any Council action.[28]

The concept of the responsibility to protect found its way into the 2005 *Summit Outcome* document, with a number of further shifts in emphasis. The *Summit Outcome* stresses that the responsibility is first and foremost one of individual states to protect their populations. In addition, the link between the concept and international crimes was solidified, as states are only called upon to protect their populations from 'genocide, war crimes, ethnic cleansing and crimes against humanity.'[29] Responsibilities are posited also for 'the international community,' but these are to 'encourage and help States' to exercise their responsibility to protect their own people, and to 'use appropriate diplomatic, humanitarian and other peaceful means…to help protect populations.'[30] Finally, under Chapter VII of the UN Charter, collective action can be taken through the Security Council, on a 'case by case basis' and 'should peaceful means be inadequate and national authorities manifestly fail to protect their populations' from the listed international crimes.[31] The member states did not take up the earlier recommendations to develop more specific criteria for military intervention. The document contains only a charge to the General Assembly to 'continue consideration of the responsibility to protect… and its implications, bearing in mind the principles of the Charter and international law.'[32]

The story we have traced so far is one of concerted norm entrepreneurship by a variety of actors. The norm was articulated and progressively refined in

[27] Ibid., para 126.

[28] Ibid.

[29] UN General Assembly, *Summit Outcome*, para.138. 'Ethnic cleansing' is not established as a distinct international crime, but it is included in the concepts of 'genocide,' 'extermination,' 'deportation or forcible transfer of population' and 'enforced disappearance' as set out *inter alia* in Arts. 6 and 7 of the Rome Statute of the International Criminal Court, UN Doc. A/CONF.183/9 (17 July 1998). Depending upon factual circumstances, it might also be a 'war crime.'

[30] *Summit Outcome*, paras. 138 and 139.

[31] Ibid., para 139.

[32] Ibid., para 139.

expert reports and in a detailed response by Secretary General Annan. Various non-governmental organizations have also been active in promoting the norm.[33] Through the negotiations of the *Summit Outcome*, the norm was brought into the inter-state arena, where it was cast into terms that resonated more explicitly with existing international law. And, as we are about to detail, the Security Council, the Secretary General, Ban Ki-Moon, and the General Assembly have since all shown support for the responsibility to protect as articulated in the *Summit Outcome*.

The UN Security Council, in 2006, adopted a resolution that endorsed the concept as expressed in the *Summit Outcome*,[34] and another invoking it with respect to the situation in Darfur.[35] In January 2009, the Secretary-General released a major report on 'Implementing the responsibility to protect.' The report elaborates on the 'three pillar' approach (primary responsibility of each state; international responsibility to build capacity to that end; and collective responsibility to act if national authorities are manifestly failing to protect) that underlies the *Summit Outcome*'s articulation of the responsibility to protect.[36] The report stresses the strict focus of the concept on genocide, war crimes, ethnic cleansing, and crimes against humanity, which firmly anchors the responsibility to protect in existing international law.[37] It also emphasizes that the responsibility to protect, as endorsed by the General Assembly in 2005, 'is an ally of sovereignty, not an adversary' and 'seeks to strengthen sovereignty, not weaken it.'[38] Hence we see a strong emphasis on the primary responsibility of each state and the international responsibility to support states in their efforts to protect their populations.[39] As well we have a conceptualization of 'sovereignty as responsibility' and an effort to distance the responsibility to protect from the controversial notion of a 'right' to humanitarian intervention.[40]

---

[33] See e.g. the recently launched (28 January 2009) *Responsibility to Protect-Engaging Civil Society*, at www.responsibilitytoprotect.org; the *Global Centre for the Responsibility to Protect*, at www.globalcentrer2p.org; the *R2P Coalition*, at www.r2pcoalition.org; and the *Asia-Pacific Centre for the Responsibility to Protect*, at www.r2pasiapacific.org.

[34] See United Nations Security Council Resolution 1674, 28 April 2006, UN Doc. S/RES/1674, para. 4 (reaffirming paras. 138 and 139 of the *2005 Outcome*); at www.un.org/Docs/sc/unsc_resolutions06.htm.

[35] United Nations Security Council Resolution 1706, 31 August 2006, UN Doc. S/RES/1706, preamble (recalling Resolution 1674, as well paras. 138 and 139 of the *2005 Outcome*); at www.un.org/Docs/sc/unsc_resolutions06.htm.

[36] *Implementing the Responsibilty to Protect*, paras. 11 & 12, and 13-66.

[37] Ibid., paras. 2 & 3, and 10 (b).

[38] Ibid., para. 10 (a).

[39] Ibid., paras. 13-48.

[40] Ibid., paras. 7 & 10 (a).

Yet, the Secretary General's report is also clear that 'sovereignty does not bestow impunity' and that there is an international responsibility to 'respond collectively in a timely and decisive manner' when a state is manifestly failing in its protective responsibility.[41] Collective enforcement measures could include targeted sanctions imposed by the Security Council, or indicated by the General Assembly under the 'uniting for peace' procedure.[42] However, as the report underscores, 'the responsibility to protect does not alter, indeed it reinforces, the legal obligations of Member States to refrain from the use of force except in conformity with the Charter.'[43] Coercive military action is reserved for 'extreme cases' and must be authorized by the Security Council 'or by regional or subregional arrangements under Article 53 [of the Charter], with the prior authorization of the Security Council.'[44]

The report offers two further observations in relation to possible military action, both of which pick up on recommendations in some of the earlier reports. First, the Secretary General's report urges the five permanent members of the Security Council to 'reach a mutual understanding' to refrain from employing or threatening the use of their veto power 'in situations of manifest failure to meet obligations relating to the responsibility to protect, as defined in paragraph 139 of the Summit Outcome.'[45] And, second, the report asks UN members to 'consider the principles, rules and doctrine that should guide the application of coercive force,' pointing out that 'the credibility, authority and hence effectiveness of the United Nations in advancing the principles relating to the responsibility to protect depend, in large part, on the consistency with which they are applied.'[46]

The Secretary General's report was presented to the UN General Assembly in July 2009. A formal plenary debate ensued, during which speakers representing all parts of the world took the floor to offer the views of member states and various groupings of states. Taken together, these interventions suggest gathering support for the responsibility to protect, especially when compared to the debates leading up to the 2005 Summit. During these earlier debates, strong support for the concept came largely from Northern countries, such as the members of the EU, Australia, Canada, Iceland, Japan, New Zealand and Norway. Several states, including some Arab states, Cuba, Iran, Pakistan, Venezuela, and Vietnam, rejected the responsibility to protect as an

41 Ibid., paras. 11 (c), 54.
42 Ibid., paras. 56-57, 63.
43 Ibid., para. 3.
44 Ibid., para. 56.
45 Ibid., para. 61.
46 Ibid., para. 62.

unacceptable intrusion into state sovereignty. Others, including Malawi speaking on behalf of the Group of African States, were more open to the idea, but were concerned that collective security might come to be defined in terms of the responsibility to protect and serve as a pretext for intervention. Yet others, such as Colombia, Indonesia, Mexico, were non-committal and called for more discussion. Some, such as Bulgaria, Chile, Russia, Tanzania, insisted on the role of the Security Council.[47] The Non-Aligned Movement (NAM) of states expressed 'its rejection of the so-called "right" of humanitarian intervention, which has no basis either in the UN Charter or in international law,' observed 'the similarities between the new expression 'responsibility to protect' and 'humanitarian intervention,' and wished 'to carefully study and consider further the expression 'responsibility to protect' and its implications on the basis of the principles of non-interference and non-intervention as well as the respect for territorial integrity and national sovereignty of States.'[48]

The 2009 plenary debate appeared to get off to a rocky start, with the President of the General Assembly, Miguel d'Escoto Brockmann of Nicaragua, prefacing the session in a 'concept note' that questioned the international community's responsibility to protect. The note echoed many of the abovementioned criticisms of the concept, warning that '[c]olonialism and interventionism used responsibility to protect arguments,' emphasizing that the responsibility to protect is solely 'a sovereign's obligation,' and arguing that the use of force provisions of the Charter would not 'cover responsibility to protect unless the situation is a threat to international peace and security.'[49] The concerns expressed by the President, especially relating to the use of force, were taken up by some participants in the plenary debate. A large majority of member states, however, were supportive of the responsibility to protect as articulated in the 2005 *Summit Outcome*, which, according to China, had provided a 'prudent description' of the concept.[50] Several areas of convergence and points of concern are worth highlighting for present purposes.

---

[47] See *Review of the Secretary-General's Report "In larger freedom: towards development, security and human rights for all"*, 6-8 April 2005, Verbatim Records A/59/PV.85 | A/59/PV.86 | A/59/PV.87 | A/59/PV.88 | A/59/PV.89 | A/59/PV.90; at www.un.org/ga/59/hl60_plenarymeeting.html#debates

[48] *Comments of the Non-Aligned Movement on the Observations and Recommendations Contained in the Report of the High-level Panel on Threats, Challenges and Change*, 28 February 2005, paras. 14-15; at www.un.int/malaysia/NAM/Positionpaper280205.doc.

[49] Office of the President of the General Assembly, *Concept note on responsibility to protect populations from genocide, war crimes, ethnic cleansing and crimes against humanity*, 17 July 2009; at http://responsibilitytoprotect.org/R2P%20programme%20%20concept%20note%20(3).pdf.

[50] See 'More than 40 Delegates Express Strong Scepticism, Full Support as General Assembly Continues Debate on Responsibility to Protect', UN GA/10849, 24 July 2009; at http://www0.un.org/News/Press/docs/2009/ga10849.doc.htm.

Almost sixty member states echoed the Secretary General's view that the responsibility to protect was anchored in existing international law.[51] For example, Sweden, speaking on behalf of the European Union and several other states, expressed its support for the Secretary General's report, and indicated that the obligations inherent in 'responsible sovereignty' were 'firmly embedded in international law.'[52] Russia noted that the language of the *Summit Outcome* was 'in line with the Charter,' while Sri Lanka indicated that 'paragraphs 138 and 139 of the 2005 World Summit Outcome were based on pre-existing norms.'[53] Jamaica, speaking for the members of the Caribbean Community (CARICOM), indicated that, notwithstanding the need to achieve consensus on the responsibility to protect, 'existing international law bestows on all of us the responsibility to prevent the crime of genocide, war crimes, ethnic cleansing and other mass atrocities.'[54]

Many states, including the members of the European Union, Benin, Costa Rica, Lesotho, Qatar, and Timor-Leste, also agreed that mass atrocities within states could constitute threats to international peace and security, such as to enable the Security Council to take collective action.[55] The United States noted, in very general terms, that collective action would '[o]nly rarely, and in extremis, ... include the use of force.'[56] In any case, as with all operational aspects of the responsibility to protect, including action through the Security Council, responsibility could arise only in relation to the international crimes identified in the *Summit Outcome*.[57]

---

[51] See Global Centre for the Responsibility to Protect, *Implementing the Responsibility to Protect*, p. 5.

[52] See Statement on behalf of the European Union by H.E. Mr. Anders Lidén, Ambassador and Permanent Representative of Sweden to the United Nations, General Assembly Debate on the Responsibility to Protect, 23 July 2009; at http://www.responsibilitytoprotect.org/EU_Sweden_ENG.pdf.

[53] See 'Delegates Weigh Legal Merits of Responsibility to Protect Concept as General Assembly Concludes Debate - Speakers Question its Effectiveness in Face of Security Council Veto Power', UN GA/10850, 28 July 2009; http://www0.un.org/News/Press/docs/2009/ga10850.doc.htm.

[54] See Statement of Raymond Wolfe to the UN General Assembly, 28 July 2009; at http://www.responsibilitytoprotect.org/CARICOM%20Statement%20on%20R2P%20as%20amended-Final.pdf.

[55] Global Centre for the Responsibility to Protect, *Implementing the Responsibility to Protect*, p. 5.

[56] Remarks by Ambassador Rosemary A. DiCarlo, at a General Assembly Debate on the Responsibility to Protect, in the General Assembly Hall, July 23, 2009, at http://responsibilitytoprotect.org/USA_ENG-1.pdf.

[57] Global Centre for the Responsibility to Protect, *Implementing the Responsibility to Protect*, p. 6.

Not surprisingly, the role of the Security Council and questions concerning recourse to military measures were nonetheless among the most controversial topics of debate. Cuba, Iran, North Korea, Pakistan, Sudan, and Venezuela echoed earlier NAM statements connecting the responsibility to protect to the controversial notion of humanitarian intervention, and warned against the risks of abuse of the concept to justify illegal interventions in states.[58] And while a majority of states emphasized the difference between the collective security-based third pillar of the responsibility to protect and (unilateral) humanitarian interventions, several of the states that were supportive of the third pillar also raised concerns about the parameters of collective action. For example, Switzerland queried who would decide whether a situation involved one of the triggering crimes,[59] while the CARICOM statement sought clarification of the circumstances in which the Security Council could resort to Chapter VII measures.[60] Several states endorsed the Secretary General's proposal that consideration be given to guidelines on the use of force. For example, the Philippines considered it 'imperative that policies, principles and rules be laid out in cases where coercive force is applied in extreme situations.'[61] Finally, a sizeable number of member states expressed concerns about Security Council paralysis, and endorsed the Secretary General's recommendation that the veto power not be used in situations involving the responsibility to protect.[62] Some statements linked progress on the responsibility to protect to calls for reforms for a more representative Security Council.[63]

On 14 September 2009, the General Assembly adopted a short and carefully balanced resolution on the responsibility to protect.[64] In it, it reaffirmed its respect for the principles and purposes of the UN Charter, recalled

---

[58] Ibid., p. 7.

[59] Déclaration de S.E. M. Peter Maurer, Représentant permanent de la Suisse auprès des Nations Unies – La mise en oeuvre de la responsabilité de protéger, 23 July 2009, p. 3; at http://www.responsibilitytoprotect.org/Switzerland_ENG_FR.pdf.

[60] See Statement of Raymond Wolfe, p. 2.

[61] Statement of H.E. Mr. Hilario G. Davide, Jr., Ambassador Extraordinary and Plenipotentiary, Permanent Representative of the Republic of the Philippines to the United Nations in New York – Thematic Debate on the Report of the Secretary-General on Implementing The Responsibility to Protect (A/63/677), 23 July 2009, p. 4; at http://www.responsibilitytoprotect.org/Philippines_ENG.pdf.

[62] See Global Centre for the Responsibility to Protect, *Implementing the Responsibility to Protect*, p. 6-7 (counting 35 states, including Costa Rica, Denmark, Malaysia, New Zealand, Norway, Rwanda, Singapore, South Africa, and Timor-Leste).

[63] Ibid. (citing CARICOM, Gambia, India, and Sudan).

[64] UN General Assembly Resolution 63/308, UN Doc. A/RES/63/308, 7 October 2009; at http://daccessdds.un.org/doc/UNDOC/GEN/N09/513/38/PDF/N0951338.pdf?OpenElement.

paragraphs 138 and 139 of the *Summit Outcome*, takes note of the Secretary General's report on implementation and the 'timely and constructive' debate on the report, and decides 'to continue its consideration of the responsibility to protect.' Revealing the reservations that some states continue to have, it was only the removal of the words 'with appreciation' from the operative paragraph taking note of the Secretary General's report that enabled adoption of the resolution by consensus.[65]

The Responsibility to Protect: A Legal Norm?

Drawing together insights from constructivist approaches to international relations and the legal theory of Lon Fuller we have developed a novel account of how international law is made, maintained or destroyed.[66] Constructivism helps us illuminate how norms emerge and shape social interaction.[67] Fuller's work provides a set of criteria of legality that enables us to identify legal norms and explain their distinctive influence.[68] Briefly put, our three-pronged framework posits that legal norms arise when shared normative understandings evolve to meet the criteria of legality, and become embedded in a practice of legality. Given the central importance of social and legal interaction in this framework, we refer to it as an 'interactional' account of international law. As we hope to illustrate in the following assessment of the responsibility to protect norm, our framework provides a richer understanding of the emergence and evolution of legal norms than an analysis that uses the customary or treaty status of a norm as the sole indicator of legality.

Shared Understandings

Social norms can only emerge when they are rooted in an underlying set of shared understandings supporting first the need for normativity, and then any particular norms that shape behavior.[69] Shared understandings are collectively held background knowledge, including social norms and practices. But these

---

[65] See Global Centre for the Responsibility to Protect, *Summary of Statements on Adoption of resolution RES A/63/L80 Rev. 1 – September 2009*; at http://globalr2p.org/media/pdf/GCR2P_Summary_of_Statements_on_Adoption_of_Resolution_on_R2P.pdf.

[66] See Brunnée and Toope, *Legitimacy and Legality in International Law*.

[67] See Ian Hurd, 'Constructivism', in Christian Reus-Smit and Duncan Snidal, eds., *The Oxford Handbook of International Relations* (Oxford: Oxford University Press, 2008).

[68] See Lon L. Fuller, *The Morality of Law*, Rev. ed. (New Haven: Yale University Press, 1969).

[69] Brunnée and Toope, *Legitimacy and Legality in International Law*, Ch. 2.

understandings do not simply exist, or spontaneously emerge as agreed among actors. They are *shared* understandings precisely because they are intersubjective – generated and maintained through social interaction. On the one hand, actors generate and promote particular understandings, whether through norm entrepreneurship or through the work of epistemic communities. Shared understandings then emerge, evolve or fade through processes of social learning.[70] On the other hand, once in existence, shared understandings shape how actors perceive themselves and the world, how they form interests and set priorities, and how they make arguments or evaluate others' arguments.[71]

It is noteworthy that the norm building process surrounding the responsibility to protect has been sensitive to the need for widely shared understandings, and to the fact that such understandings must be cultivated over time.[72] Textual representations of a norm can be helpful in this process, but they cannot themselves be taken as reflective of a social norm. It is important, therefore, that the *Summit Outcome* has not been treated as the culmination of the norm building process, but rather as a platform for further normative interaction and deliberation. The Secretary General's report on the implementation of the responsibility to protect clearly reflects the recognition of the need for wider and deeper support for the norm that was delineated in the *Summit Outcome*, as well as for further elaboration and clarification of its meaning. The 2009 General Assembly debate on the Secretary's report provides a window on states' views and so allows, with all due caution, an assessment of the currently shared normative ground. The almost universal participation in the debate, either directly or through endorsement of group statements, is particularly significant in this context.

A full review of the interventions in the debate is beyond the scope of this article. But it is safe to conclude that the understanding of the responsibility to protect that is outlined in paragraphs 138 and 139 of the *Summit Outcome* is shared by a growing number of states from all parts of the world.[73] As we noted earlier in this article, the members of the African Union had endorsed

---

[70] Alexander Wendt, *Social Theory of International Politics* (Cambridge: Cambridge University Press, 1999); Etienne Wenger, *Communities of Practice: Learning, Meaning, and Identity* (Cambridge: Cambridge University Press, 1998).

[71] Emanuel Adler and Steven Bernstein, 'Knowledge in Power: The Epistemic Construction of Global Governance', in Michael Barnett and Raymond Duvall (eds.), *Power in Global Governance* (Cambridge: Cambridge University Press, 2005).

[72] For a detailed discussion, see Ramesh Thakur and Thomas G. Weiss, 'R2P: From Idea to Norm, and Action?' *Global Responsibility to Protect*, 1/1: 22-53 (2009).

[73] Global Centre for the Responsibility to Protect, *Summary of Statements*, pp. 10-11 (detailing the patterns of support in Africa, Asia and Pacific, Latin America and the Caribbean, the Middle East, and Eastern and Western Europe).

the responsibility to protect at a regional level long before its inclusion in the *Summit Outcome*. In the lead-up to the 2005 Summit, they reaffirmed their commitment to the principle in a common position on UN reform.[74] More generally speaking, while concerns about abuses of the concept linger, the number of states that are categorically opposed to its collective action aspects, including use of force through the Security Council as a last resort, appears to be shrinking.[75] It is also noteworthy that the NAM statement offered on the occasion of the debate was considerably softer than the earlier statements of the movement. The statement merely notes 'mixed feelings' about the implementation of the responsibility to protect, and 'concerns' about its possible abuse beyond the four crimes listed in the *Summit Outcome*, 'to legitimize unilateral coercive measures or intervention in the internal affairs of States.'[76] Furthermore, it has been noted that many of the 118 NAM member states 'appeared to break with tradition by not explicitly aligning themselves with the NAM statement.'[77]

The emphasis of the continuing debate appears not to be on challenging the concept of the responsibility to protect as such, but on refining it, especially as it relates to the use of force. Indeed, seen through the lens of our conceptual framework, the proposals in the Secretary General's report, as well as many of the interventions in the General Assembly debate, seem at least in part designed to strengthen the legality of the norm.

The Criteria of Legality

Legal norms are rooted in shared social understandings. Such understandings may be largely procedural in nature, such as rules that govern international institutions or decision-making processes, or they may be more substantive and value-laden, as in the case of the emerging responsibility to protect norm.

---

[74] See African Union (AU), *The Common African Position on the Proposed Reform of the United Nations: The Ezulwini Consensus*, March 7-8, 2005, AU Doc. Ext/EX.CL/2 (VIII).

[75] Cuba, Nicaragua, Pakistan, Sudan, the People's Republic of Korea, and Venezuela are the most vocal of these states. See International Coalition for the Responsibility to Protect, *Report on the General Assembly Debate on the Responsibility to Protect.*, 15 September 2009, pp. 7-8; at http://responsibilitytoprotect.org/ICRtoPGAdebate.pdf.

[76] See Statement by Egypt on behalf of the Non-Aligned Movement, Agenda Item 44 and 107: "Integrated and coordinated implementation of and follow-up to the outcomes of the major United Nations conferences and summits in the economic, social and related fields; Follow-up to the outcome of the Millennium Summit: report of the Secretary- General," p. 1; at http://www.responsibilitytoprotect.org/NAM_Egypt_ENG.pdf.

[77] See Global Centre for the Responsibility to Protect, *Implementing the Responsibility to Protect*, p. 4.

However, shared understandings alone do not make law.[78] Many social norms exist that never reach the threshold of legal normativity. We have already suggested that this threshold is marked by adherence to specific criteria of legality. Lon Fuller set out eight such criteria, which apply to both individual rules and systems of rule-making. Legal norms must be general, prohibiting, requiring or permitting certain conduct. They must also be promulgated, and therefore accessible to the public, enabling actors to know what the law requires. Law should not be retroactive, but prospective, enabling actors to take the law into account in their decision-making. Actors must also be able to understand what is permitted, prohibited or required by law – the law must be clear. Law should avoid contradiction, not requiring or permitting and prohibiting at the same time. Law must be realistic and not demand the impossible. Its requirements of actors must remain relatively constant. Finally, there should be congruence between legal norms and the actions of officials operating under the law.[79]

The responsibility to protect norm as articulated in the *Summit Outcome* addresses some of these legality requirements, but falls short on others. The inclusion of the responsibility to protect in the *Outcome* serves some aspects of the promulgation requirement. While it did not promulgate the norm into law, it did publicize the foundations upon which a legal norm would grow and set the parameters for further normative debate. In turn, the fact that the *Outcome* tied the responsibility to protect to a set of established international crimes speaks to a number of the legality requirements. Compared to the formulations of triggering events in the ICISS and High Level Panel reports, the *Outcome*'s linking of the responsibility to existing legal categories significantly enhances the clarity of the triggering events and scope of the norm.[80]

The linkage also ensures the norm's consistency with established international law – a point that was stressed in the Secretary General's report and by several participants in the Assembly debate – thereby addressing the requirements of non-contradiction and constancy over time. Indeed, individual states' responsibilities to protect their own populations from the listed crimes as well as the international responsibilities to assist and, if necessary, to take collective action through the Security Council, are grounded inter alia in the

[78] Brunnée and Toope, *Legitimacy and Legality in International Law*, Ch. 3.

[79] Colleen Murphy, 'Lon Fuller and the Moral Value of the Rule of Law', *Law and Philosophy* 24: 239-262, pp. 240-241 (2005).

[80] But see Carlo Focarelli, 'The Responsibility to Protect Doctrine and Humanitarian Intervention: Too Many Ambiguities for a Working Doctrine', *J. Confl. & Sec. L.* 13: 191-213 (2008).

law of state responsibility.[81] In limiting the responsibility to protect to 'genocide, war crimes, ethnic cleansing and crimes against humanity,' the *Outcome* tied the responsibility to protect to norms that are widely considered to have both *erga omnes* effect and *jus cogens* status.[82]

If this assessment is correct, much of the responsibility to protect is a specific articulation of the general consequences that international law attaches to the violation of *jus cogens* and *erga omnes* norms.[83] Notably, by virtue of their *erga omnes* effect, states already owe the human rights obligations underlying the responsibility to protect not only to persons under their jurisdiction, but also to all states. By the same token, all states already have a legal interest in the protection of individual states' populations against these grave human rights abuses. In the face of such abuses, all states could invoke the responsibility of the perpetrating state, and could demand that the abuses stop. If the state perpetrating the abuses refuses to comply, all states are further entitled to take 'lawful measures' to compel compliance.[84]

General international law underscores that third states' concerns over extreme human rights abuses within an individual state are not unwarranted interventions in internal affairs, but the legitimate pursuit of collective legal interests. But what of the greatest innovation of the responsibility to protect, the idea that third states not only have legal interests but also legal responsibilities? A closer look reveals that here too the responsibility to protect against 'genocide, war crimes, ethnic cleansing and crimes against humanity' rests on the foundations of the law of state responsibility. In the case of *jus cogens* violations, the law of state responsibility instructs that states are not merely entitled to demand that they stop but are under an obligation to cooperate to bring them to an end.[85] Again, therefore, the responsibility to protect concept makes explicit what international law already requires.

---

[81] See International Law Commission (ILC), Draft Articles on Responsibility of States for Internationally Wrongful Acts, in *Report of the International Law Commission on the Work of Its Fifty-third Session,* UN GAOR, 56th Sess., Supp.No. 10, 43, UN Doc. A/56/10 (2001).

[82] See also Ekkehard Strauss, 'A Bird in the Hand is Worth Two in the Bush – On the Assumed Legal Nature of the Responsibility to Protect', Global Responsibility to Protect 1: 291-323 (2009). (As noted above, however, 'ethnic cleansing' is not a separate international crime, but falls within a number of established categories.)

[83] See generally Christian Tams, *Enforcing Obligations Erga Omnes in International Law* (Cambridge: Cambridge University Press, 2005); and see Ian Scobbie, 'The Invocation of Responsibility for the Breach of 'Obligations under Peremptory Norms of General International Law',' *EJIL* 13: 1201-1220 (2002).

[84] ILC, Draft Articles on Responsibility, Articles 48 & 54.

[85] Ibid., Article 41.

The *Outcome* also tracks the current state of the law on the use of force. It does not seek to introduce any new 'right' – or responsibility – of military intervention for individual states. Rather, it keeps recourse to force firmly in the hands of the Security Council. The document leaves open, however, whether collective action 'in accordance the Charter, including Chapter VII' presupposes that a situation involving the listed crimes must first be found to constitute a threat to international peace and security, whether all such situations would constitute threats to peace and security, or whether the Security Council can intervene whenever a state is 'manifestly failing' to protect their populations. If the determination of a threat to peace and security does remain a threshold requirement, then the responsibility to protect will be tied to a deliberately fluid and broadly political decision-making criterion. It also remains unclear to what extent the Security Council has an obligation to intervene if necessary to protect populations from the listed crimes,[86] a proposition roundly rejected by some key states.[87] The *Summit Outcome*'s reference to 'case-by-case' decisions on the use of force would seem to suggest there is no such obligation. Rather, it maintains space for political assessments and tends to weaken the legality of the responsibility to protect as regards the requirements of generality, clarity and constancy over time. Concerns regarding the generality of the norm are also heightened by the limited membership of the Security Council, and the role of the five permanent members in its decision-making, notably through their veto.

In light of these weaknesses of the responsibility to protect as articulated in the *Summit Outcome*, it is of interest that many of the interventions in the 2009 General Assembly debate raise legality concerns, especially about the use of force element of the responsibility to protect. Furthermore, the main proposals for further development of the principle would all serve to strengthen the legality of the norm. For example, the calls for a more representative Security Council speak to the concern about generality. The Swiss question who would decide whether a crisis situation involved a triggering crime speaks to the clarity requirement, as well as to the delineation between legal and political space. The same is true for CARICOM's request for clarification on the circumstances in which the Security Council could resort to collective

[86] See Stephen J. Toope, 'Does International Law Impose a Duty upon the United Nations to Prevent Genocide?' *McGill Law Journal* 46: 187-194 (2000); and see Louise Arbour, 'The Responsibility to Protect as a Duty of Care in International Law and Practice', *Review of International Studies* 34: 445 (2008).

[87] Notably, the United States took this position during the April 2005 General Assembly debates on Secretary General's *In Larger Freedom* report. See U.N. Doc. A/59/PV.87, p. 23.

action. In turn, the strong emphasis, in the Secretary General's Report and in several states' plenary statements, on the need for guidelines on the use of force underscores the importance of generality, clarity and constancy. Guidelines, such as those proposed by ICISS or the High Level Panel, would significantly enhance the legality of the norm by subjecting case-by-case decisions to over-arching criteria that identify the extreme and exceptional cases to which military intervention should be restricted. They would also highlight cases in which force should in fact be used, and demand a reasoned justification of inaction. Finally, the call for non-use of the veto in cases involving one of the listed crimes is also related to legality considerations. The veto power for the five permanent members undercuts the generality of protective force option, and weakens the potential for consistent decision-making by the Council.

The Practice of Legality

We have not yet addressed the last criterion of legality, the requirement that official action be congruent with existing law. So as to avoid repetition, we will blend our consideration of congruence, as a criterion of legality, into our investigation of the last step in determining the legal force of the responsibility to protect, deciding whether or not the practice of legality supports the existence of a legal norm. If there is no congruence between norm and action, no practice of legality, we will have to conclude that the responsibility to protect has not yet emerged as a legal norm.

Fuller, whose work was preoccupied with national legal systems, emphasized the need for 'reciprocity' between officials and citizens in the creation and sustenance of all law.[88] He illustrated that what is often assumed to be a vertical relationship (of authority and subordination) actually has strong horizontal features,[89] a proposition that makes his work particularly relevant to international law. Reciprocity, in Fuller's conception, means that law-givers must be able to expect that citizens will 'accept as law and generally observe' the promulgated body of rules.[90] However, in order for these rules to be able to guide their actions, they must meet the requirements of legality. Therefore, conversely, citizens must be able to expect that the government will abide by

[88] Fuller, *The Morality of Law.*

[89] Ibid.

[90] Lon Fuller, 'Human Interaction and the Law', in Lon Fuller, *The Principles of Social Order,* Kenneth Winston (ed.) (Durham, N.C.: Duke University Press, 1981), p. 235.

and apply these rules, that the actions of officials will be congruent with posited law, and consonant with the requirements of legality.[91]

The reciprocity that underpins law, then, is deeper than the exchange flowing from the calculation of material interests. When the eight criteria of legality are met, actors will be able to reason with rules because they will share meaningful standards. In international society, the deeper sense of reciprocity that we just described is even more relevant because states are both subjects and lawmakers. To the extent that international law is created without congruence with shared norms and the criteria of legality, neither commitment to law nor a sense of obligation amongst states will be generated. The central insight is that, in international law, the kind of reciprocity that we are speaking of is created and maintained collectively. To be sure, not all members of international society must be engaged in this enterprise. International law can withstand individual defiance so long as a solid majority of actors works to uphold legality. But when explicit rules are unrelated to how states and other international actors actually behave, commitment to law cannot arise or is eventually destroyed.

The fact that reciprocity requires collective effort also serves to underscore why claims to legal 'exceptionalism' by powerful states can be so corrosive. Some states will be actively resentful when confronted with such claims, or with other failures to meet the requirements of legality. This dynamic was well illustrated by the strong reactions to US assertions of a right to preventive self-defence that went beyond the generally accepted bounds of the right to self-defence.[92] The same is true for the 2003 intervention in Iraq by a US and UK-led 'coalition of the willing,' which was tenuously justified on the basis of purported Security Council authorization.[93] The NATO intervention in Kosovo also raised concerns among many states about some states arrogating to themselves a right to intervene outside of the existing rules on the use of force.[94] These examples, all of which strain the legality requirements imposed

[91] Fuller, *The Morality of Law*.

[92] See Jutta Brunnée and Stephen J. Toope, 'The Use of Force: International Law After Iraq', *International & Comparative Law Quarterly* 53: 785-806 (2004). What is more, since the right was tied to unilateral assessment of emerging threats, it ultimately did not contain a rule that could be generally applied. See also Richard B. Miller, 'Justifications of the Iraq War Examined', *Ethics & International Affairs* 22: 43-67 (2008), pp. 52-53 (noting that '[p]reventive war doctrine is not generalizable to situations of parity between states').

[93] See United Nations Security Council Press Release SC 7705, 'Security Council Holds First Debate on Iraq since Start of Military Action; Speakers Call for Halt to Aggression, Immediate Withdrawal', 26 March 2003, at www.un.org/News/Press/docs/2003/sc7705.doc.htm.

[94] See Jules Lobel and Michael Ratner, 'Bypassing the Security Council: Ambiguous Authorizations to Use Force, Cease-Fires and the Iraqi Inspection Regime', *American Journal of International Law* 93: 124-154 (1999) pp. 130-134.

by the existing rules on the use of force, form part of the experience that has led many developing countries to be suspicious of the third pillar of the responsibility to protect.

The considerations inherent in the congruence requirement have obvious salience for the responsibility to protect and the use of protective force through the Security Council. As we have seen, the norm as it currently stands fails on some of the traits of legality that would enhance its ability to guide decision-making. But it also falls short on the congruence requirement. International practice so far has not invoked the responsibility to protect to justify collective recourse to force. Past practice under the banner of protective force (or 'humanitarian intervention') has been notoriously uneven. Hence, many states and other observers do not expect the Security Council to apply the responsibility to protect norm with any consistency. Rather, the expectation is that a body in which powerful states hold veto rights will always produce politically and strategically motivated action and inaction. Indeed, the congruence requirement instructs that it would not be enough to adopt a General Assembly or Security Council resolution that concretizes the collective responsibility to protect through guidelines on the use of force or an undertaking by the permanent members not to exercise their veto. Even if the norm's legality were to be further developed along these lines, the responsibility to protect will not emerge as a global legal norm unless there also emerges a practice that consistently upholds the norm and adheres to the requirements of legality.[95]

Conclusion

The responsibility to protect, including its potential for collective action, is increasingly supported by globally shared understandings. However, the norm falls short on several of the legality criteria that we highlighted in this article, notably on generality, clarity, consistency, and constancy over time. Furthermore, given the inconsistent practice on protective use of force, no practice of legality can be said to have evolved. Nonetheless, the current discourse confirms that the *Summit Outcome* provided an accurate snapshot of the emerging norm, and a well-crafted platform for efforts to build up its

[95] The same applies at a regional level. Observers have noted, for example, that the AU's practice in relation to the responsibility to protect enshrined in its Constitutive Act 'does not reflect a clear commitment' to the norm. See Kwesi Aning and Samuel Atuobi, 'Responsibility to Protect in Africa: An analysis of the African Union's Peace and Security Architecture', *Global Responsibility to Protect* 1: 90-113 (2009), p. 113.

legality. Continuing debates over the parameters for collective action reveal concerted efforts to strengthen the legality of the emerging norm.

If these efforts to promote a legal responsibility to protect were to succeed, decision-making in the Security Council would be significantly affected. Resistance to the further evolution of a legal responsibility to protect is not, therefore, likely to be limited to members of the NAM who fear the erosion of a hard-won sovereignty. The evolution of the responsibility to protect into a legal norm would shrink the space for political assessments in cases involving failures to protect populations against grave crimes, likely prompting some of the veto-holding powers to demur from a hard norm as well. Security Council decisions would have to meet the requirements of the responsibility to protect, and would be measured against the criteria of legality. For better or for worse, efforts to promote the emergence of a collective legal responsibility to protect raise sensitive questions about the role of law and politics in Security Council decision-making. Proponents of the norm face a lot of hard work ahead.

The Responsibility to Protect and International Law

Alex J. Bellamy and Ruben Reike

Abstract
The article evaluates the relationship between the Responsibility to Protect (RtoP) principle and international law. We argue that although the principle is best understood as a political commitment to implement already existing legal commitments, the RtoP is not devoid of legal content as some of its critics claim. The principle contains two sets of legal responsibilities. The first – responsibilities owed by a state towards its own population – are well-established customary principles in international law. The second – responsibilities owed by states to populations in other states – are much less well established. We argue that although RtoP does not in itself create new legal duties, states already have international legal responsibilities that relate directly to the principle's second pillar. Moreover, we identify the emergence of nascent legal thinking which suggests that a wider set of legal duties might emerge in the future.

Keywords
responsibility to protect; international law; genocide convention; war crimes; crimes against humanity; United Nations

At the 2005 World Summit, states unanimously declared that they had a 'Responsibility to Protect' (RtoP) their populations from genocide, war crimes, ethnic cleansing and crimes against humanity and that they 'stood ready' to step in to prevent these crimes and protect endangered populations should the host state manifestly fail to fulfill its protection duties. This commitment was unanimously reaffirmed by the UN Security Council in 2006 (Resolution 1674) and reiterated by an overwhelming majority of states that contributed to the General Assembly's debate in July 2009.[1]

It is widely understood that the relationship between the RtoP principle and international law requires further clarification.[2] On the one hand, a

[1] Global Centre for the Responsibility to Protect, 'Implementing the Responsibility to Protect: The 2009 General Assembly Debate: An Assessment', GCR2P Report, August 2009.

[2] A point recognised by the UN Secretary-General's Special Adviser, Edward Luck, among others. See Edward C. Luck, 'The United Nations and the Responsibility to Protect', *Stanley Foundation Policy Analysis Brief,* August 2008.

number of academics and policy advisers have argued that RtoP represents a new legal norm that provides a basis for legitimising coercive interference in the domestic affairs of states which are unable or unwilling to protect their populations from genocide or mass atrocities. For example, Alicia Bannon argued that 'the [2005 World] Summit agreement strengthens the legal justification for limited forms of unilateral and regional action – including military action – if the United Nations fails to act to protect populations from genocide and other atrocities'.[3] The following year, Stephen John Stedman, a senior advisor to former UN Secretary-General Kofi Annan, argued that Annan's reform agenda for the UN had included, 'a new norm, the responsibility to protect, to legalize humanitarian intervention' and then claimed that the Summit had succeeded in establishing 'a new norm to legalize humanitarian intervention'.[4] Others dispute these views. Indeed, most legal commentators agree that RtoP is not yet an international legal norm because it lacks clarity and has not been appropriately legislated.[5] In addition, Ekkehard Strauss has argued that the General Assembly resolution that gave effect to the global consensus on RtoP in 2005 is a non-binding recommendation for Member States rather than a statement of law. Whilst acknowledging that General Assembly resolutions may provide evidence of customary international law when accompanied by general practice and *opinio juris*, he pointed out that such resolutions cannot create *new* law by themselves.[6] It is also worth noting that at least one prominent international lawyer argues that it is 'dangerous' to conceive RtoP in terms of a legal norm because that would involve redefining sovereignty, enabling self-interested coercive intervention, and expanding the scope for potential intervention.[7]

This article aims to clarify this problematic relationship between RtoP and international law. Overall, it accepts Strauss' view that the World Summit

---

[3] Alicia L. Bannon, 'The Responsibility to Protect: The UN World Summit and the Question of Unilateralism', *The Yale Law Journal*, 115 (2006), p. 1158.

[4] Stephen John Stedman, 'UN Transformation in an Era of Soft Balancing', *International Affairs*, 83/5 (2007), pp. 933 and 938.

[5] Especially Carsten Stahn, 'Responsibility to Protect: Political Rhetoric or Emerging Legal Norm?', *American Journal of International Law*, 101/1 (2007), p. 102.

[6] Ekkehard Strauss, 'A Bird in the Hand is Worth Two in the Bush – on the Assumed Legal Nature of the Responsibility to Protect', *Global Responsibility to Protect*, 1/3 (2009).

[7] See Jose E. Alvarez, 'The Schizophrenias of R2P', Panel Presentation at the 2007 Hague Joint Conference on Contemporary Issues of International Law: Criminal Jurisdiction 100 Years After the 1907 Hague Peace Conference, The Hague, The Netherlands, 30 June 30 2007 p. 12. Available at: http://www.asil.org/pdfs/r2pPanel.pdf.

agreement did not create new law. The RtoP is best understood, therefore, as a political commitment to act upon shared moral beliefs, much of which is embedded in already existing international law.[8] That is not say, however, that RtoP is devoid of legal content. In relation to the legal responsibilities of states the RtoP principle contains two broad sets of commitments. The first involve the state's responsibilities towards its own population. These responsibilities are deeply embedded in existing international law, much of which is considered *jus cogens*. The second set of commitments relate to the responsibility of the international community to take measures to assist states in trouble or to prevent genocide and mass atrocities and/or protect imperiled populations when the host state is manifestly failing to do so. These commitments are much less well defined legally. In relation to this second set of responsibilities, former American Ambassador John Bolton was broadly correct to argue that, unlike the responsibility of the state towards its own population which is legal in nature, the responsibilities of the international community are chiefly moral and political, and therefore not of a legal nature. There is, according to Bolton, therefore a significant difference between the legal quality of the two sets of commitments contained within the RtoP principle.[9] However, Bolton's line of argument is not *entirely* correct and it is possible to identify legal duties to assist states to fulfill their responsibilities. In addition, former UN High Commissioner for Human Rights, Louise Arbour, argues that we can see in the recent International Court of Justice ruling in the *Bosnia vs. Serbia* case an emerging legal duty to prevent genocide. Whilst Arbour's argument may be premature, it points towards an emerging area of legal innovation that may strengthen the application of RtoP over time. In this vein, it is worth noting that the International Law Commission (ILC) is also exploring the question of whether international organisations have relevant legal responsibilities.[10]

This paper proceeds in two main parts. The first briefly sets out the 2005 agreement on RtoP and charts its background. The second focuses on the two sets of legal responsibilities associated with RtoP – those that States have towards their own populations and the legal responsibility of States to address

---

[8] A similar view is expressed by Centre for Conflict Resolution, *Preventing Genocide and the Responsibility to Protect: Challenges for the UN, Africa, and the International Community*, policy advisory group seminar report, 13-15 December 2007.

[9] Letter from John R. Bolton, the representative of the United States of America to the United Nations, to President Ping, president of the UN General Assembly, 30 August 2005.

[10] Third Report on Responsibility of International Organizations, A/CN.4/533, para. 10 (13 May 2005).

situations in other countries – in relation to the four crimes associated with the RtoP.

RtoP: From Idea to Norm

One of the few real achievements of the UN's 2005 World Summit was the adoption of the 'responsibility to protect' (RtoP) principle. As agreed by UN Member States, the RtoP principle rests on three equally important and non-sequential 'pillars'. First, the responsibility of the state to protect its population from genocide, war crimes, ethnic cleansing and crimes against humanity, and from their incitement. Second, the international community's duty to assist the state to fulfill its responsibility to protect. Third, the international community's responsibility to take timely and decisive action, through peaceful diplomatic and humanitarian means and, if that fails, other more forceful means, in a manner consistent with Chapters VI (pacific measures), VII (enforcement measures) and VIII (regional arrangements) of the UN Charter, in situations where a state has manifestly failed to protect its population from the four crimes.[11] In April 2006, the UN Security Council reaffirmed RtoP and indicated its readiness to adopt appropriate measures where necessary (Resolution 1674, 28 April 2006). In early 2009, the Secretary-General issued a report on implementing the RtoP. The Secretary-General's report was subsequently discussed by the General Assembly in July 2009. Most states that contributed to the dialogue welcomed the Secretary-General's report, reaffirmed their commitment to the 2005 agreement and endorsed the three pillars of RtoP. Subsequently, the General Assembly adopted a unanimous resolution noting the Secretary-General's report and deciding to continue its consideration of the RtoP.[12]

RtoP's intellectual and political origins lay in older ideas about 'sovereignty as responsibility' and their rearticulation in various forms in the 1990s as a response to the commission of genocide, mass atrocities and forced displacement in that decade. Sovereignty has always entailed both rights and responsibilities. Even theorists most associated with the defence of unbridled sovereign power conceded this point. Thomas Hobbes, for example, insisted that the sovereign's authority was based on an unwritten contract between the state and the

[11] A/60/L.1, 20 September 2005, paras. 138-140. See Ban Ki-moon, *Implementing the Responsibility to Protect: Report of the Secretary-General*, A/63/677, 12 January 2009.

[12] A/63/L.80, 14 September 2009.

individual whereby the individual sacrificed his/her natural freedom in return for security. This entitled the sovereign to take whatever measures it thought necessary for the preservation of the peace, but the contract was broken if the sovereign posed an existential threat to the individual.[13] Between the eighteenth and twentieth centuries, this idea was enumerated as the principle of 'popular sovereignty' – the idea that sovereignty derives from 'the people', who have a fundamental right to determine their own form of government. First enunciated in the English, American and French revolutions, this idea provided the basic legitimising principle for decolonisation and opposition to white minority rule.[14] Indeed, in the aftermath of the Second World War this idea became one of the basic organising principles of world politics.[15] Although it left as many questions as it answered (who are 'the people'? how is the people's will to be determined?), popular sovereignty rests on the idea that the state is responsible to the people and has a duty of care towards them. In other words, sovereignty entails domestic responsibilities as well as rights.

These ideas were given new impetus in the 1990s as a result of the emergence of a number of decidedly 'uncivil' wars and developed in two different contexts – a discussion about sovereign responsibilities in the face of internal displacement and a debate about the so-called 'right' of humanitarian intervention. The contemporary idea of sovereignty as responsibility was developed by the UN's Special Representative on Internally Displaced Persons (IDPs), Francis Deng and Roberta Cohen, a Senior Fellow at the Brookings Institution, in the 1990s.[16] Their principal challenge was how to persuade governments to improve protection for IDPs and they developed the idea of sovereignty as responsibility to fit this purpose.[17] The concept's starting point was recognition that the primary responsibility for protecting and assisting IDPs lay with the host government.[18] No legitimate state, they argued, could quarrel with

---

[13] Thomas Hobbes, *Leviathan* (Oxford: Oxford University Press, 1996).

[14] On its origins see Mlada Bukavansky, *Legitimacy and Power Politics: The American and French Revolutions in International Political Culture* (Princeton, NJ: Princeton University Press, 2002).

[15] Brad R. Roth, *Governmental Illegitimacy in International Law* (Oxford: Oxford University Press, 2000).

[16] See for example Roberta Cohen and Francis M. Deng, *Masses in Flight: The Global Crisis of Internal Displacement* (Washington DC: The Brookings Institution, 1998), Francis M. Deng, 'The Impact of State Failure on Migration', *Mediterranean Quarterly*, 15/4: 16-36 (2004). See also Thomas G. Weiss and David A. Korn, *Internal Displacement: Conceptualization and Its Consequences* (New York: Routledge, 2006).

[17] Deng, 'Impact of State Failure on Migration', p. 20.

[18] Cohen and Deng, *Masses in Flight*, p. 275.

the claim that they were responsible for the well-being of their citizens and in practice no governments did in fact quarrel with this proposition. Where a state was unable to fulfil its responsibilities, it should invite and welcome international assistance.[19] Such assistance helped the state by enabling it to discharge its sovereign responsibilities and take its place as a legitimate member of international society.[20] During major crises, troubled states faced a choice: they could work with international organisations and other interested outsiders to realise their sovereign responsibilities or obstruct those efforts and sacrifice their good standing and sovereign legitimacy.[21] As such, sovereignty as responsibility focused on the responsibilities of host governments and maintained that effective and legitimate states were the best way to protect vulnerable populations. This left unanswered the problem of what to do when a state refuses to request assistance or itself commits genocide and mass atrocities, pitting a sovereign's right to non-interference—enshrined in Articles 2(4) and 2(7) of the UN Charter—against a sovereign's putative responsibilities.

This dilemma was most pointed in relation to the question of humanitarian intervention and in the midst of the highly contentious global debate about the legitimacy of NATO's 1999 intervention in Kosovo, the concept of sovereignty as responsibility was picked up by UN Secretary-General Kofi Annan.[22] Mindful of the apparent contradictions between the rights and responsibilities of sovereignty, Annan challenged international society to develop a way of reconciling the twin principles of sovereignty (and protection of self-determination) and fundamental human rights. That challenge was taken up by the Canadian government, which created the International Commission on Intervention and State Sovereignty (ICISS). Chaired by Gareth Evans and Mohammed Sahnoun, the Commission coined the phrase 'RtoP', set out the case for it, and focused on developing ideas in relation to humanitarian intervention.[23]

Although UN Member States adopted the language of RtoP, they chose not to adopt the ICISS' recommendations wholesale and to frame the new principle around the idea of sovereignty as responsibility. As Edward Luck has

[19] Deng, 'Impact of State Failure on Migration', p. 20.

[20] Francis M. Deng, Sadikiel Kimaro, Terrence Lyons, Donald Rothchild and I. William Zartman, *Sovereignty as Responsibility: Conflict Management in Africa* (Washington DC: The Brookings Institution, 1996), p. 1.

[21] Ibid., p. 28.

[22] Kofi Annan, 'Two Concepts of Sovereignty', *Economist*, 18 September 1999.

[23] International Commission on Intervention and State Sovereignty, *The Responsibility to Protect* (Ottawa: IDRC, 2001).

argued, it is important to not confuse what we would like the RtoP principle to be with *what it actually is.*[24] In particular, Member States rejected the ICISS' calls for RtoP to include criteria to guide decision-making about when to intervene; a code-of-conduct for the use of the veto by the permanent members of the Security Council; and the potential for coercive interference in the domestic affairs of states not authorised by the UN Security Council. In short, contrary to the views of those like Bannon and Stedman (see above) there is nothing in the 2005 World Summit agreement that creates—or tries to create—*new law* in relation to the RtoP.

But we should not succumb to the view that the RtoP principle that emerged from the 2005 World Summit was too weak or insubstantial to make a positive contribution to strengthening global humanitarianism, or that it is unencumbered with legal responsibilities. First, the World Summit clarified the principle's scope. At the request of Pakistan, it was agreed that RtoP applies to genocide, war crimes, ethnic cleansing and crimes against humanity. Each of these have fairly precise legal meanings grounded in existing international law. Second, the World Summit clarified relevant roles and responsibilities. In line with the doctrine put forth by Deng and Cohen, all states have a primary responsibility to their own populations. All other states have a responsibility to assist their peers in fulfilling this primary responsibility. Should a state manifestly fail in its responsibility, the various bodies of the UN in partnership with relevant regional arrangements have a responsibility to use whatever means they determine as necessary and appropriate. Significantly, all measures should be consistent with the UN Charter. Third, the agreement clarified that there is no such thing as an 'RtoP event or crisis' in that there is no moment at which something becomes relevant to RtoP. A state's responsibility does not appear and evaporate; nor does the world's responsibility to assist and support that state or the Security Council's responsibility to take all necessary means when appropriate. In other words, it is not the nature of the responsibility that changes, but the most appropriate means of preventing genocide, war crimes, ethnic cleansing and crimes against humanity and protecting vulnerable populations in any given situation. Finally, it is important to stress that as a product of the largest ever gathering of heads of state and government, the agreement produced by the 2005 World Summit carries immense political weight.

---

[24] See Edward C. Luck, 'The Responsible Sovereign and the Responsibility to Protect', *Annual Review of United Nations Affairs 2006/2007* (New York: Oxford University Press, 2008), vol. 1, pp. xxxiii-xliv.

This brings us to the relationship between RtoP and international law. Although RtoP cannot be considered a legal norm in its own right, and it is unlikely that the principle as it is structured now could become a legal norm, the RtoP is embedded in international law in that some of the responsibilities associated with RtoP are enumerated in existing law. The remainder of this article focuses on this issue.

RtoP and Legal Responsibilities

The first part of the relationship between RtoP and international law relates to the legal responsibilities that the principle places on States and international organisations. As we mentioned in the introduction, RtoP comprises two, quite distinct, sets of responsibilities: the 'pillar one' responsibilities owed by a State to its own populations and the 'pillars two and three' responsibilities of States as members of the international community to assist their peers and take action to prevent genocide and mass atrocities and protect vulnerable populations when the host state is manifestly failing to do so. There is a distinct difference in the legal quality of these two sets of responsibilities – the first is generally considered *jus cogens*, and the second is barely a legal duty at all. To understand how this distinction was arrived at, it is worth briefly considering the US position on RtoP as expressed by its UN Ambassador, John Bolton, in the pre-summit negotiations in 2005.

John Bolton – a renowned anti-UN hawk – took up position as America's Ambassador to the UN on 3 August 2005. On arrival, he announced his intention to begin renegotiating the world summit document from scratch. Starting on 29 August – less than three weeks before the summit – he began issuing a series of communiqués (referred to as 'Dear Colleague' letters) calling for the redrafting of hundreds of paragraphs (including the RtoP paragraphs) and the deletion of many others from the draft text intended for adoption at the 2005 World Summit. Bolton's problems with RtoP itself were relatively minor but he emphasised an important distinction between the two sets of responsibilities implied by the principle. He argued that whilst the US accepted that states had the primary responsibility to protect their own populations and that the international community had a responsibility to act when the host state permitted or perpetrated atrocities, it was important to recognise that 'the responsibility of the other countries in the international community is not of the same character as the responsibility of the host, and we thus want to avoid formulations that suggest that the other countries are inheriting the same responsibility as the host state has'.[25] He continued, 'the [UN] Charter has never been interpreted as creating a legal obligation for Security Council members to enforcement action in various cases involving serious breaches of international peace'. Thus, he argued that the international community and UN Security Council were not *legally* obliged to protect endangered civilians, whereas states were legally obligated to protect their own populations. As such, he successfully demanded a change to the wording of Paragraph 139 of the Outcome Document, which replaced a proposed 'obligation' on the part of the international community with a (moral) 'responsibility'. As Bolton flatly explained, 'We do not accept that either the United Nations as a whole, or the Security Council, or individual states, have an obligation to intervene under international law'. Bolton also counseled that the Security Council must have the freedom to decide the most appropriate course of action on a case-by-case basis.[26]

In the analysis that follows, we argue that Bolton's characterisation of the legal qualities of the two sets of responsibilities points to an important substantive difference but that it is not entirely accurate to caricature the international community's responsibilities as entirely devoid of legal content. Bolton's position overlooked the existence of legal responsibilities to assist states in the implementation of their existing obligations under International Humanitarian Law (pillar two of RtoP). It also overlooked the highly contentious emergence of ideas about the legal responsibility to prevent genocide (pillar three) and the responsibilities of international organisations (pillar three).

The Primary Responsibility: The State and Its Population

The primary responsibility of the state was set out unambiguously by Member States in the paragraph 138 of the World Summit Outcome Document. States unanimously agreed that:

> 'Each individual State has the Responsibility to Protect its populations from genocide, war crimes, ethnic cleansing and crimes against humanity. This responsibility entails the prevention of such crimes, including their incitement, through appropriate and necessary means. We accept that responsibility and will act in accordance with it'.

---

[25] Letter from John R. Bolton, the Representative of the United States of America to the United Nations to President Ping, President of the UN General Assembly, 30 August 2005.

[26] Ibid.

As the UN Secretary-General noted, this solemn pledge was 'remarkable for its clarity, simplicity and lack of qualifications of caveats'.[27] He went on to maintain that this 'first pillar' of the RtoP rested 'on long-standing obligations under international law'. Although these first pillar responsibilities are well established in international law, and the four crimes associated with RtoP (genocide, war crimes, ethnic cleansing and crimes against humanity) are clearly prohibited, the precise nature of the *acts* constituting these four crimes and the scope of the state's responsibility to prevent them and protect vulnerable populations is clearer in relation to genocide and war crimes than in relation to crimes against humanity and ethnic cleansing. Indeed, ethnic cleansing has no definitive legal definition and the precise nature of crimes against humanity is open to debate.

The legal responsibility of states in relation to genocide is clearly codified in the 1948 *Convention on the Prevention and Punishment of the Crime of Genocide*, which has 138 State Parties and is generally considered to be *jus cogens* and therefore part of customary international law.[28] For our purposes, the Convention has three points of particular interest – the prohibition of genocide, the clear definition of the crime, and articulation of the duty to prevent it and punish the perpetrators. Article 1 of the Convention prohibits the crime of genocide, and establishes the duty of states to actively prevent the crime and punish the perpetrators.[29] Article 2, meanwhile, provides the definitive definition of genocide that has been subsequently adopted by the International Criminal Tribunals for former Yugoslavia and Rwanda (ICTY, ICTR) and Rome Statute of the International Criminal Court (ICC). Although this definition has been criticised as too restrictive in applying only to the destruction of national, ethnic, racial and religious groups, it is generally accepted as authoritative.[30] The one element of the regime that remains contested is the precise scope of the state's responsibility to prevent genocide and punish the perpetrators. The question of whether this involves duties pertaining to genocides committed in other countries is dealt with later. For now, it is worth noting that until relatively recently it remained unclear what states were legally

[27] Ban Ki-moon, *Implementing the Responsibility to Protect*, para. 13.

[28] See Caroline Fournet, *The Crime of Destruction and the Law of Genocide: Their Impact on Collective Memory* (Aldershot: Ashgate, 2007), p. 99 and Jan Wouters and Sten Verhoeven. 2005. 'The Prohibition of Genocide as a Norm of *Ius Cogens* and Its Implications for the Enforcement of the Law of Genocide'. *International Criminal Law Review* 5/3 (2005), p. 405.

[29] William Schabas, *Genocide in International Law: The Crimes of Crimes* (Cambridge: Cambridge University Press, 2000), p. 2.

[30] On the criticism see Martin Shaw, *What is Genocide?* (Cambridge: Polity, 2006). On its status see Wouters and Verhoeven, 'The Prohibition of Genocide', p. 403.

obliged to do within their own territory beyond desisting from the commission of genocide. Some clarity on this was provided by the ICJ in *Bosnia vs. Serbia* where it found that the Article 1 obligation to prevent genocide requires that states 'employ all means which are reasonably available to them'.[31] This suggests that not only is there a clear legal pillar one duty to prevent genocide, there is also emergent jurisprudence defining the scope of that duty.

In similar vein, International Humanitarian Law (IHL) provides a strong legal foundation for the responsibility of states to protect their populations from war crimes. The relevant law here is both well-defined and well-established, and places clear legal obligations on States. The relevant law also includes pillar 2 responsibilities to assist others in fulfilling their legal duties, which we will come to later. War crimes are enumerated in IHL, which restricts and limits the methods, means and tactics of warfare and protects people that are not actively participating in armed conflict.[32] There are several slightly different definitions of war crimes, but the most accepted contemporary account can be found in Article 8(2) of the Rome Statute, which claims to reflect customary international law.[33] According to the Statute, a 'war crime' comprises (a) grave breaches of the 1949 Geneva Conventions [and their subsequent Protocols] such as willful killing, torture, causing of great suffering or extensive destruction not justified by military necessity and (b) other serious violations of the laws and customs applicable in armed conflict, such as attacks on civilians, humanitarians and peacekeepers, ethnic cleansing, the use of rape as a weapon of war, forced starvation, and the use of weapons that cause unnecessary suffering. To be labeled a 'war crime' warranting international jurisdiction, these acts should be committed on a widespread and systematic basis, and given that RtoP applies only to the most serious and extensive of violations, it is fair to apply this standard to RtoP too.[34] It is widely agreed that these basic standards apply to both international and intra-state war and that

---

[31] See Mark Gibney, 'Genocide and State Responsibility'. *Human Rights Law Review* 7/4 (2007), p. 772 and Marko Milanovic, 'State Responsibility for Genocide: A Follow-Up'. *European Journal of International Law* 18/4 (2007), p. 686.

[32] Beth Van Schaack and Ronald Slye. *International Criminal Law and its Enforcement* (New York: Foundation Press, 2007), p. 106.

[33] On differences see Yoram Dinstein, *The Conduct of Hostilities under the Law of International Armed Conflict* (Cambridge: Cambridge University Press, 2004), p. 229. On the customary law point see Kirsch 2002, p. xiii Philippe Kirsch, 'Foreword', K. Doermann (ed.), *Elements of War Crimes under the Rome Statute of the International Criminal Court: Sources and Commentary* (Cambridge: Cambridge University Press, 2002), p. xiii.

[34] Lawrence Woocher, 'Developing a Strategy, Method and Tools for Genocide Early Warning', Report for the office of the Special Advisor to the UN Secretary General on the Prevention of Genocide, 2006.

the prohibition of 'grave breaches' of these rules is a peremptory rule with *jus cogens* status.[35] Indeed, this view has been confirmed by both the ICJ and ILC.[36] Unlike the Genocide Convention, IHL sets out a wide range of positive duties that extend beyond the duty to refrain from committing war crimes. These include duties to punish the perpetrators of violations, care for the sick and wounded, cooperate with the ICRC on certain matters, and take steps to protect the civilian population. Often overlooked is the fact that IHL also contains a duty to ensure respect for the law which is relevant to pillars two and three of RtoP. This is further discussed below.

The third group of crimes related to RtoP is crimes against humanity. As we mentioned earlier, the crime of 'ethnic cleansing' has not been prohibited in its own right but the acts associated with ethnic cleansing (forced displacement of civilians) are prohibited as war crimes (above) and crimes against humanity. Whilst international law relating to genocide and war crimes provides a sound legal foundation for pillar one of RtoP and establishes peremptory duties on the part of states, the law relating to crimes against humanity is less clear, because there is no specialised convention that clarifies their scope and establishes a duty to prevent them and punish the perpetrators.[37] As such, the law relating to crimes against humanity remains largely uncodified.[38] The category of crimes against humanity was first mentioned in the London Charter (Article 6) establishing the International Criminal Tribunal for the prosecution of major war criminals in the aftermath of the Second World War. The Charter defined crimes against humanity as:

> [N]amely, murder, extermination, enslavement, deportation, and other inhumane acts committed against any civilian population, before or during the war, or persecutions on political, racial or religious grounds...whether or not in violation of the domestic law of the country where perpetrated (Article 6(c)).

---

[35] This view is held, for example, by judges Rafael Nieto-Navia and Antonio Cassese. See Antonio Cassese, 'On the Current Trends towards Criminal Prosecution and Punishment of Breaches of International Humanitarian Law', *European Journal of International Law* 9/1 (1998), p. 6 and Rafael Nieto-Navia, Rafael, 'International Peremptory Norms (Jus Cogens) and International Humanitarian Law', 2001, p. 24. Accessed 26 September 2008. Available at http://www.iccnow.org/documents/WritingColombiaEng.pdf.

[36] See Dietrich Schindler, 'International Humanitarian Law: Its Remarkable Development and its Persistent Violation', *Journal of the History of International Law* 5/2 (2003), p. 180 and International Law Commission (ILC) 'Responsibility of States for Internationally Wrongful Acts', 2001. Accessed 25 September 2008. Available at http://untreaty.un.org/ilc/texts/instruments/english/draft%20articles/9_6_2001.pdf.

[37] Phyllis Hwang, 'Defining Crimes Against Humanity in the Rome Statute of the International Criminal Court'. *Fordham International Law Journal* 22/2 (1998), p. 488.

[38] Luck, 'The United Nations and the Responsibility to Protect', p. 4.

Broadly similar definitions were subsequently used by the Charter for the Far East Military Tribunal (Article 5(c)), the statutes of the ICTY (Article 5) and ICTR (Article 3) and the Rome Statute (Article 7). The Rome Statute provides the most definitive recent account, and it is worth noting that 120 States voted in favour of the Statute—and its interpretation of crimes against humanity—in 1998. The Statute defined crimes against humanity as 'any of the following acts when committed as part of a widespread or systematic attack directed against any civilian population, with knowledge of the attack:

a. Murder;
b. Extermination;
c. Enslavement;
d. Deportation or forcible transfer of population;
e. Imprisonment or other severe deprivation of physical liberty in violation of fundamental rules of international law;
f. Torture;
g. Rape, sexual slavery, enforced prostitution, forced pregnancy, enforced sterilisation, or any other form of sexual violence of comparable gravity;
h. Persecution against any identifiable group or collectivity on political, racial, national, ethnic, cultural, religious, gender, or other grounds that are universally recognised as impermissible under international law,
i. Enforced disappearance of persons;
j. The crime of apartheid;
k. Other inhumane acts of a similar character intentionally causing great suffering, or serious injury to body or to mental or physical health.

Accordingly, crimes against humanity must be part of a systematic or widespread attack which is directed against a civilian population.[39] Although the legal history of crimes against humanity is shorter than that of genocide and war crimes, there is broad consensus that the crimes enumerated here are not only a core part of customary international law, but are also peremptory and *jus cogens*.[40] However, because there is no specialised convention on crimes against humanity, states have no specific duties beyond the duty to refrain from committing such crimes, such as duties to prevent their commission. The 108 states that are parties to the ICC have a legal duty to investigate alleged crimes against humanity and punish the perpetrators but there are no obvious generalised legal duties beyond this.

---

[39] Hwang, 'Defining Crimes Against Humanity', p. 467.

[40] Luck, 'The United Nations and the Responsibility to Protect', p. 5 and Yoram Dinstein, 'Crimes Against Humanity after Tadic', *Leiden Journal of International Law* 13 (2000), p. 376.

It is clear, therefore, from the preceding discussion that the state's pillar one responsibility to protect its population from genocide, war crimes, ethnic cleansing and crimes against humanity is embedded in customary international law. Indeed, it is fair to conclude that the first pillar of RtoP is *jus cogens*. As such, in this context RtoP is best understood as a political commitment to implement and act in accordance with the already existing legal obligations that states owe to their own populations and—importantly—to the populations of countries they deploy their armed forces into. Much less clear, however, is the legal quality of the responsibilities enumerated by pillars two and three of RtoP. Although John Bolton was correct to argue that there is a substantive difference between the legal quality of the state's responsibility to its own population and the international community's residual responsibilities, it is not wholly accurate to argue that the responsibilities set out in pillars two and three are entirely devoid of legal content.

The Responsibility of the International Community

This section briefly examines the second set of responsibilities enumerated by RtoP – those attached to the international community. As agreed by Member States in 2005, the international community's responsibilities relate to assisting the state to fulfill its responsibility to protect (pillar two) and taking timely and decisive action when a state is manifestly failing to protect its population from the four crimes (pillar three). As such, we will first consider the legal quality of the pillar two responsibility, before shifting to pillar three. Finally, we will briefly discuss the emergence of work on the legal responsibilities of international organisations, focusing on the UN.

RtoP's second pillar is set out in both paragraphs 138 and 139. As interpreted by the UN Secretary-General, and endorsed by the General Assembly, it comprises four main elements: (a) encouraging states to meet their pillar one responsibilities; (b) helping them to exercise this responsibility; (c) helping them to build their capacity to protect; (d) assisting States 'under stress before crises and conflicts break out'.[41] Although this is predominantly a political commitment, it is not entirely devoid of legal content. The Genocide Convention and IHL in particular place a number of obligations on States to 'encourage' and 'assist' others in relation to 'ensuring' compliance with the law. However, these duties are much less well defined than the pillar one obligations noted above.

---

[41] Ban, *Implementing the Responsibility to Protect,* para. 28.

We noted earlier that in *Bosnia v. Serbia*, the ICJ ruled that states are obliged to take all reasonable measures to prevent genocide and punish the perpetrators, within the bounds of existing international law. Debate has since focused on the question of whether this creates a legal duty for the Security Council to authorise intervention in cases of genocide—a subject I will return to later in relation to pillar three. However, the state's obligation to take all reasonable measures to prevent genocide is not limited to military intervention within the confines of existing international law. Indeed, in the case at hand, the ICJ found that Serbia had political, military and financial influence over the Bosnian Serb army and sufficient information about the potential for genocide in Srebrenica and yet took no action to prevent the genocide.[42] The Court argued that whilst states are not obliged to use coercive measures or to actually succeed in preventing genocide, they must be able to show that when furnished with influence and information they have taken the initiative and attempted to prevent genocide. At the very least, therefore, the international community's pillar two responsibility to 'encourage' states to fulfill their RtoP includes a *legal* obligation to take positive action to prevent genocide on the part of states that have influence and information.

IHL identifies a wider range of pillar two responsibilities with respect to ensuring compliance and preventing the commission of war crimes. Indeed, the obligation of states to both abide by the law and to ensure that others do likewise is a core part of the Geneva Conventions. Article 1 of the four 1949 Geneva Conventions establishes duties 'to respect and to ensure respect for the present Convention in all circumstances'. While the precise scope of this legal duty 'to ensure respect' for IHL is unclear, some ICRC officials contend that the *travaux preparatoires* indicate that the intention was to ensure that parties 'do everything they could to ensure universal compliance with the humanitarian principles underlying the Conventions'.[43] Legal commentators typically argue that the Conventions established a clear duty of states to use non-military means to prevent and halt the commission of war crimes and to bring the perpetrators to justice. Measures specifically identified by commentators include the use of private and public diplomacy, meetings of the High Contracting Parties and the use of treaty committees to report on non-compliance, and—more controversially—the adoption of more coercive measures such as travel restrictions, mandatory sanctions and

---

42 ICJ, *Bosnia v Serbia*, para. 425.

43 Laurence Boisson de Chazournes and Luigi Condorelli, 'Common Article 1 of the Geneva Conventions Revisited: Protecting Collective Interests', *International Review of the Red Cross*, 837 (2000), pp. 67-87.

embargoes.[44] In addition to diplomatic and other measures aimed at encouraging compliance with IHL (reflecting the first element of RtoP's second pillar), the duty to 'ensure respect' for IHL could also be reasonably assumed to extend to two other elements of RtoP's second pillar: helping states to exercise their RtoP and assisting them to build the necessary capacity. It could be argued, therefore, that states with the capacity to do so, have a legal obligation to provide assistance to others to this end. This may include the provision of training and education on IHL, cooperation and oversight in multinational operations, and assistance with building requisite capacities (for example in the military justice sphere).

This brings us to pillar three – the international community's responsibility to take timely and decisive action in situations where a host state is manifestly failing to protect its population from genocide, war crimes, ethnic cleansing and crimes against humanity. As we noted earlier, there is nothing in the RtoP principle that expands the *rights* of states to interfere coercively in the domestic affairs of other states. The question here is whether the principle creates a legal *duty* to take coercive measures on the part of those with the authority to do so (i.e. the UN Security Council). John Bolton's position that no such duty exists is broadly supported by international lawyers but it is worth noting three recent developments that might alter that fact in the coming decades: (1) the identification of state responsibilities by the ILC; (2) the effect of RtoP and the ICJ's ruling in *Bosnia vs. Serbia* on the legal responsibilities of the UN Security Council; (3) the emerging idea that international organisations have legal responsibilities. Two things should be stressed at this point. First, these are new and emergent ideas that depend on a very progressive reading of the law. Second, these ideas focus on creating responsibilities for states operating within the current framework of laws. They do not imply changes to the law governing the use of coercion, for example. We will briefly consider each in turn.

State responsibilities. It has been suggested that the duty to ensure compliance with IHL may be further strengthened and translated into a legal responsibility to take coercive measures by Article 41 of the ILC's Draft Articles on the Responsibility of States for Internationally Wrongful Acts.[45] Article 41 sets out the responsibility of states to halt violations of peremptory norms of international law. Thus, it insists that 'States shall cooperate to bring an end through

[44] Dietrich Schindler, 'International Humanitarian Law: Its Remarkable Development and its Persistent Violation'. *Journal of the History of International Law* 5/2 (2003), p. 175.

[45] By Luck, 'The United Nations and the Responsibility to Protect', p. 5. See ILC, Draft Articles on the Responsibility of States for Internationally Wrongful Acts, 2001, available at http://untreaty.un.org/ilc/texts/instruments/english/commentaries/9_6_2001.pdf

lawful means any serious breach within the meaning of Article 40'. As the prohibition of war crimes and crimes against humanity have the status of *jus cogens*, Article 41 would seem to require that states take lawful measures to halt their commission. Thus, as the UN Secretary-General's Special Adviser, Edward Luck, explained, 'there are some indicators that, when a state commits a serious breach of a peremptory norm, the international community should cooperate to bring the breach to an end using lawful means'.[46] However, the question of whether Article 41 establishes a positive duty of States to cooperate to halt the perpetration of war crimes and crimes against humanity – including by adopting coercive measures through the UN Security Council when other peaceful means are inadequate – remains contested. To assume that such an obligation exists would, in Luck's opinion, represent an extremely progressive and wide interpretation of international law.[47]

The UN Security Council's responsibilities. It has also been suggested recently that a combination of the RtoP principle and the ICJ's ruling in *Bosnia vs Serbia* goes some way towards establishing a legal duty to intervene on the part of the UN Security Council, its permanent members especially.[48] Although it might be premature to speak of a specific legal obligation to intervene militarily, the emergence of such a duty is important because it places legal obligations on states and creates the potential for legal redress if those obligations are not satisfied.

It is well known that the 1948 Genocide Convention not only prohibits genocide but establishes a duty to prevent and punish it (Article 1). This duty to prevent genocide is widely understood to be a principle of customary international law.[49] However, it was never clear whether this general duty to prevent genocide amounted to a legal obligation to intervene to halt specific genocides. On the one hand, the US State Department in 1994 explained its reluctance to use the term genocide to refer to what was happening in Rwanda on the grounds that 'there are obligations which arise in connection with that term',[50] and Malaysia argued that the permanent members of the Security Council had violated their Genocide Convention obligations by not authorising enforcement action against the tormentors of Bosnia's Muslims.[51]

---

[46] Luck, 'The United Nations and the Responsibility to Protect', p. 5.

[47] Ibid.

[48] Louise Arbour, 'The Responsibility to Protect as a Duty of Care in International Law and Practice'. *Review of International Studies* 34/3: 445-58 (2008).

[49] William Schabas, *Genocide in International Law: The Crime of Crimes* (Cambridge: Cambridge University Press, 2000), p. 500.

[50] Cited in Ibid., p. 495.

[51] Ibid., p. 492.

On the other hand, in 2004 the US argued that labeling the crisis in Darfur as genocide created no specific legal obligations.[52] Although some legal scholars have argued that Article 1 imposes a duty on the UN and its member states to act (including through military intervention) wherever a genocide takes place,[53] the majority view seemed to support former US Secretary of State Colin Powell's assertion that the Convention's language did not impose such a wide-ranging obligation.[54] However, important new light was shed on this issue by the ICJ's 2007 ruling in the *Bosnia v. Serbia* case.

As we noted earlier, the Court found that Serbia was not guilty of genocide but had violated its Article 1 obligation to prevent and punish the crime of genocide. The ICJ found that, whilst states are not obliged to succeed in their efforts to prevent genocide, they 'must employ all means which are reasonably available to them to do so'.[55] Of course, it remains to be seen what measures may be thought to be 'reasonably available' to states in given situations. It is unlikely that each individual state now has a responsibility to intervene militarily to end genocide, and it should be remembered that measures to end genocide must be consistent with international law, which prohibits the use of force except in self-defence or with the express authorisation of the UN Security Council.[56] However, it has been argued by the former UN High Commissioner for Human Rights, Louise Arbour, that the ruling—especially when taken in conjunction with RtoP—imposes specific responsibilities on the members of the UN Security Council, and the permanent members especially.[57] The UN Security Council has the legal authority to authorise armed intervention whenever it identifies a threat to international peace and security. Moreover, as the world's leading military powers, permanent members of the Security Council have the military capacity to intervene

---

[52] Paul D. Williams and Alex J. Bellamy, 'The Responsibility to Protect and the Crisis in Darfur', *Security Dialogue*, 36/1 (2005), p. 31.

[53] Stephen J. Toope, 'Does International Law Impose a Duty upon the UN to Prevent Genocide?', *McGill Law Journal*, 46/1: 187-94 (2000).

[54] Jerry Fowler, for example, argued that 'the language of the [Genocide] Convention does not provide any indication that such an extensive obligation was contemplated. Indeed it would be quite bizarre to think that the drafters intended in 1948 to make intervention in the internal affairs of other states obligatory'. Jerry Fowler, 'A New Chapter of Irony: The Legal Definition of Genocide and the Implications of Powell's Determination', in Samuel Totten and Eric Markusen (eds.), *Genocide in Darfur: Investigating the Atrocities in the Sudan* (London: Routledge, 2006), p. 131.

[55] In Milanovic, 'State Responsibility for Genocide: A Follow-Up', p. 686.

[56] Mark Gibney, 'Genocide and State Responsibility', *Human Rights Law Review*, 7/4 (2007), p. 767.

[57] Arbour, 'The Responsibility to Protect as a Duty of Care in International Law'.

to halt genocide. Thus armed with both the authority to intervene and the capacity to do so, it could be argued that armed intervention to halt genocide falls well within the scope of 'reasonably available' measures for permanent members of the Security Council. This is not to say, of course, that armed intervention will be the most appropriate course of action in every case. And it should be noted that this line of argument depends on a very liberal interpretation of the law. However, a combination of the RtoP principle and the *Bosnia v. Serbia* ruling indicate an emerging legal duty to intervene to prevent and halt genocide. In the future, states that are victims of genocide might test this proposition by bringing the permanent members of the Security Council to the ICJ charged with failing to take reasonably available measures to prevent genocide.

Responsibilities of International Organisations. In addition to its work on the responsibilities of States, the ILC has also begun developing draft articles on the responsibilities of international organisations. Among those, is draft Article 8 relating to the existence of a breach of an international obligation. The third report on this issue argued that international organisations, like states, should be held legally accountable for internationally wrongful acts – i.e. acts that violate international obligations. The report found that if it was assumed that international law requires States and other entities to prevent genocide, and that the UN had been in a position to prevent the Rwandan knowledge (recall the influence and information tests noted by the ICJ), failure to act would have represented a breach of the legal obligation. Difficulties relating to decision-making, the report argued, could not exonerate the UN.[58] The UN, of course, famously recognised its failure to prevent the Rwandan genocide as a failure of the whole UN system. The ILC's draft articles suggest the possibility that this failure may have been legal in nature, though one prominent international lawyer has chided the ILC's interpretation as 'absurdly premature and not likely to be affirmed by state practice'.[59]

Conclusion

From the preceding analysis, it is clear that states have a peremptory legal responsibility to protect their populations from genocide, war crimes, ethnic cleansing and crimes against humanity that is derived from customary

[58] A/CN.4/553, para. 10.
[59] Jose E. Alvarez, 'The Schizophrenias of R2P'.

international law generally considered to be *jus cogens*. In other words, RtoP's first pillar is a peremptory norm of international law. Although John Bolton was correct to point out that these responsibilities were of a different quality to a state's responsibility towards its own population, it is not the case that the responsibilities enumerated in pillars two and three are entirely devoid of legal content. In particular, states have a legal duty to take peaceful measures to prevent genocide whenever they have relevant influence and information and an obligation to use peaceful means to ensure compliance with the laws of war. Such measures may include pillar two activities aimed at 'encouraging' states to comply through diplomatic means and enabling compliance through training and capacity building, as well as pillar three activities in accordance with international law. These obligations have been largely overlooked, but it is important that international efforts by agencies such as the ICRC to ensure compliance with IHL be recognised as a core component of implementing the RtoP and that states provide requisite support in line with their legal duties. Finally, whilst nothing in the RtoP principle widens the scope for coercive interference in the domestic affairs of states, it is important to recognise that emerging trends spearheaded by the ILC and ICJ may see the evolution of a legal duty to respond decisively to genocide and mass atrocities that inheres on Member States generally, the Security Council in particular, and the UN system as a whole – though we remain a long way from reaching consensus on this point.

The Responsibility to Protect: A Legal and Rights-based Perspective

Dorota Gierycz

Abstract
This article analyses the responsibility to protect from a legal and rights-based perspective. It shows that the responsibility to protect populations from genocide, war crimes, ethnic cleansing and crimes against humanity is rooted in existing International Human Rights Law (IHRL) and International Humanitarian Law (IHL). These crimes fall under the jurisdiction of the International Criminal Court (ICC) and evoke serious international legal consequences under all circumstances, also if tried by national courts. Protection of the individual against atrocities is a primary responsibility of states. However, if a state is unable or unwilling to exercise its protection obligations, these shift to international organisations, including the United Nations or any other authority controlling the territory and its population. The article further analyses various protection tools available within the UN human rights machinery, in particular the Human Rights Council (HRC) and the Office of the High Commissioner for Human Rights (OHCHR) and concludes that they could play a much stronger role in preventing and addressing the atrocities and that the most important obstacle in this respect is the prevailing institutional gap between human rights and security matters within the UN. The article concludes that the responsibility to protect clause adopted by consensus by the 2005 World Summit in its Outcome Document (GA Resolution A/60/1) constitutes an important commitment towards implementing these universal rights and obligations which are lacking enforcement and continue to be violated, especially in armed conflicts. It also identifies research and policy recommendations that may facilitate operationalisation of this important clause.

Keywords
human rights; responsibility to protect; International Humanitarian Law; protection of civilians; peace-keeping; United Nations.

Introduction

The World Summit Outcome document adopted by resolution A/60/1 of the UN General Assembly (GA) on 24 October 2005 contains provisions on the responsibility to protect populations from genocide, war crimes, ethnic cleansing and crimes against humanity (paragraphs 138 and 139).[1] It was

[1] '2005 World Summit Outcome', UNGA Res.60/1, 16 September 2005.

agreed by consensus among all participating member states. It explicitly states that each individual state has the responsibility to protect its populations from these atrocities, and that such providing protection entails prevention and the exercise of responsibility. The text further spells out obligations of the international community to 'help States to exercise this responsibility' (Para. 138) through the United Nations, using peaceful means, in accordance with Chapters VI and VII of the Charter, or collective action, in a timely and decisive manner through the Security Council, should peaceful means be inadequate and national authorities manifestly fail to protect their populations (Para. 139).

The provisions of the World Summit regarding the responsibility to protect (the protection clause) were reaffirmed in UN Security Council resolutions 1674 (28 April 2006) on the protection of civilians in armed conflict and 1706 (31 August 2006) calling for the deployment of a UN peacekeeping force to Darfur.

While adoption of the clause has been generally welcomed, views on its practical utility are divided. Although most believe that it provides greater practical opportunities to act, to prevent or respond decisively to 'future Srebrenicas and Rwandas',[2] others claim that it weakens the prospects for operational application of the concept.[3]

The World Summit Outcome document was adopted as a General Assembly (GA) resolution. Under international law, approval by the GA has a different consequence from a treaty that becomes effective through a required number of ratifications. The former is recommendatory rather than binding.[4] However, this particular document has high political and moral significance, in particular since the commitments were undertaken by the world leaders and it addresses such a fundamental issue as the obligation to provide protection from genocide, war crimes, ethnic cleansing, and crimes against humanity.

The obligations reflected in the clause stem from well established rules and principles of customary and treaty international human rights law (IHRL) and international humanitarian law (IHL), and these are universally binding.

---

[2] Todd Lindberg, 'Protect the people', *Washington Times*, 27 September 2005; Alex J. Bellamy, 'Whither the Responsibility to Protect? Humanitarian Intervention on the 2005 World Summit', *Ethics and International Affairs*, 20/2: 143-169 (2006).

[3] Michael Byers, 'High Ground Lost on UN's Responsibility to Protect', *Winnipeg Free Press*, 18 September 2005; Bellamy, 'Whither the Responsibility to Protect?'

[4] Henry J. Steiner, Philip Alston and Ryan Goodman, *International Human Rights in Context: Law, Politics, Morals*, 3rd edn. (Oxford: Oxford University Press, 2008), p. 152.

Thus, the provisions in the outcome document constitute their reflection, not the source of the obligation. It is therefore important to revisit the existing set of legal standards, institutional structures and the jurisprudence underpinning the clause from the rights-based perspective to see how they better can be understood and applied by various actors (primarily states) under the protection obligations proclaimed by the World Summit.

A review of main underlying protection standards and obligations could also contribute to a better understanding of the nature of the responsibility to protect – to recognise it as a means of protection of the person, rooted in universal human rights standards, and not a military doctrine aimed at justifying intervention.

This general recognition of protection standards included in IHRL and IHL does not translate itself into their equally universal application. They are, however, increasingly used as the concrete point of reference against which to judge the conduct of states. Moreover, they have provided the legal foundations for the creation of international criminal courts and tribunals, including the ICC, and have contributed to the emerging culture of accountability and international justice.

Even though human rights remain formally valid in times of armed conflict, the means of actual protection through national and international human rights bodies are rather limited. Moreover, some state parties to major human right treaties fail to fulfil their protection obligations towards their own populations as well as towards others affected by armed conflict, by opposing international protection measures in the context of the Security Council.

At the core of the problem is the gap between human rights and security issues within the UN framework (the Human Rights Council and OHCHR and the Security Council and political and security departments in the UN Secretariat) and in the policies of states. Although the interdependency between the two has been emphasised by former Secretary-General Kofi Annan[5] and the HCHR, Sergio Vieira de Mello,[6] the UN human rights machinery is not a part of the mainstream activities of the Security Council.

[5] Kofi Annan, *In Larger Freedom: Towards Development, Security and Human Rights for All*, A/59/2005, 21 March 2005.

[6] '...The signal political failure of our era is the failure to understand the security threat posed by gross violations of human rights, and the failure to achieve practical consensus in acting against such a threat.....The time has arrived for all states to redefine global security – to put human rights at the center of this concept.' Sergio Vieira de Mello, 'Only Member States can Make the UN Work', *Sur International Journal on Human Rights*, No.1, 2004, pp. 161-164, www.surjournal.org/eng.

The clause on responsibility to protect may provide a new framework for better integration of these two key pillars.

The responsibility to protect under IHRL

International human rights law (IHRL) is a set of rules established by convention or custom, codified in international treaties and national bills of rights and focused on the protection of the individual.[7] The human rights system has been based on the responsibility of states as the main actors in the international arena and bearers of human rights obligations under international law. IHRL, in principle, applies both in times of war and peace.[8]

The term human rights appear infrequently in the UN Charter, and most such references[9] have a 'promotional' character relating specifically to the Charter's purposes or goals, not actions. Only the right to equal protection receives specific mention in the Charter (Art. 1.3, 13.1.b; 55). Despite these limitations, the Charter has served as the point of departure for further elaboration of human rights standards: in the 1948 Universal Declaration on Human Rights (UDHR),[10] the two human rights covenants of 1966: the International Covenant on Civil and Political Rights (ICCPR) with 164 state parties, and the International Covenant on Economic, Social and Cultural Rights (ICESCR) with 160, and a host of human rights treaties of more limited focus that have been ratified by most countries of the world.[11]

---

[7] Manfred Nowak, *Introduction to the International Human Rights Regime* (Leiden: Martinus Nijhoff, 2003).

[8] The International Court of Justice (ICJ), in its broadly cited Advisory Opinion stated: 'The protection of the ICCPR does not cease in times of war…' Although there is a possibility of derogation of certain provisions in times of emergency, the right to life, prohibition of torture and slavery are not subject of derogation. For details see ILC, 58th session, 1 May – 9 June and 3 July – 11 August 2006. See also Nowak, *Introduction to the International Human Rights Regime*; Steiner, Alston and Goodman, *International Human Rights in Context.*

[9] Preamble, Arts. 1.3, 13.1, 55, 56, 62.2 and 68; see Steiner, Alston and Goodman, *International Human Rights in Context*, p. 135.

[10] The UDHR became in the meantime a part of customary law. Steiner, Alston and Goodman, *International Human Rights in Context*, p. 137.

[11] They include the 1948 Convention on the Prevention and Punishment of Genocide with 140 State parties, the 1951 Convention Relating to the Status of Refugees with 144, the 1966 Convention on the Elimination of Racial Discrimination (CERD) with 173, the 1979 Convention on the Elimination of All Forms of Discrimination against Women (CEDAW) with 185, the 1984 Convention against Torture (CAT) with 146, the 1989 Convention on the Rights of the Child (CRC) with 193, the 1990 International Convention on the Protection of Rights of All Migrant Workers (CRMW) with 40, and the two latest conventions from 2006,

They contain provisions reflecting customary law and voluntarily undertaken binding treaty obligations. The high number of ratifications of such instruments like the Covenants, the Convention on Genocide, CAT, CRC, CEDR as well as the universal ratification of the 1948 Geneva Conventions[12] puts state parties under concrete obligations as to implementation. If taken seriously and conscientiously implemented at the national level, those instruments could have prevented most of the atrocities committed and helped to effectively address others, if necessary with the assistance of the international community.

The protection obligations of states under these instruments include general and specific provisions aimed at certain groups (women, or vulnerable groups like children, Internally Displaced Persons – IDPs, or persons with disabilities), or the nature of crimes (genocide, torture, forced disappearances).

General protection obligations

The general positive obligations of a state to protect and promote the human rights of all, without distinction or discrimination, including the right to life, liberty and security of person and the explicit ban of torture, cruel, inhumane and degrading treatment, and slavery are spelled out in the UDHR.[13] The two Covenants have further developed those obligations in the form of treaties, making some obligations more precise. The ICCPR obliges state parties to respect and ensure the rights to 'all individuals within its territory and subject to its jurisdiction…' not only its citizens, but includes refugees, or migrant workers, groups particularly vulnerable to abuses in practice (Art. 2.1)[14]. If the existing legislation is not sufficient to fulfil this obligation, state parties are to adopt proper legislative measures (Art. 2.2), and, if the rights are violated, to ensure an effective remedy and its enforcement by competent authorities (Art. 2-3).

Convention on the Rights of Persons with Disabilities, with 45 and International Convention on the Protection of All Persons from Enforced Disappearance, with 7 state parties; Sandy Ghandi (ed), Blackstone's Statutes, *International Human Rights Documents,* 6th edition, (Oxford University Press, 2008), Steiner, Alston and Goodman, *International Human Rights in the Context.*

[12] Steiner, Alston and Goodman, *International Human Rights in Context.*

[13] Universal Declaration of Human Rights (UDHR), Preamble, Articles 2-4; International Covenant on Civil and Political Rights (ICCPR), Preamble, Articles 1-9; *International Human Rights Documents,* pp. 10, 39-40.

[14] Bertrand G. Ramcharan, 'Contemporary Human Rights Ideas', *Global Institutions,* 2008.

Special protection obligations

Internally Displaced Persons (IDPs), children and women are disproportionally affected by violent conflict and atrocities. A host of international regulations (including treaties,[15] declarations and resolutions of the United Nations) addresses their protection requirements and related obligations of states and other stake holders.

Protection of Internally Displaced Persons (IDPs)
The Guiding Principles on Internal Displacement (1997) state the primary duty and responsibility of national authorities to provide protection and humanitarian assistance to IDPs within their jurisdiction (Principle 3). These principles reiterate their right to be protected against arbitrary displacement (Principle 6), genocide, murder, summary executions, enforced disappearances, indiscriminate attacks, starvation as a method of combat, use to shield military objectives (Principle 10), as well as against rape, mutilation, degrading treatment, gender-specific violence, forced prostitution, slavery, sexual exploitation, forced labour of children (Principle 11) and their recruitment into any armed forces (Principle 13) – the crimes that fall under the ICC terms of genocide, war crimes, ethnic cleansing and crimes against humanity.

Protection of children
The Convention on the Rights of the Child (CRC) of 1989, with 193 state parties, comprises a catalogue of state obligations to ensure the best interest of the child and protect her/his rights, such as the right to live (Art. 6), protection against all forms of sexual exploitation (prostitution, coercion, pornography) (Art. 34); abduction, traffic or sale of children (Art. 35); torture, cruel treatment, capital punishment or life sentence (Art. 37, a).[16] The CRC also includes the obligation to protect children in armed conflicts, in particular to prevent their recruitment as soldiers (Art. 39) – the provision fully developed in the Optional Protocol on the Involvement on Children in Armed Conflicts (2000). The ICC Statute lists the recruitment of children under age 15 as a war crime.

Protection of women and girls against gender-based violence
Numerous international instruments relate to the protection of women and girls against gender-based violence, but there is no specific treaty/convention

---

[15] Ibid., p. 5.

[16] Similar provisions are contained in the 1993 Vienna Declaration (Para. 21) adopted by the UN World Conference on Human Rights (WCHR).

addressing the issue. Most comprehensive is the 1993 Declaration on the Elimination of Violence against Women, adopted by consensus by the UN General Assembly (GA res. 59/167) in the aftermath of the WCHR in Vienna. Although some of its provisions constitute a part of customary law, the Declaration is binding only politically, not legally. On the other hand, the value of the GA consensus declaration is that states themselves have adopted the text, and thus stated the minimum obligations resulting from it. It carries more weight than, for example, recommendations issued by expert bodies.

Other instruments include the Geneva Conventions of 1949 and the Additional Protocols of 1977; the Refugee Convention of 1951 and the Protocol of 1967; the Convention on the Elimination of Discrimination against Women (CEDAW) of 1979 and the General Recommendation 19 on Violence against Women of 1992, and the Optional Protocol of 1999; the CRC of 1989 and the two Optional Protocols of 2000; the Rome Statute of the ICC and Security Council Resolutions on women and peace 1325 (2000) and 1820 (2008).

Despite all these instruments and numerous efforts aimed at eradicating violence against women at national and international levels, rape and other forms of sexual violence against women are still massively employed in war- and post-war countries.

Protection against genocide, torture and forced disappearances

Genocide, torture and forced disappearances are subject to specific international instruments: the Convention on the Prevention and Punishment of the Crime of Genocide (1948) with the Convention against Torture and Other, Inhuman or Degrading Treatment or Punishment (CAT) (1984, GA res. 39/46) with 144 state parties, and the Convention on the Protection of All Persons from Enforced Disappearance (2006).[17] They are included in the Statute of the ICC. All the three instruments reflect international customary law in most of their provisions. They do not allow immunities; the statute of limitations does not apply; they fall under universal jurisdiction and involve increased states' obligations to cooperate.

The Conventions put clear and strong protection obligations on states to treat genocide, torture and forced disappearances as crimes under their legal system, to prevent them, under all circumstances, address them if they occur and bring the perpetrators to justice, irrespective of their standing in society, and provide redress to the victims. CAT includes a specific provision that there

[17] These crimes and related protection obligations are also addressed in the ICCPR, 1949 Geneva Conventions, and the 1993 Vienna Declaration and Programme of Action.

should be no admission of any statement made under torture (Art. 15) and no extradition or expulsion if there is danger of torture in the country of destination (Art. 3).

International Treaty Bodies

The main human rights treaties have associated monitoring bodies (committees) composed of independent experts to oversee their implementation, with authority to interpret the treaty.[18] Some human rights treaties (ICCPR, CEDAW, CRC) require state parties to submit periodic reports on their implementation to treaty monitoring bodies. Such reports are increasingly accompanied by independent 'shadow reports' prepared by civil society. The reports, combined with comments, conclusions and recommendations of these bodies provide information useful for assessing the situation in the country, not least the status of protection.

The specific aspects of work of the committees differ. The CERD has an early warning system to prevent serious violations of the Convention.[19] Some other committees (ICCPR, CEDAW, CRC, and CAT) are equipped with complaints procedures, based on separate Optional Protocols, allowing them to receive individual complaints or communications on violations of the treaty in question. Such complaints could have a direct bearing on the state's responsibility to protect.

International Treaty Bodies provide some information on the implementation of protection obligations by respective state parties. The nature of their work and its timeframe predispose them to identify issues and patterns of violations for early warning use, to prevent further deterioration of the situation, more than providing immediate intervention. With the adoption of the responsibility to protect clause, the Treaty Bodies could be encouraged to generate and analyse the relevant material systematically, aiming to identify threats and suggest preventive measures within their mandates.

[18] They include Human Rights Committee (for ICCPR), the Committee on Economic, Social and Cultural Rights (for ICESCR), Committee against Torture (for CAT), Committee on the Elimination of Discrimination against Women (for CEDAW), Committee on the Elimination of Racism and Racial Discrimination (for CERD), Committee on the Rights of the Child (for CRC), Committee on Migrant Workers (for ICRMW), Committee on the Rights of Persons with Disabilities (for CRPD) and Committee on Enforced Disappearances (for CPAFD).

[19] Its recent warnings have concerned *inter alia* Darfur, Israel and Laos. See also Olivia Ball and Paul Gready, '*The No-Nonsense Guide to Human Rights*' (New Internationalist: Oxford, 2006).

Responsibility of the power in control

The responsibility to protect rests with the authorities controlling the territory, in the first place the states. There are however, circumstances in which a state (delete-many) may be unable or unwilling to exercise its protection obligations, such as when:

- The government (central authority) is too weak to exercise its constitutional powers; it has lost control over all or part of the territory and cannot prevent negative consequences (violence) for the population or parts of it;
- National laws, policies, and judicial practices contradict international human rights standards and violate rights of people instead of protecting them (institutionalised racial, gender or ethnic inequalities);
- The state and its agents actively and massively violate the human rights of people (torture, extra judiciary killings, disappearances, kidnappings).[20]

When states fail to protect their people from human rights violations and atrocities, the responsibility shifts to international organisations, including the United Nations.[21] Like other controlling powers (including a formally recognised occupying power), it is bound, to protect the inhabitants and respect IHL and IHRL.[22] The decision of the International Court of Justice (ICJ) in the *Case Concerning Armed Activities on the Territory of the Congo*, of December 2005, affirms this principle and demonstrates its relevance. The ICJ ruled that Ugandan forces occupying the Ituri district in the Democratic Republic of Congo (DRC) are obliged to respect all the human rights treaties to which Uganda is party. Moreover, as the occupying power, Uganda was obliged under Article 43 of The Hague Regulations of 1907[23] to take all measures in its power to restore, and ensure, as far as possible, public order and safety in the occupied area, while respecting the laws in force in the DRC.

[20] Siobhan Wills, 'The Responsibility to Protect by Peace Support Forces under International Humanitarian Law', *International Peacekeeping*, 13/4, December 2006, p. 477.

[21] Andrew Clapham, *Human Rights Obligations of Non-State Actors* (Oxford: Oxford University Press, 2006), p. 111; see also Annan, *In larger freedom* (para.135).

[22] The applicability and role of the Covenant in times of armed conflict was affirmed by the UN Human Rights Committee in General Comment 29, stating that the ICCPR applies also in situations of armed conflicts to which the rules of IHL are applicable. 'While in respect of certain Covenant rights more specific rules of IHL may be specifically relevant...both spheres of law are complementary, not mutually exclusive' (General Comment 31).

[23] Art. 43: 'The authority of the legitimate power having in fact passed into the hands of the occupant, the latter shall take all measures in his power to restore and ensure as far as possible, public order and safety, while respecting unless absolutely prevented, the laws in force in the country'.

This obligation comprised the duty to secure respect for the applicable rules of international human rights law and international humanitarian law, to protect the inhabitants of the occupied territory against acts of violence and not to tolerate such violence by any third party including rebel groups acting on their own account.[24] Thus, the Court found Uganda responsible not only for acts of its military, but also that it had failed to stop violence that resulted in 100,000 deaths and 500,000 displacements that took place while the Uganda Peoples Defence Force stood by and did not attempt to protect civilians.[25]

This opinion is especially relevant to ongoing violent conflicts in many parts of the world where parties in *de facto* control of certain regions – governmental forces or non-state actors – attempt to evade their responsibility for protecting civilian populations, claiming lack of knowledge of ongoing atrocities, inability to act, or disowning any responsibility in view of actions of other parties in conflict. As the responsibility to protect rests with *any* power effectively controlling the territory and is not limited to legal occupation, it applies to international forces as well as non-state actors.

The general comment of the UNHRC of 2004, on Article 2, of ICCPR goes in the same direction, emphasising protection obligations of 'those within the power of effective control of the forces of a state party acting outside its territory, regardless of the circumstances in which such power or effective control was obtained, such as forces constituting a national contingent of a state party assigned to an international peace-keeping or peace-enforcement operation'.[26]

In sum, any controlling power, including the UN, is responsible for protection of the inhabitants and for any violations of IHRL and IHL committed by its forces or agents.

Responsibility for major crimes under international law and jurisdiction

Protection against genocide, war crimes, ethnic cleansing and crimes against humanity – this is where the obligations of protection by the states and/or

[24] ICJ, *Case Concerning Armed Activities on the Territory of the Congo: Democratic Republic of Congo v Uganda,* 19 December 2005, Para. 217.

[25] Wills, 'The Responsibility to Protect by Peace Support Forces under International Humanitarian Law'. The case constitutes a useful example of convergence between the regimes of human rights law and international humanitarian law which strengthen basis for responsibility to protect in practice.

[26] General Comment No. 31, UN Doc. CCPR/C/2/1/Rev.1/Add.13, 21 April 2004, para. 10.

other controlling powers resulting from the IHRL and IHL[27] can be particularly great and intertwined. Many of today's human rights crimes violate both sets of laws, evoking protection obligations in all circumstances, by all actors.

These crimes fall under the jurisdiction of the International Criminal Court (ICC) established by the Rome Statute in 1998[28] to address the 'most serious crimes of concern to the international community', including genocide, crimes against humanity, war crimes and the crime of aggression.[29] They are defined under Article 6 (Genocide), Article 7 (Crimes against humanity) and Article 8 (Wars crimes) of the Statute. However, ICC has jurisdiction only over its state parties and those referred to its jurisdiction by the UN Security Council. It is complementary to national criminal jurisdictions.

These crimes evoke serious international legal consequences under all circumstances, also if tried by national courts. Genocide and crimes against humanity are considered crimes under all circumstances, whether in time of peace or war; neither immunities nor status of limitations apply; they fall under universal jurisdiction with an obligation of local trial or extradition; they involve increased international obligations on states to cooperate; and are not to be subject to amnesty.

Although these crimes carry individual responsibility, they may have multiple legal implications. Violations by individuals may also implicate states or other controlling powers, if these have been responsible for either condoning such crimes or not fulfilling their protection obligations. This point is particularly important in today's global world with increasingly influential non state actors in international relations, who exercise significant power over the lives of other people and thus should be accountable for their actions. Although

---

[27] For definition of IHRL, see above; IHL – the Four Geneva Conventions of 1949 and 1977 Additional Protocols define minimum standards for international and non-international armed conflicts to regulate the methods of conducting hostilities, the treatment of combatants and protection of civilians. The four Geneva Conventions of 1949 have gained the strength of customary law. They also achieved universal ratification in 2006 (Steiner, Alston and Goodman, *International Human Rights in Context*). Their common Art. 3 contains provisions which apply to non international conflicts and include most basic rights such as freedom from torture, murder, mutilation, and cruel treatment.

[28] Rome Statute of the International Criminal Court, UN doc. A/Conf.183/9, 17 July 1998.

[29] The crime of aggression can be addressed by the ICC once the provision has been adopted in accordance with its Articles 121 and 123 defining the crime as being consistent with the relevant provisions of the UN Charter and setting out the conditions for exercising jurisdiction of this provision. Due to the sensitivity of the issue the UN has not been able to agree on the definition of 'aggression' for decades.

their legal responsibility is often blurred and their status differs from state actors, there is a tendency to make them accountable for their behaviour, in particular the crimes included under the Statute of the ICC.[30]

The provisions of the ICC Statute, including definitions of crimes, draw heavily on the customary and statutory IHR and IHRL and the work of jurisprudence. Many see a growing convergence, or at least 'cross-fertilisation', between the rules relating to and the elements of many war crimes, and the rules and interpretations relating to human rights protection (the right to life, freedom from torture, and the right to a fair trial) which could strengthen the coherence of the overall legal protection system to the benefit of the individual.

The ICC has benefited especially from the work of the International Criminal Tribunal for the Former Yugoslavia (ICTFY), established by Security Council Resolution 808 (1993), which has prosecuted persons responsible for serious violations of international humanitarian law committed in the territory of the former Yugoslavia since 1991 on the basis of both customary and conventional law. Its work has contributed to expanding the jurisprudence related to rape in wartime and its final recognition as a crime against humanity; better definition of torture and elements of genocide; and the elaboration of a doctrine of command responsibility, subsequently fully defined in the Rome Statute.

The struggle to end impunity[31] in cases of most serious international crimes has given a new meaning to the universality principle, allowing national third party courts (neither courts of countries in which violations took place, nor international tribunals) to deal with such charges in exceptional circumstances, when the justice system of the country where the violations took place is unable or unwilling to proceed. Spain should be given due credit in this respect. The Spanish courts ordered the arrest of Augusto Pinochet during his visit to London in 1998,[32] and followed up by undertaking the litigation and sentencing in Spain of an Argentinean citizen for crimes against humanity that had been committed in Argentina.[33] Courts in other countries followed suit. That the case of Darfur was referred to the ICC by the Security Council, although Sudan is not a party to the ICC, and the extradition of Charles

[30] See Rosalyn Higgins, *Problems and Process: International Law and How We Use It*, (Oxford: Clarendon Press, 1994), p. 5.

[31] Dorota Gierycz, 'Transitional Justice – Does It Help or Does It Harm?', Oslo, NUPI Working Paper 737, 2008.

[32] Naomi Roht-Arriaza, *The Pinochet Effect: Translational Justice in the Age of Human Rights* (Philadelphia, PA: University of Pennsylvania Press, 2005).

[33] The case of Adolfo Scilingo, http://www.asil.org/-ilib/2005/04/ilib050426.htm#j3

Taylor on the order of the Special Court for Sierra Leone, demonstrate a new and important aspect of universal justice.

UN Human Rights Machinery

The three pillar concept

The United Nations Human Rights Machinery has a considerable potential for addressing the responsibility to protect. It includes the UN Human Rights Council and its Special Procedures, Human Rights Commissioner as well as various treaty bodies to monitor the implementation of the human rights treaties discussed above. After major protection failures in Srebrenica and in Rwanda, and facing a similar crisis in Darfur, Secretary-General Kofi Annan made a serious attempt to revive this apparatus, to make it more relevant and responsive to gross violations of human rights.

In his report *In larger freedom: towards development, security and human rights for all* (A/59/2005), Annan stated that development, security and human rights are all imperative, interdependent and mutually reinforcing, 'we will not enjoy development without security, we will not enjoy security without development, and we will not enjoy either without respect for human rights' (Para. 17). The report called for high level and sustainable UN engagement in human rights; a more active role for the High Commissioner for Human Rights in the deliberations of the Security Council and of the proposed Peace-building Commission; the incorporation of human rights into decision-making and discussion throughout the work of the organisation (Para.144).

Further, the report acknowledged that the UN technical support to human rights promotion in the field 'is of little value where the principle of protection is being actively violated', and stressed the need for a greater human rights field presence during times of crisis to provide timely information to UN bodies (Para. 143) so they could prepare a crisis response and contribute to conflict prevention.

This three pillar concept constitutes an unprecedented attempt to integrate human rights into the work of the UN on an equal footing with security and development, and to provide the human rights machinery with conditions for operating in the mainstream of its activities, in close correlation with the Security Council. If implemented, that concept could have created the conditions for a consolidated, systemic UN approach to enacting the principle of the responsibility to protect. Certainly, in view of the ongoing discussions on the responsibility to protect, the concept could be revisited and given proper attention.

Unfortunately, the concept encountered firm resistance from member states as well as from various parts of the UN system, and has gradually faded away. Some parts of the human rights machinery, however, like the UN High Commissioner for Human Rights (HCHR)[34] and that office and the Commission on Human Rights, converted into the Human Rights Council, have been considerably strengthened in the context of the overall UN reform.[35]

The UN High Commissioner for Human Rights

The reforms clearly strengthened the protective functions of the OHCHR. In order to ensure timely and systematic response to gross violations of human rights, the rapid response unit was established;[36] UN human rights field offices were expanded and provided with a stronger protection mandate focused on support for human rights defenders, national protection systems, and on countering impunity for past and ongoing serious human rights violations. Subsequently, the Secretary-General's Policy Committee decision 2005/24 on human rights in integrated missions further strengthened human rights components, and introduced obligatory periodic and thematic public reporting on the situation on the ground. Such public reports coming from all field missions can provide broader information otherwise rarely available to member states. If included in the mainstream work of the UN, the Security Council in particular, they could offer a more complete and realistic picture of the country and conflict under consideration, including elements of early warning against possible atrocities. In practice, however, this is not the case. Although reports are generally accessible, they are seen as part of the human rights domain and as such are rarely used by other parts of the UN system. Moreover, in some countries the reports are perceived as 'counterproductive', unnecessarily taking up 'sensitive' issues and antagonising host countries and certain other governments. Thus they may be less regular and more 'selective'. Despite such shortcomings, regular field reporting on the human rights situation plays an important awareness raising role, and could be further used in the context of the responsibility to protect.

---

[34] GA res. 48/141 of 1993. The UNHCHR is appointed by the Secretary-General with the approval of the General Assembly.

[35] As per HCHR's Strategic Management Plan, 2006-2007. In late 2007 there were 7 regional and 15 country HR offices, in addition to human rights advisers on some UN country teams and human rights officers at some UNDP offices.

[36] Annual report of UNHCHR Louise Arbour to the General Assembly, A/26/36.

Human Rights Council, 2006

The Human Rights Council (GA resolution 60/251) is mandated *inter alia* to 'contribute through dialogue and cooperation, towards the prevention of human rights violations and respond promptly to human rights emergencies', 'address the situations of violations of human rights, including gross and systematic violations, and make recommendations thereon' and promote effective coordination and the mainstreaming of human rights within the UN system (Art. 3).[37]

The Human Right Council has at its disposal various measures to address gross violations of human rights once its members so decide. It can hold special sessions, public debates or use its Special Procedures, including the appointment of thematic human rights rapporteurs and working groups, country specific rapporteurs, or Special Representative of the SG. As of 2007 there were over 40 thematic mechanisms, and four working groups. The special rapporteurs – especially in such areas as torture, extrajudicial executions,[38] enforced disappearances, arbitrary detentions, and violence against women – are particularly well placed to assess the facts on the ground and, if necessary, alert the Council to ongoing gross violations of human rights, or suggest means of prevention once they note the first symptoms. Being independent, they can make public statements on the issues, request fact-finding on the ground, denounce violators, collect data, engage in dialogue with governments, or demand an emergency session of the Council. Their reports provide first-hand information, which is often utilised more by NGOs than by the UN system. Special Procedures can play an important role in preventing, addressing and responding to gross violations of human rights.

The Human Rights Council can also collect valuable information related to the responsibility to protect through its review and investigative procedures. It has introduced a new peer review mechanism – Universal Periodic Review (UPR) of each state – enabling analysis of its entire human rights record, including the treaty obligations and commitments emanating from UN conferences and summits. The Council could make a conscious effort to include the responsibility to protect as one of the leading topics/questions in these enquiries.

[37] See also Ramcharan, 'Contemporary Human Rights Ideas'.

[38] The Special Rapporteur on Extrajudicial Arbitrary and Summary Executions tried to alert the international community to the forthcoming genocide in Rwanda (1993), albeit unsuccessfully.

The Council has inherited from the Human Rights Commission the procedure of confidential examination of communications[39] dealing with alleged violations of human rights, which it applies with minor modifications. This can also be relevant to the responsibility to protect, although, in view of the procedural requirements, more as a means of information collection and long-term prevention than for immediate protective action.

It is difficult to assess the role of the Human Rights Council with regard to the responsibility to protect. The time since its creation has been too short, expectations too high and the attempts to distance it from the Human Rights Commission often unrealistic. While the Council has contributed to dialogue, and addressed some aspects of the responsibility to protect through Special Procedures, it has generally failed in exercising the responsibility to protect in the case of Darfur.[40] As a political body it has suffered from similar obstacles as those encountered by other parts of the UN intergovernmental structure.

Conclusions and recommendations

There can be no doubt as to the universal and unconditional nature of the legal obligation reflected in the World Summit Outcome Document of 2005 to protect populations from genocide, war crimes, ethnic cleansing and other crimes against humanity. This obligation is primarily binding on states, but also, if these are unable to act, on intergovernmental organisations and other actors exercising control over a given territory, and is rooted in existing customary and statutory IHRL and IHL.

However, the clause has not been translated into action, either by states or the UN Security Council. The Security Council is its own master, and, judging from the recent experiences of with Darfur or Zimbabwe, it cannot be relied upon to uphold the promise 'never again'. Neither are there indications that the Council will be prepared to relax its procedures in accordance with suggestions of the International Commission on Intervention and State Sovereignty (ICISS)[41] for intervention in the name of the responsibility to

---

[39] The Commission has dealt with alleged violations through the procedure of confidential examination of communications (complaints) in situations of human rights violations requiring attention of the Commission, under the 1503 procedure named after ECOSOC res. 1503 (1970) which established this procedure. Steiner, Alston and Goodman, *International Human Rights in Context*, p. 812.

[40] UN press release SG/SM/10794, 12 December 2006.

[41] Report of the International Commission on Intervention and State Sovereignty (ICISS), *The Responsibility to Protect*, 2001.

protect. While some minor departures can be noted in the practice of the Council to authorise robust action under Chapter VII in response to gross violations of human rights, there has been no major shift from its traditional mandate of linking any intervention to a 'threat to peace' and defining the latter in a rather narrow manner.

The responsibility to protect clause needs to be recognised as an opportunity to give force to the implementation of the underlying human rights instruments, which too often remain on paper or are not supported by sufficient national legislation and enforcement. Two sets of measures – concerning research, and concerning policy – might help in achieving momentum towards implementing the responsibility to protect clause.

Research recommendations:

- Identification of key human rights standards and instruments most relevant to the responsibility to protect, and their publication in a handbook
- Comprehensive review of states' records in these areas in line with the clause (legislative, administrative, and judicial measures, and their conduct related to emergencies and armed conflict)
- Analysis of states' voting patterns in the UN HRC, human rights treaty bodies and the Security Council (based on case studies)
- Assessment of the OHCHR's role and capacity (field and HQ) to act on the responsibility to protect
- Analysis of the established and possible links between the UN human rights machinery and the Security Council (reporting, briefings, early warning)
- Review of the three-pillar concept and a tailoring of its possible application to the responsibility to protect.

Policy recommendations:

- Regular submission of information relevant to the responsibility to protect by all UN human rights review mechanisms (in particular UPR, Special Procedures) and treaty bodies
- Regular, high-level involvement of the OHCHR in Security Council debates on cases related to the responsibility to protect
- Submission of special reports by the OHCHR to the Security Council in cases involving the responsibility to protect.

International Law and the Responsibility to Protect: Clarifying or Expanding States' Responsibilities?

Jennifer M. Welsh and Maria Banda

Abstract

The Responsibility to Protect (R2P) invokes one of the most powerful moral and legal terms in contemporary international politics – namely, responsibility. The nature of the relationship between R2P and international law and morality, however, remains contested, giving rise to questions lying at the core of R2P's normative foundations. What is the source of R2P? To whom is this responsibility attributable, and under what circumstances? Does R2P give rise to legal obligations? Such questions challenge International Relations (IR) theorists to look beyond their discipline for more insightful tools and methods of analysis. In this article, we apply a broadened theoretical framework to explain the ongoing controversy about R2P. In Part II, we borrow tools from moral philosophy to identify the source and the bearer of the responsibility to protect in today's international society. In Part III, we draw on international legal scholarship to analyse whether R2P has emerged as a 'new' norm of customary international law. We find that international endorsement of R2P has helped to clarify existing obligations in international law, but that intrinsic ambiguities in its articulation currently limit R2P's capacity to entrench new obligations for states to protect strangers. At the same time, our finding that R2P is an example of 'soft law' leads us to conclude that R2P can nonetheless exert significant influence on how states interpret their legal obligations and, in the coming decade, it may also help catalyse diplomatic efforts to reform the international architecture for preventing and responding to mass atrocities.

Keywords

responsibility to protect; sovereignty; jus cogens; norms; erga omnes; extraterritorial; Summit Outcome Document; Genocide Convention; soft law

R2P invokes one of the most powerful moral and legal terms in contemporary international politics – namely, responsibility. As such, it would be surprising if the last decade of conceptual and diplomatic work in support of R2P had *not* had important effects on the content and interpretation of international law. Yet, as previous and current issues of this journal have shown, the nature of the relationship between international law and the principle of the Responsibility to Protect remains contested.[1] We argue that the core of the controversy can

[1] See, for example, Ekkehard Strauss, 'A Bird in the Hand is Worth Two in the Bush – On the Assumed Legal Nature of the Responsibility to Protect', *Global Responsibility to Protect*,

be reduced to two related questions: 1) what is the source and who is the bearer of the responsibility to protect in today's international society; and 2) has that responsibility become a 'new' legal norm? Both of these questions challenge International Relations (IR) analysts to broaden their disciplinary frame of reference. The first requires consultation and application of tools from moral philosophy, in order to more clearly attribute responsibilities. The second challenges Constructivist IR scholars[2] who study the evolution of norms to interact more deliberately with legal arguments about the development of custom. Unlike most IR accounts of normative change, which tend to analyse norms as a homogeneous form – and, hence, which often have difficulty explaining why some norms are more likely to generate consensus, or controversy, than others – international law is premised on heterogeneity and a hierarchy of normative forms. Principles, norms, and rules of customary law are 'protean': i.e. they reflect different degrees of legal standing, command varying levels of support, and leave an uneven imprint on international practice.[3] We believe that while endorsement of the principle of R2P has helped to clarify existing obligations in international law, ambiguities concerning who, precisely, has the responsibility to protect, as well as uncertainty over the strength of the political commitment expressed for R2P, currently limit its capacity to entrench new obligations for states in terms of protection. Instead, as an example of 'soft law', R2P's contribution to the prevention of mass atrocity crimes is twofold: a powerful reminder to states of their legal obligations; and a catalyst for reform and innovation to the international architecture for protection (which includes international and regional organisations;

1/3: 291-323 (2009); and Sheri P. Rosenberg, 'Responsibility to Protect: A Framework for Prevention', *Global Responsibility to Protect*, 1/4: 442-477 (2009). For an analysis of the legal status of the various aspects of R2P, see also Carsten Stahn, 'Responsibility to Protect: Political Rhetoric or Emerging Legal Norm', *American Journal of International Law*, 101/1: 99-120 (2007).

[2] For examples of general Constructivist scholarship, see Alexander Wendt, *Social Theory of International Politics* (Cambridge: Cambridge University Press, 1999); and Jeffrey Checkel, 'The Constructivist Turn in International Relations Theory', *World Politics*, 50/2: 324-348 (1998). For examples of Constructivist analysis of norms, see Martha Finnemore and Kathryn Sikkink, 'International Norm Dynamics and Political Change,' *International Organization*, 52/4: 887-917 (1998); Nina Tannenwald, *The Nuclear Taboo: The United States and the non-use of nuclear weapons since 1945* (Cambridge: Cambridge University Press, 2007); and Thomas Risse-Kappen et al, eds., *The Power of Human Rights: International Norms and Domestic Change* (Cambridge: Cambridge University Press, 1999).

[3] R.R. Baxter, 'International Law in "Her Infinite Variety"', 29, *International Comparative Law Quarterly* (1980), 563.

agencies; NGOs; and governments) with a view to making such obligations more effective.

I. Contemporary understandings of R2P

As originally conceived, the primary purpose of the Responsibility to Protect was to avoid inaction by the international community when genocidal acts or massive human rights violations are occurring inside the frontiers of a sovereign state, and the state in question is unable or unwilling to halt them.[4] But proponents of the principle have also insisted that it is designed to remind states of the responsibilities they have for the safety and well-being of their citizens. As described in the UN Secretary-General's 2009 report, R2P consists of three components or 'pillars'.[5] Pillar One, drawing on pre-existing legal obligations,[6] is the responsibility of individual states to protect their own populations (whether nationals or not) from genocide, war crimes, ethnic cleansing, and crimes against humanity. Pillar Two calls on the international community (acting through the UN system and partner organisations) to help states fulfill these responsibilities. Finally, Pillar Three specifies that if the state in question is 'manifestly failing' to protect its population, UN Member States have a residual responsibility to respond collectively, in a 'timely and decisive manner,' using the full range of diplomatic and – if necessary – military tools.

This articulation suggests that R2P sits at the intersection of three different legal regimes: sovereign equality;[7] the use of force and non-intervention;[8]

---

[4] For background, see Gareth Evans, *The Responsibility To Protect: Ending Mass Atrocity Crimes Once and For All* (Washington, D.C.: Brookings Institution, 2008).

[5] Ban Ki-Moon, *Implementing the Responsibility to Protect,* A/63/677, 12 January 2009.

[6] For a detailed discussion of the elements of international human rights law giving rise to this state responsibility, see Rosenberg, 'Responsibility to Protect', 447-459.

[7] The core elements of sovereignty were codified in a series of international documents, including the 1933 Montevideo Convention on the Rights and Duties of States (Article 1), UN Charter (Article 2), and UNGA Declaration on Principles of International Law Concerning Friendly Relations Among States. The International Court of Justice (ICJ) observed in 1949 that 'between independent States, respect for territorial sovereignty is an essential foundation of international relations' (*Corfu Channel* case, ICJ Reports 1949, 4), which it reaffirmed four decades later by referring to the 'fundamental principle of state sovereignty on which the whole of international law rests'.(*Military and Paramilitary Activities in and against Nicaragua* (Nicaragua v. United States), ICJ Reports, 1986, para. 263).

[8] Article 2.4 of the UN Charter expressly prohibits member-states from using (or threatening) force against each other, with two exceptions: self-defence (Article 51) and military measures

and the protection of civilians. The protection of civilians regime – which is also the most recently codified – consists not only of human rights law, but also humanitarian law, international criminal law, and refugee law. It has evolved through milestones such as the 1948 Universal Declaration of Human Rights (UDHR); four Geneva Conventions and two Additional Protocols on international humanitarian law in armed conflict; the 1948 Convention on the Prevention and Punishment of the Crime of Genocide (the Genocide Convention); the two 1966 International Covenants – on Civil and Political (ICCPR) and Social, Economic and Cultural Rights (ISECR); the 1998 Rome Statute establishing the International Criminal Court (ICC), and the Ottawa Convention on landmines.[9]

What sets this body of 'international protection law'[10] apart from the rules governing sovereignty and the use of force is its referent: the rules making up the protection regime are fundamentally concerned with protecting not state borders, but individuals. Thus, while the protection rules are negotiated by governments at the international level, the resulting laws codify the most fundamental of all social contracts: the obligations owed by each state to its citizens. States have been less willing, however, to undertake comparable obligations for the protection of strangers. Indeed, the legal nature of these extraterritorial obligations is more ambiguous – particularly since the Draft Articles on State Responsibility require State A (the extraterritorial state) to have played a contributing role in the wrongful conduct of State B before it can be attributed responsibility.[11] As we show below, fleshing out the extraterritorial responsibilities of states with respect to the protection of individuals

---

authorized by the Security Council under Chapter VII (and, by extension, regional organizations under Chapter VIII) in response to 'any threat to the peace, breach of the peace or act of aggression.' The architects of the UN Charter acknowledged in 1945 that military action may be necessary under exceptional circumstances and thus sought to strike a balance between the sovereignty and equality of individual states, and the collective international responsibility for the maintenance of international peace and security. The former is reflected in the Principles of the UN (Article 2.1, 2.4, and 2.7) and the latter in Chapter VII (Articles 39 to 51) and the powers vested in the Security Council.

[9] It also includes 'softer' laws like the UN Guidelines on Internally Displaced Persons and the Guiding Principles on Humanitarian Assistance.

[10] In using this phrase, we recognize that R2P draws on, but is not identical to, the rules on the protection of civilians. As Strauss notes, the protection of civilians is a notion which pertains to the context of armed conflict, while the mass atrocity crimes encompassed by R2P can be committed outside such situations. In addition, the protection of civilians agenda deals with a broader set of crimes than the specific four identified in the 2005 Outcome Document statement of R2P. See Strauss, 'A Bird in the Hand', p. 305.

[11] *Draft Articles on the Responsibility of States for Internationally Wrongful Acts, Report of the ILC on the Work of its Fifty-third Session,* UNGA, 56th Session, Supp. No. 10, UN Doc A/56/10

from mass atrocity crimes requires an engagement with both moral philosophy and recent jurisprudence relating to the Genocide Convention.

II. The Source and Bearer of the International Responsibility to Protect

While responsibility is a contested concept in the philosophical and legal literature,[12] it can be defined most simply as 'actions or forbearances that one is deemed bound to perform or observe'.[13] This definition suggests that any complete account of responsibility should clarify the source of these duties (or reasons that they have been generated). One of the earliest statements of R2P, the Report of the International Commission on Intervention and State Sovereignty (ICISS),[14] failed to take on this task directly. The Commissioners spent the bulk of their time outlining the conditions under which the principle of non-intervention may be overridden in the name of protecting human rights,[15] and less time answering the fundamental question of why there is a prospective *international* responsibility to protect.[16] As philosopher Kok-Chor Tan observes: 'The report seems to take it for granted that there is a default responsibility to protect, and the only obstacle to the performance of this responsibility is the principle of nonintervention.'[17]

(2001). For the particular discussion on attribution in these Articles, see James Crawford, *The International Law Commission's Articles on State Responsibility: Introduction, Text and Commentaries* (Cambridge: Cambridge University Press, 2002), Articles 16-18.

[12] One of the clearest expositions of the concept can be found in Peter Cane, *Responsibility in Law and Morality* (Oxford: Hart Publishing, 2002).

[13] Toni Erskine, 'Introduction: Making Sense of "Responsibility" in International Relations – Key Questions and Concepts', in Toni Erskine, ed., *Can Institutions Have Responsibilities? Collective Moral Agency and International Relations*, (Houndmills, Basingstoke: Palgrave, 2003), p. 11 (fn. 1). See also the distinctions between various kinds of responsibility in David Miller, 'Distributing Responsibilities', *The Journal of Political Philosophy*, 9/4: 453-471 (2001).

[14] ICISS, *The Responsibility to Protect*, Report of the International Commission on Intervention and State Sovereignty (Ottawa: IDRC, 2001).

[15] The report lays out six criteria which would make infringement of the principle of non-intervention permissible: just cause (referring to severity of atrocity), right intention, last resort, proportionality, reasonable prospects of success, and proper authority. See *The Responsibility to Protect*, p. xii.

[16] For more on this gap, and an argument for locating the source of responsibility in natural law, see William Bain, 'Responsibility From Where?: Theorising the Obligation to Rebuild'. Paper presented to the Workshop on the Ethics of Post-Conflict Reconstruction, Centre for International Studies, University of Oxford, 26 June 2008.

[17] Kok-Chor Tan, 'The Duty to Protect', in Terry Nardin and Melissa Williams, eds., *Humanitarian Intervention. NOMOS ILVII* (New York: New York University Press, 2006), pp. 84-116 (p. 88).

Nonetheless, if one mines the separate passages of the ICISS report a bit further – along with subsequent statements by R2P's authors and supporters – it is possible to piece together a reasonably clear account of the source of responsibility. The clue can be found in the Commissioners' appeals to universal human rights and 'common humanity'.[18] In fact, the ICISS report launches its analysis by talking not about states, but rather about human rights and human security:

> Millions of human beings remain at the mercy of civil wars, insurgencies, state repression and state collapse. This is a stark and undeniable reality, and it is at the heart of all the issues with which this Commission has been wrestling. What is at stake here is not making the world safe for big powers, or trampling over the sovereign rights of small ones, but delivering practical protection for ordinary people, at risk of their lives, because their states are unwilling or unable to protect them.[19]

The logic runs as follows: though a crisis begins with a challenge to individual rights through persecution and violence, the scale of the atrocities inflicted upon those individuals affects us *collectively*, through the international harm principle. To commit genocide or engage in ethnic cleansing is to fail to treat people *as humans*, thereby threatening humanity's values and interests.[20] This is what generates the moral responsibility for members of the international community to act in ways that might otherwise be seen as an infringement of non-intervention and the principle of third-party neutrality. As Tan puts it: 'If the right of the offending state to nonintervention may be overruled in the name of human rights, so too … may the right of other states to stay disengaged.'[21]

Thus, if we focus on the duty-generating character of universal human rights,[22] and agree on the force of the principle of common humanity, we can overcome the problem of the missing source for the international community's remedial responsibility to protect. But this still leaves the account of responsibility incomplete. A second issue is the lack of clarity as to who within the

---

[18] *The Responsibility to Protect,* p. 2. Gareth Evans has reinforced this view with his statement that 'the case for R2P rests simply on our common humanity'. See 'The Responsibility to Protect: An Idea Whose Time Has Come … and Gone?' *International Relations*, 22/3:283-98 (2008).

[19] *The Responsibility to Protect,* p. 11.

[20] The international harm principle is laid out by Larry May in *Crimes Against Humanity: A Normative Account* (Cambridge: Cambridge University Press, 2005).

[21] Tan, 'The Duty to Protect', p. 90.

[22] *Ibid.*, pp. 92-3. For another compelling account which suggests that rights imply duties, see Henry Shue, 'Limiting Sovereignty', in Jennifer M. Welsh, ed., *Humanitarian Intervention and International Relations* (Oxford: Oxford University Press, 2004), pp. 11-28.

international community bears this remedial responsibility. In the ICISS report, the appeal to the international community is a very general one, leaving us – in Tan's words – with an 'imperfect duty' to protect.[23] This ambiguity has two potential effects. First, the diffuse responsibility can make it easier for states and international organisations to shirk their obligations. Ironically, then, an unallocated responsibility to protect risks encouraging inaction on the part of other states rather than the rampant interventionism that many critics of R2P fear. Second, an imperfect duty does not provide suffering citizens within a state any real claim against the international community. To put it another way, a duty of protection is asserted, but no corresponding liability for a failure to protect.[24] The problem is not only one of unfulfilled expectations, but also of the absence of mechanisms for holding the international community accountable retrospectively for its failure to play its remedial role.

It should be noted here that the strategy of deriving the responsibility to protect from existing obligations in international law was not pursued by the Commissioners, suggesting that the principle for them was predominantly a moral and political imperative. However, we argue that an international responsibility for protection (i.e., an extraterritorial responsibility) could be derived through three fundamental concepts: *jus cogens*; obligations *erga omnes;* and, universal jurisdiction (or what we call the 'universality principle').[25]

Not all international laws protecting individual rights are equally robust—and neither are the expected measures that other states can take when these rules are violated. So, for example, governments might condemn a denial of the freedom of speech or fair trial within another country, but they will rarely go beyond diplomatic rebukes.[26] Violations of peremptory rules of

---

[23] Tan, 'The Duty to Protect', p. 95.

[24] Drawing on Hohfeld, David Rodin describes R2P as a 'liberty right'. See 'The Responsibility to Protect and the Logic of Rights', in Oliver Jutersonke and Keith Krause, eds., *From Rights to Responsibilities: Rethinking Interventions for Humanitarian Purposes* (Geneva: Programme for Strategic and International Security Studies, 2006), pp. 45-60 (p. 55). If A has a right against B, this is equivalent to B having a duty to honour A's right. But if B has no duty, that means that B has a liberty, i.e. B has a choice of whether or not to honour A's right.

[25] For examples of this kind of legal approach, see Louise Arbour, 'The responsibility to protect as a duty of care in international law and practice', *Review of International Studies,* 34/3: 445-458 (2008); and Rosenberg, 'The Responsibility to Protect', p. 450. Both authors rely on the *Case Concerning the Application of the Convention on the Prevention and Punishment of the Crime of Genocide (Bosnia and Herzegovina v. Serbia and Montenegro),* in which the International Court of Justice found Serbia in violation of Article 1 of the Convention, for failing to prevent genocide in the territory of another state. The case is discussed further below.

[26] Alain Pellet, 'State sovereignty and the protection of fundamental human rights: an international law perspective,' *Pugwash Occasional Papers,* I:i (2000).

international law, or *jus cogens,* however, are treated differently.[27] Such norms give rise to a special kind of obligations, or obligations *erga omnes*, which, rather than being owed to a specific state, are owed to the international community as a whole.[28] Thus, if it can be determined that R2P is linked to principles of *jus cogens,* its extraterritorial demands may be more onerous. As such, the source of international responsibility (and obligation) may fall in the category *erga omnes*, and a failure to protect may trigger a variety of forms of redress.[29]

Extraterritoriality is also embedded in the final, though contested, principle of universality, which is most closely associated with peremptory rules forbidding war crimes, crimes against humanity, and genocide. Under universal jurisdiction, any state's courts can prosecute and punish such violations irrespective of where they may have occurred, and irrespective of state sovereignty. To date, only a handful of international treaties place a legally-binding obligation on the ratifying states to exercise universal jurisdiction.[30] No such *treaty* requirement exists with regard to genocide and crimes against humanity, but universal jurisdiction is increasingly being applied even in these cases as a matter of customary law or domestic legislation.[31] This practice remains contested, with the opponents worrying about judicial 'tyranny'[32] and the proponents, in contrast, contending that universal jurisdiction is the foundation of a universal responsibility for protection.[33]

[27] Rules of *jus cogens* (Lat.: 'compelling law') are so fundamental that they cannot be modified or displaced by a treaty, i.e. 'a norm accepted and recognised by the international community of States as a whole as a norm for which no derogation is permitted and which can be modified only by a subsequent norm of general international law having the same character' (1969 Vienna Convention on the Law of Treaties, Article 53).

[28] Barcelona Traction case (Belgium v Spain) (Second Phase), ICJ Rep 1970, 3 [33]. Beyond genocide, *erga omnes* norms are said to include slavery, apartheid or racial discrimination, and piracy—giving every state a right to complain about, prosecute, and punish their commission.

[29] One limitation in using the framework of violations of *jus cogens/erga omnes* is that it will not apply when the violator is not a state. These concepts address issues in the context of state-to-state responsibility only. We are grateful to Dapo Akande for raising this point.

[30] Examples include the Geneva Conventions, the Convention Against Torture, and the Inter-American Convention on Forced Disappearance of Persons (binding only within OAS). It is disputed whether the Genocide Convention (particularly Article VI) can be interpreted more broadly to include universal jurisdiction.

[31] E.g. British House of Lords decision in 1998/9 to extradite General Pinochet and Belgium's conviction of Rwandan nuns in 2001 for complicity in genocide.

[32] Henry Kissinger, 'The Pitfalls of Universal Jurisdiction,' *Foreign Affairs* (July/August 2001).

[33] Kenneth Roth, 'The Case For Universal Jurisdiction,' *Foreign Affairs* (September/October 2001).

Given the above observations, it is logical to focus our discussion of legal responsibility on the 1948 Genocide Convention, which incorporates notions of both *jus cogens* and universality.[34] As the ICJ observed in its Advisory Opinion on the Convention: 'In such a convention, the contracting States do not have any interests of their own; they merely have, one and all, a common interest, namely, the accomplishment of those high purposes which are the *raison d'être* of the convention.'[35] Since the drafting of the Genocide Convention, it has been acknowledged that all contracting parties have an obligation to prevent and punish genocidal acts occurring within their territory; more recently, with the case of Srebrenica, this obligation has been alleged to extend beyond the territorial state to other neighbouring states (in this instance, Serbia's failure to prevent genocide in Bosnia).[36] As Arbour shows in her analysis of the case, the responsibility invoked by the ICJ is essentially one of due diligence: Serbia had not taken all the measures that were reasonably available to it to prevent genocide.[37] In its judgment, the Court insists that if a 'State has available to it means likely to have a deterrent effect on those suspected of preparing genocide, or reasonably suspected of harbouring specific intent *(dolus specialis)*, it is under a duty to make such use of these means as the circumstances permit.'[38] In addition, in reasoning which appears to borrow from domestic law (both criminal and tort law) the ICJ claims that responsibilities to act are triggered when a state has a reasonable degree of knowledge about impending crimes: 'a State's obligation to prevent, and the corresponding duty to act, arise at the instant that the State learns of, or should normally have learned of, the existence of a serious risk that genocide will be committed.'[39]

---

[34] Convention on the Prevention and Punishment of the Crime of Genocide, 9 December 1948, in Adam Roberts and Richard Guelff, eds., *Documents on the Laws of War,* 3rd edition (Oxford: Oxford University Press, 2000), pp. 179-194.

[35] International Court of Justice, Advisory Opinion on *Reservations to the Genocide Convention,* ICJ Reports 1951, 15 at 23.

[36] International Court of Justice, *Case Concerning the Application of the Convention on the Prevention and Punishment of the Crime of Genocide (Bosnia and Herzegovina v. Serbia and Montenegro.* General List, no. 91, 26 February 2007. Available at http://www.icj-cij.org/docket/files/91.13685.pdf (henceforth referred to as 'ICJ Judgment'). This was the first time that state responsibility (as opposed to individual responsibility) had been the subject of ICJ judgment with respect to the Genocide Convention.

[37] Arbour, 'The responsibility to protect', pp. 451-52. See ICJ Judgment, para. 430.

[38] ICJ Judgment, para. 431.

[39] *Ibid.* For discussion of the analogy with domestic torts law, see Arbour, 'The responsibility to protect', p. 452; and Rosenberg, 'The Responsibility to Protect', pp. 466-67.

But while the above interpretation of the jurisprudence on the Genocide Convention suggests a trend toward the acceptance of positive state obligations to protect populations from mass atrocities within another state's jurisdiction, we are still left with an incomplete picture. More specifically, the law remains unclear as to which states will have that obligation to act in precise circumstances. Do these obligations apply equally to all signatories to the Convention, or do special circumstances (for example, the historical links between the countries concerned, geographic proximity, or material ability of particular states) make this obligation a variable – or even optional – one?[40] This issue is magnified when we consider that the Responsibility to Protect, as currently articulated, does not specify what the responsibility actually requires, in terms of concrete action.

To have true remedial responsibility, as philosopher David Miller reminds us, is for a particular agent (or particular agents) to have a particular duty to put the wrong right – to be designated to carry a responsibility that is not shared equally among all.[41] Again, ICISS did not fully consider how this allocation of responsibility might occur, beyond concluding that the UN Security Council is the appropriate body to authorise any international response to a situation in which a state is failing in its protection responsibilities.[42] To reiterate the problem: R2P's invocation of responsibility is not based on the idea that a state or group of states has a duty to intervene on behalf of a group of people whose unjust suffering it has helped to cause. Instead, as suggested above, R2P (temporarily) transfers responsibility from the primary state to the 'international community' based on the severity of the atrocity

[40] There is also ambiguity concerning the obligations associated with the other crimes mentioned in the 2005 Outcome Document, namely war crimes, crimes against humanity, and ethnic cleansing. Unlike genocide, there is no international treaty that contains an explicit obligation on States to prevent these crimes. However, the four Geneva Conventions dealing with the laws of war (1949) contain a common provision, Article 1, whereby states accept an obligation not only to respect but also 'to ensure respect' for the Conventions. While this Common Article 1 is regarded as a bedrock provision for the Geneva Conventions, there has been little analysis of the scope of these obligations to ensure respect.

[41] David Miller, 'The Responsibility to Protect Human Rights', Paper presented to the International Symposium on Justice, Legitimacy, and Public International Law, University of Bern, 15-17 December 2006.

[42] ICISS did consider principles such as proximity and capability in its discussion of mobilizing the political will to act in crises involving the commission of mass atrocities. See *Responsibility to Protect*, p. 70. Commissioners were also fully aware of the objections to reliance on the Security Council (for example, the slowness of the Council's decision-making; the under-representation of key regions; and the political nature of vetoes of the five permanent members). Nonetheless, they preferred this solution to the alternative of unregulated unilateralism.

(i.e., the violation of *jus cogens*), urgency of needs, and the failure of the 'host' state to act.

So which agents could be identified as bearing the remedial international responsibility to protect? The ICJ judgment in the case of *Bosnia v. Serbia* offers some enticing suggestions on how these extraterritorial responsibilities might be allocated, referring to states which are, for example, geographically close to the events in question or which have special political ties with the country where genocidal acts are about to occur.[43] But we have yet to see a full interpretation of this jurisprudence beyond the confines of this particular case, or consideration of its implications. Furthermore, there are some difficulties in following Arbour's strategy of drawing from the law of torts, since concepts such as knowledge and proximity (which create a duty of care) do not apply to innocent bystanders in many legal systems, but only to those individuals who have *by their behaviour* set into motion a chain of events. In short, there must be an element of causal responsibility at work.[44]

Moral philosophers, however, in their discussions of collective responsibility, have begun to consider a series of principles which might assist in the process of allocating responsibility, including the geographical proximity of an agent to those in need of care or protection, the special capacities of a particular agent (such as expertise or strength), and the existence of historic or special links between an agent and those in need of care or protection.[45] To see how these principles might work in practice, we posit a hypothetical case of a humanitarian crisis occurring in Kenya, which threatens to lead to mass atrocity crimes – and which the current government is unable to contain. There are

---

[43] ICJ judgment, para. 430.

[44] See J. Henderson , JR. & R. Pearson, *The Torts Process* (1981), pp. 506-08. A more productive source of reasoning may be the so-called Good Samaritan Laws. In common law systems, a bystander may choose to act in aid of a stranger; in civil law systems, however, there is a duty of rescue. Given these differential duties, we might say that R2P stands in an undefined space between duty and option to help. For the legal doctrine prevailing in U.S. states (no duty to aid or rescue strangers), see Jay Silver, 'The Duty to Rescue: A Reexamination and Proposal,' *William & Mary Law Review* 26: 424 (1985); R.J. Lipkin, 'Beyond Good Samaritans and Moral Monsters: An Individualistic Justification of The General Duty to Rescue,' *UCLA Law Review* 31: 267 (1983). For a comparison of the doctrine in civil law systems, see Feldbrugge, 'Good and Bad Samaritans: A Comparative Survey of Criminal Law Provisions Concerning Failure to Rescue,' *American Journal of Comparative Law* 14 (1966); and Damien Schiff, 'Samaritans: Good, Bad and Ugly: A Comparative Law Analysis,' *Roger Williams University Law Review* 77: 11 (2005).

[45] See Miller, 'Distributing Responsibilities'; Tan, 'The Duty to Protect'; and James Pattison, 'Whose Responsibility to Protect? The Duties of Humanitarian Intervention', *Journal of Military Ethics*, 7/4: 262-83 (2008).

several options for attributing responsibility to act. First, geographical proximity might suggest that the closest neighbours – perhaps Tanzania or Uganda – have the remedial responsibility to act in the first instance, since they are likely to respond quickly and have 'local knowledge' as to what kind of measures might be most effective. (This is in fact what Tanzania did, when faced with massive human rights violations in neighbouring Uganda, in the late 1970s.) Alternatively, one might look to more powerful states – such as regional hegemons Nigeria and South Africa, or Western powers such as the U.S., France, or UK – which are capable of projecting significant military strength overseas in a relatively short period of time. (Examples of this practice would include U.S. intervention in Somalia, British intervention in Sierra Leone, or French intervention in Cote d'Ivoire.) Or, finally, we might consider historic linkages among states in a particular community as the key driver in identifying the agent of remedial responsibility.[46] African states have appealed to this rationale in arguing that interventions on the continent should be carried out by the African Union (AU), rather than Western states, because 'African solutions to African problems' have a better chance of long-term success. This logic was also a motivating factor in France's (late) intervention during the Rwandan genocide, as well as in the appeals for the U.S. to exercise leadership in addressing the humanitarian crisis in Liberia.

As evident from the above, these principles point in different directions, and there is no obvious method of determining which should have the greatest weight. Furthermore, each of these principles has its drawbacks, making it impossible, as Miller argues, to establish *a priori* a general theory as to which should be applied in each case. Examining the third criterion, for example, one could argue that an intervening power from the regional neighbourhood is likely to have a particular agenda of its own (including partiality towards particular factions within the target state's society) that would complicate its exercise of remedial responsibility. The same could be said of the principle of geographic proximity, which might give regional hegemons a license to interfere – a point that has also been made in arguments against regional collective security arrangements. It is worth remembering that one of the key rationales supporting multilateral action is the belief that it is less likely to be motivated by narrow ideological or national interests than unilateral action.

In sum, while the principles identified above have the potential to help allocate the international responsibility to protect by creating reasonable

[46] Miller refers to this as the 'communitarian principle'. See 'Distributing Responsibilities', p. 462.

expectations about who should act in a given situation, they ultimately do no more than identify *possible* bearers of responsibility. They still cannot definitively create an obligation on the part of any particular agent to act, and therefore cannot yet help us to implement remedies should there be a failure to act. In this respect, the 2005 Summit Outcome Document, which ties the responsibilities inherent in R2P explicitly to the UN (and the Security Council), could be interpreted as a welcome move. Indeed, Arbour suggests that the Council, because of the power wielded by its members, should have a more onerous responsibility to protect than other actors in international society.[47]

But there is another way of looking at Article 139, which suggests that serious gaps will remain in both the exercise of responsibility and the ability to hold particular agents accountable for failures to protect. By formulating the Responsibility to Protect as it does in Article 139, the Outcome Document narrows the vehicle for implementing collective responsibility. It is no longer the challenging framework of common humanity which creates the moral responsibility, but rather the specific political commitment of states to act through the UN to address potential or real atrocities. Furthermore, by assigning the collective responsibility to the UN, responsibility is less likely to be distributed down to where it needs to be felt and exercised: by individual states. There is a well-worn tradition – illustrated by the Rwandan tragedy – of states allowing the UN to take remedial action and then acknowledge fault when its efforts are ineffective, without following suit themselves. But so often, when critics claim that the 'UN has failed', they really mean that particular Member States have failed – both in terms of carrying out explicitly defined obligations or of summoning the political will to act. Nowhere was this more apparent than in the case of non-intervention in Rwanda, or the breakdown of the sanctions regime against Saddam Hussein's Iraq.

It should also be remembered that the Council's role in *authorising* actions designed to fulfill international responsibilities cannot and should not be confused with the role of actually *fulfilling* such responsibilities. In order to do the latter, the Security Council would need to apply an accepted procedure for distributing responsibilities to particular states, organisations, and agencies in international society – perhaps using some of the guiding principles discussed above – as well as a formula for cost-sharing. Such a systematic approach does not yet figure in the Council's working procedures. Moreover, there is still no indication of what should transpire if there is failure by the Permanent Five to come to agreement on what action should be taken to respond to crises.

---

[47] Arbour, 'The responsibility to protect', p. 453.

None of this is to suggest that the UNSC should not play a leading role in efforts to operationalise the international community's remedial responsibility to protect. As suggested earlier, both regional organisations and neighbouring states can have high stakes in efforts to address a humanitarian crisis and could easily be perceived by some of the parties in the target country as highly biased in their actions. In other words, proximity cannot be the ultimate trump in terms of distributing responsibility. Moreover, any ethical framework for thinking about who/what should bear the international community's remedial responsibility needs to take *some* account of the existing allocations of responsibility in international society. This pragmatic injunction does not assume that the existing allocation is in all cases necessarily morally superior; it simply recognises that current arrangements have acquired the status of a 'social fact', and are therefore guiding (to some extent) the expectations and actions of both those who are vulnerable and those who are in a position to help.[48]

III. R2P and Customary International Law

Analysis of the source and the bearer of the responsibility to protect does not exhaust the legal questions raised by the principle. Indeed, of equal – and arguably greater – importance is the issue of what kind of principle R2P represents. In short, has it become a *legal* norm?

By placing normative concepts at the centre of their research agenda, Constructivists have enriched IR theory and expanded its explanatory potential.[49] Constructivist notions of norm entrepreneurship, norm socialization, and related theories of social movements have found their application across a variety of political phenomena for which the previously dominant theories of international relations, Realism and Neo-Liberalism, had no readily available analytical models: the abolition of slavery, nuclear and chemical weapons bans, human rights trials, to name but a few. The ideas of norm-building and norm-acceptance developed in Constructivist literature are often indistinguishable from the legal concepts of law-creation and compliance. While the notion that the end-point for many successful norms is institutionalization (usually through law)[50] has now become widely accepted in IR literature,[51]

---

[48] For an elaboration on this argument, see Robert E. Goodin, *Protecting the Vulnerable: A Re-Analysis of Our Social Responsibilities* (Chicago: University of Chicago Press, 1985), p. 125.

[49] *See supra* note 2.

[50] Finnemore and Sikkink, 'International Norm Dynamics and Political Change.'

[51] Kenneth W. Abbott et al., 'The Concept of Legalization', *International Organization* 54/3 (2000): 401-19.

Constructivists have yet to engage with international legal scholarship in their research. In their pioneering work on norm dynamics, Finnemore and Sikkink, for instance, urged IR scholars to consider legal theories of change, singling out in particular the importance of "[u]nderstanding which norms will become law ('soft' law as well as 'hard' law) and how, exactly, compliance with those laws comes about."[52]

From the perspective of theorising about R2P, this inquiry is critical: if not all law-like norms are destined to become binding law, then the process of institutionalization and "legalization" will not necessarily create a norm that is legally enforceable in the international arena. The creation of international rights and correlative duties, then, hinges on both the form that legalization takes and the extent to which so-called 'soft laws' (a notion we return to below), without being legally binding, might affect the interpretation of neighboring norms or influence actor behavior.

While the original ICISS report did not explicitly call for legal reform to enshrine R2P, the Commissioners did leave the impression that international morality and international law should be more closely aligned. Those 'norm entrepreneurs' who have consistently advanced the notion of R2P, such as Evans and Arbour (both cited above) affirm the principle as a new international norm, well on its way to becoming a rule of customary international law.[53] However, those working closely in the office of former UN Secretary General Kofi Annan in the run-up to the 2005 World Summit insist that his goal was not to develop new law, but rather to strengthen the implementation of existing international humanitarian law, such as the Genocide Convention. In Annan's view, R2P was to be a new phrase in the lexicon of international relations, calling for implementation of existing commitments.[54]

This latter understanding of R2P has resonance with a variety of states, which, for very different reasons, oppose the crystallisation into law of responsibilities to prevent and respond to mass atrocities. So, for example, states that have been consistently wary of R2P – for fear that it could erode sovereignty and permit excessive intervention – reject legal interpretations that suggest that the principle has evolved into a new customary rule. The U.S. has been similarly unenthusiastic about creating new legal obligations in the more

---

[52] Finnemore and Sikkink, 'International Norm Dynamics and Political Change,' pp. 915- 6.

[53] Evans, 'The Responsibility to Protect', p. 286; and Arbour, 'The responsibility to protect', pp. 447-8.

[54] Bruce Jones, 'Implementing "In Larger Freedom"', in Paul Heinbecker and Patricia Goff, eds., *Irrelevant or Indispensable? The United Nations in the 21st Century* (Waterloo: Wilfred Laurier University Press, 2005), pp. 33-40 (p. 36).

specific area of humanitarian intervention, as indicated by the diplomacy of former U.S. ambassador to the United Nations, John Bolton, in the weeks prior to the September 2005 Summit. In a statement on the draft text for the Summit he argued that:

> [T]he international community has a responsibility to act when the host state allows such atrocities. But the responsibility of the other countries in the international community is not of the same character as the responsibility of the host ... We do not accept that either the United Nations as a whole, or the Security Council, or individual states, have an obligation to intervene under international law.[55]

This question of whether R2P has indeed transitioned from the world of norms into the ambit of law has important implications for both theory and practice. First, the progression from the purely normative to the legal realm can increase the reputational costs of violation of a principle, particularly if certain states perceive themselves as members of an international society structured by the rule of law.[56] Second, as Finnemore notes, insofar as states' coercive powers exist to enforce the law, states may be more likely to use such powers when the norms which have been violated are legal.[57] The law also demands a special form of justification which emphasises precedents and practice over national interest and preferences; therefore, legal rules may exert a greater 'compliance pull' because of the legitimacy associated with the obligations they outline.[58] Finally, and most importantly, legal obligations (as opposed to moral responsibilities) trigger specific remedies if they are not fulfilled, including, in some cases, the legal liability of the wrongful party.[59]

So does the inclusion of R2P in the Outcome Document represent a moment of legalisation? In answering this question, it is crucial to distinguish between two sets of norms: those which oblige states to refrain from certain

---

[55] Letter from Ambassador John Bolton, Permanent Representative of the United States of America to the United Nations (30 August 2005). Available online at http://www.reformtheun.org.

[56] For a discussion of this conception of international society, see Hedley Bull, *The Anarchical Society* (New York: Columbia University Press, 1977); and Andrew Hurrell, *On Global Order: Power, Values, and the Constitution of International Society* (Oxford: Oxford University Press, 2007).

[57] Martha Finnemore, 'Are Legal Norms Distinctive?' *New York University Journal of International Law and Politics* 32: 699-705 (2000), pp. 703-05.

[58] Kenneth W. Abbott and Duncan Snidal, 'Hard and Soft Law in International Governance,' International Organization, 54/3: 421-456 (2000). See also Thomas Franck, *The Power of Legitimacy Among Nations* (Oxford: Oxford University Press, 1990).

[59] Rosenberg, 'Responsibility to Protect', p. 446.

actions that jeopardize their populations (negative duties), and those which mandate a response to violations of that obligation (positive/affirmative duties). With respect to the first category of norms, our analysis suggests that a great deal of legalization has already occurred. With respect to the second set of norms, the situation is more complex.

In Articles 138 and 139 of the 2005 Summit Outcome Document we did see a declared commitment on the part of states to act in ways not explicitly provided for in the UN Charter.[60] But the status of that statement as a legal instrument is contested, as the UN General Assembly is not a law-making body with powers under the Charter to pass legally-binding rules.[61] The fact that the Assembly lacks these powers does not mean that its statements are necessarily without any effect. A consensus of the Assembly, as the world's most representative body, is a reasonable proxy for the existence of the international *opinio juris* on a given issue. Where accompanied by consistent state practice, the Assembly's pronouncements may reveal the existence, or the formation, of rules of customary international law. Assembly declarations and resolutions may also provide an obligatory source of international law in certain circumstances. The Universal Declaration on Human Rights, for instance, originally a non-binding declaration much like the Outcome Document, became the forerunner of international human rights covenants and, eventually, an element of customary law.[62] Absent substantial evidence of state practice, however, the proposition that Assembly declarations can create binding laws is controversial.[63] Thus, for example, no UN Member State at this stage could be hauled before the ICJ or the ICC on the basis of its failure to implement in Darfur the solemn promise made in the Outcome Document. The only legal grounds for action could be found in existing treaty or customary obligations, of which the Outcome Document may only offer some evidence.

---

[60] It is also significant that the language of the document was echoed in subsequent Security Council Resolutions on the Protection of Civilians in Armed Conflict. See, e.g., S/RES/1674, 28 April 2006; S/RES/1706, 31 August 2006; S/RES/1814, 15 May 2008; and S/RES/1894, 11 November 2009.

[61] The areas which are an exception to this are UN finances and internal operations.

[62] For a discussion of the Assembly's legal competency see Rosalyn Higgins, *The Development of International Law through the Political Organs of the United Nations* (Oxford: Oxford University Press, 1963); and Obed Y. Asamoah, *The Legal Significance of the Declarations of the General Assembly of the United Nations* (The Hague, 1966).

[63] On UN Resolutions generally, see Blaine Sloan, 'General Assembly Resolutions Revisited (Forty Years Later)', *British Yearbook of International Law,* 58: 39-150 (1987). For a different view, see Bin Cheng, 'United Nations Resolutions on Outer Space: 'Instant' International Customary Law?' *5 Indiana Journal of International Law*, 23 (1965), reprinted in Bin Cheng, ed., *International Law: Teaching and Practice* (London: Stevens, 1982).

In our view, the Outcome Document is best categorised as an instance of 'soft law'.[64] According to Christine Chinkin, law of this kind is written in general – and sometimes qualified – language, which leaves interpretation open to political contestation. As a result, it does not create precise legal rights and obligations. Articles 138 and 139 fit Chinkin's definition of soft law given their open-ended, malleable language and the fact that their implications have engendered considerable controversy.

While not legally binding, soft laws are still legally relevant in two main ways. First, soft laws interact in complex ways with the hard rules of law. For instance, soft laws can signal the direction of future legal developments, act as a precursor to binding treaties, or 'harden' into custom over time by mobilising state practice or providing evidence of *opinio juris*.[65] They may also help shape legal interpretation of existing rules by emphasising particular normative understandings and rules of international conduct. This function of soft law is particularly important in the area of humanitarian intervention where the UN Charter (and international law generally) offers conflicting principles.[66] Articles 138 and 139, given their virtually unanimous endorsement, can be accepted as an authoritative interpretation of the Charter's provisions on sovereignty, human rights, and the use of force. Thus, even if the Outcome Document is not legally enforceable *per se*, it does represent an important step in the evolution of international protection law.

These legal implications of soft-law instruments are highly contested. Treaties and international custom require state consent; soft laws are adopted without the strictures of formal treaty negotiation and ratification. If soft laws were given the same legal effect as hard rules, they could bind unwilling states to norms to which they had never consented. Not surprisingly, many states refute the existence of soft laws in order to prevent them from hardening into enforceable rules, while other states assert that these principles carry immediate or universal effect not in and of themselves, but as a restatement of existing custom or a reflection of an emerging consensus.[67] That similar arguments were raised during the World Summit negotiations suggests that the delegates

---

[64] See Christine Chinkin, 'The Challenge of Soft Law: Development and Change in International Law', *International and Comparative Law Quarterly*, 38/4: 850-66 (1989).

[65] Alan Boyle contends that 'soft' provisions may be binding if they inform court decisions or resolve conflicts between hard laws. See 'Some Reflections on the Relationship of Treaties and Soft Law', *International and Comparative Law Quarterly*, 48/4: 901-913 (1999).

[66] Adam Roberts, 'Humanitarian Action in War', *Adelphi Papers* No. 305 (London: International Institute of Strategic Studies, 1996).

[67] On hardening in general, see Kenneth W. Abbott et al., 'The Concept of Legalization', *International Organization*, 54/3: 412 (2000).

were aware of the possibility that the Outcome Document could eventually carry legal effect—whether directly or indirectly (as an interpretive tool). The most likely channel is by aiding in the crystallisation of customary international law on the protection of civilians.

Conclusion

R2P is not a rule of hard law which fits neatly into one single regime: it is a soft-law norm located at the nexus of three broad legal regimes which, by themselves, do not offer a definitive answer on the nature of states' responsibilities in the face of mass atrocities. Yet, as we have illustrated, R2P itself suffers from indeterminacy – most notably in terms of the bearer and precise nature of the international community's remedial responsibility under 'Pillar Three'. The implications of this ambiguity are evident in the fact that although R2P has been invoked in a variety of humanitarian crises since the 2005 World Summit (such as Darfur, Kenya, Gaza, Sri Lanka, and Burma), the principle has not generated sufficient 'compliance pull' to produce timely and coordinated international action. Indeed, during some of these crises there was significant contestation as to whether R2P *should* be invoked at all.

There is little doubt that R2P has become a central piece of the vocabulary used by members of international society in highlighting humanitarian crises and debating the appropriateness of an international response. To paraphrase Constructivists, it has become a 'social fact'. Whether it will move beyond that discussion, and establish new legal obligations for states, remains uncertain. Our analysis has demonstrated that R2P is likely to continue to have an uneasy relationship with international law. Its primary function today is to remind all states of the obligations they have to their own citizens and to clarify the extra-territorial responsibilities they have to strangers. In the coming decade, it may also help to catalyse diplomatic efforts to improve upon the international architecture for preventing and responding to mass atrocities.

Feminist Reflections on the Responsibility to Protect

*Hilary Charlesworth**

Abstract
This paper offers a feminist analysis of the responsibility to protect principle. It outlines some themes in feminist scholarship in international law and then uses these to explore the idea of a responsibility to protect. The paper argues that, despite some resonance with feminist concerns, the doctrine has been developed in a limited context, effectively privileging male elites and masculine modes of reasoning.

Keywords
Responsibility to protect, International law, Feminist theory, Intervention, Discrimination, Violence against women

Introduction

The identification and promotion of the 'responsibility to protect' principle over the last decade provides a case study of the techniques of modern international law-making. International law is a complex mix of normative and justificatory principles, a brew aptly captured by Martti Koskenniemi in his description of international legal argument as an oscillation between utopian and apologetic positions.[1] Unlike most national legal systems, the political roots of international law are constantly on display and it is difficult to avoid moral and philosophical debate in discussing its scope. The development of the responsibility to protect doctrine illustrates the power of a strong normative concept in responding to massive atrocities, accompanied by an apparently concrete set of conditions for its operation, an edgy acronym, R2P,[2] and energetic, experienced and well-resourced norm-entrepreneurs.

* Thanks to Susan Harris Rimmer for her comments on this paper.

[1] Martti Koskenniemi, *From Apology to Utopia: The Structure of International Legal Argument* (Cambridge and New York: Cambridge University Press, 2006).

[2] Gareth Evans suggests that the shorthand term R2P was devised 'under the universal cultural influence of *Star Wars* and its engagingly determined little droid R2-D2': Gareth Evans,

This paper investigates the implications of the responsibility to protect principle from a feminist perspective. Such an approach is generally marginalised in mainstream international law discourse and it is also absent from discussions of the responsibility to protect doctrine. The paper argues that the responsibility to protect has developed without adequate attention to the lives of women. The principle also depends on gendered accounts of the value of military intervention in international affairs that limit the possible responses to atrocities.

The idea that states have a responsibility to protect their populations was first articulated by the International Commission on Intervention and State (ICISS) in 2001. The ICISS was established by the Canadian government to respond to a challenge identified by United Nations (UN) Secretary-General Kofi Annan at the UN Millennium Summit in 2000. Annan had reflected on two political and moral disasters of the preceding decade: the failures to prevent the genocide in Rwanda in 1994 and the slaughter of civilians in a UN safe haven in Srebrenica in Bosnia in 1995. He observed the strength of the concept of state sovereignty as a major barrier to action, one that inevitably undermined any external claim to 'humanitarian' intervention. Annan called for new ways of thinking about sovereignty to avert situations 'that offend every precept of our common humanity'.[3] The Commission articulated the principle of responsibility to protect as a way of short-circuiting the long-standing debate between proponents of a right to intervene in states on humanitarian grounds on the one hand and protectors of maximum state sovereignty on the other.[4] Sovereignty was conceptualised as responsibility rather than authority.[5] The notion of responsibility to protect was designed to change the perspective in responding to mass atrocity from that of the prospective interveners or resisters to that of the victims of the atrocities.[6] The responsibility to protect a population rests, first, with a state. If a state is unable or unwilling to protect its citizens, then the responsibility moves to the international community collectively.

The Responsibility to Protect: Ending Mass Atrocity Crimes Once and For All (Washington: The Brookings Institution, 2008), p. 5.

[3] Kofi Annan, *Millennium Report of the Secretary-General of the United Nations,* A/54/2000, 3 April 2000.

[4] International Commission on Intervention and State Sovereignty (ICISS), *The Responsibility to Protect* (Ottawa: IDRC, 2001); see also Evans, *The Responsibility to Protect,* pp. 38-43.

[5] Ramesh Thakur, *The United Nations, Peace and Security* (Cambridge: Cambridge University Press, 2007), p. 255.

[6] Evans, *The Responsibility to Protect,* p. 40.

The responsibility to protect principle gained momentum through its endorsement by a High-Level UN Panel on Threats, Challenges, and Change in 2004, preparing for the UN's sixtieth anniversary in 2005.[7] The panel spoke of an 'emerging norm that there is a collective international responsibility to protect, exercisable by the Security Council authorizing military intervention as a last resort, in the event of genocide and other large-scale killing, ethnic cleansing or serious violation of international humanitarian law which sovereign governments have proved powerless or unwilling to prevent.'[8] Kofi Annan then embraced the principle in his report to the 2005 World Summit.[9] The principle's significance was consolidated by inclusion in the UN General Assembly's World Summit Outcomes document.[10] Each iteration of the principle altered its coverage and emphasis.[11] For example, the 2005 version omits reference to the ICISS proposal that permanent members of the Security Council should refrain from using their veto in cases of intervention if their own national security interests were not compromised. Another change from the ICISS report, which linked the operation of the responsibility to protect to the broad category of occasions of 'serious harm', was to tie it to the occurrence of four international crimes: genocide, war crimes, ethnic cleansing and crimes against humanity.[12]

As UN Secretary-General, Ban Ki-moon has supported and developed the responsibility to protect concept, appointing a special adviser on the topic, Edward Luck. Ban Ki-moon has set out to 'operationalise' the principle,

---

[7] Gareth Evans, the Co-Chair of the ICISS, was a member of the High-Level Panel.

[8] High Level Panel on Threats, Challenges, and Change, *A More Secure World: Our Shared Responsibility* (New York: United Nations, 2004), p. 106 para. 203.

[9] *In Larger Freedom: Towards Development, Security and Human Rights for All*, A/59/2005, 21 March 2005, para. 135.

[10] '2005 World Summit Outcome', A/RES/60/1, 24 October 2005, paras. 138-139. For the politics of the negotiations behind this document, see Alex Bellamy, 'Whither the Responsibility to Protect? Humanitarian Intervention and the 2005 World Summit', *Ethics and International* Affairs, 20/2: 143-69 (2006); Gareth Evans, 'From Humanitarian Intervention to R2P', *Wisconsin International Law Journal*, 24/3: 703-22 (2006).

[11] See Nicholas Wheeler, 'A Victory for Common Humanity? The Responsibility to Protect after the 2005 World Summit'. paper presented at The UN at Sixty: Celebration or Wake?', University of Toronto, 6-7 October 2005. Gareth Evans argues however that the various formulations are not significantly different: Evans, *The Responsibility to Protect*, p. 47.

[12] This change was proposed by Pakistan in order to prevent the concept being used by strong countries against weaker ones: Anne Orford, 'Jurisdiction without Territory: From the Holy Roman Empire to the Responsibility to Protect', *Michigan Journal of International Law*, 30/3: 981-1015 (2009), p. 1006.

elaborating it as consisting of three 'coequal and mutually reinforcing' pillars: the responsibility of individual states to protect their population from the four international crimes; the responsibility of the international community to assist states to meet this responsibility; and the responsibility of the international community to take timely and decisive collective action under the UN Charter if states are not meeting their individual responsibilities to their citizens.[13]

The responsibility to protect principle has encountered tough resistance politically, particularly from some developing states.[14] Despite its uncertain political and legal status, formulation of the responsibility to protect doctrine allows lawyers, politicians and civil society to feel that they are actively resisting injustice. The principle's strength comes from its rejection of a rule of might and its commitment to a higher norm of protection. At the same time, the reception of the principle demonstrates the way that invocations of notions of state sovereignty become a standard realist counter-move to undercut utopian ambitions.

Gareth Evans, the tireless campaigner for the responsibility to protect, regards the imprimatur of international lawyers as significant in the recognition of the principle because 'international law, unlike its domestic counterpart, is capable of evolving through practice and commentary as well as through formal instruments and judicial decisions'.[15] And yet he is ambivalent about the place of law in the concept, which is explicitly moral.[16] International lawyers have approached the responsibility to protect principle warily. Some are attracted to its grand humanitarian vision, but acknowledge that the doctrine is at best *de lege ferenda*, an emerging principle of international law that as yet has no independent legal status.[17] Others are sceptical of the concept of a responsibility to protect, regarding it as a reincarnation of the controversial idea of humanitarian intervention; a carapace for oppressive

---

[13] Ban Ki-moon, *Implementing the Responsibility to Protect*, A/63/677, 12 January 2009.

[14] See Evans, *The Responsibility to Protect*, pp. 52-3; Office of the President of the General Assembly, *Concept Note on the Responsibility to Protect Populations from Genocide, War Crimes, Ethnic Cleansing and Crimes against Humanity*, 17 July 2009.

[15] Evans, *The Responsibility to Protect*, p. 44.

[16] Ibid., pp. 146-47.

[17] See, for example, Jutta Brunée and Stephen Toope, 'Norms, Institutions and UN Reform: The Responsibility to Protect', *Journal of International Law & International Relations*, 2/1: 121-37 (2005), p. 133; Carsten Stahn, 'Responsibility to Protect: Political Rhetoric or Emerging Legal Norm?', *American Journal of International Law*, 101/1: 99-120 (2007); Ekkehard Strauss, 'A Bird in the Hand is Worth Two in the Bush: On the Assumed Legal Nature of the Responsibility to Protect', *Global Responsibility to Protect*, 1/3, 291-323 (2009).

interference by strong states into weak ones.[18] The legal debate has centred on the relationship of the principle to state sovereignty: whether it is consistent with sovereign statehood, or whether it interferes with sovereignty in a fundamental way.

There is now a considerable literature on the idea of the responsibility to protect. It has been explored and critiqued from many angles: for example, does the concept create a moral hazard, encouraging resort to violence by oppressed groups because of the expectation of intervention on their behalf by the international community?;[19] does it ignore the concerns of the global South and simply legitimate colonial patterns of intervention?;[20] does it produce an international community with almost unfettered powers of intervention?[21] A relatively unexplored dimension of the principle by both advocates and critics is, however, its relationship to sex and gender.

Feminist scholarship in international law

The aim of feminism is to advance the equality of women. Feminist scholarship is inspired by this political project, but has proposed many different, and sometimes contradictory, ways of describing and understanding women's inequality. Feminist theories inevitably rest on a tension between their role analysing the masculinity of disciplinary knowledge and their role as a response to political feminist goals. For this reason they often incur not only the wrath of the traditional academy because of their overtly political ends, but also the ire of feminist activists because they engage with the male-dominated world of theory.[22] In a legal context, feminist theory has been described as 'an analysis of the exclusion of (some) women's needs, interests, aspirations, or attributes from the design or application of the law.'[23]

[18] See, for example, José E. Alvarez, 'The Schizophrenias of R2P', paper presented at The Hague Joint Conference on Contemporary Issues of International Law, 30 June 2007.

[19] Alan J. Kuperman, 'The Moral Hazard of Humanitarian Intervention: Lessons from the Balkans', *International Studies Quarterly*, 52/1: 49-80 (2008).

[20] David Chandler, 'The Responsibility to Protect? Imposing the "Liberal Peace"', *International Peacekeeping*, 11/1: 59-81 (2004), p. 68.

[21] Orford, 'Jurisdiction without Territory', pp. 1013-1015.

[22] Elizabeth Grosz, 'A note on essentialism and difference' in Sneja Gunew (ed.), *Feminist Knowledge: Critique and Construct* (London and New York: Routledge, 1990), p. 332.

[23] Denise Réaume, 'What's Feminist about a Feminist Analysis of Law?', *Legal Theory* 2/4, 256-299 (1996), at p. 271.

Feminist scholars have argued that international law generally is both sexed and gendered, challenging the assumption that international law offers a rational detached universal form of justice. One way that feminist scholars make this argument is to investigate where women are located in international law – what roles are they assigned, and what benefits does international law offer them? This can be understood as a question about sex in the sense that it is interested in women as distinct from men in a biological sense.[24] Another feminist technique is to ask how the idea of gender shapes international legal concepts.[25]

Where are the women in international law? We could note, first, that there is a disproportionate representation of men in the institutions of international law. The International Court of Justice, the premier judicial body of the international legal system, has in 2010 no woman among the fifteen elected judges. Only one woman, Dame Rosalyn Higgins, has ever been elected to the Court, and one woman, Professor Suzanne Bastid, has been appointed as a judge *ad hoc*. The International Law Commission, established under the UN Charter, a prestigious body of forty-five jurists, has three women members in 2010. The UN Secretariat is dominated by men, as are the expert committees monitoring the human rights treaties of the UN. One important exception to this is the International Criminal Court, which has eleven women judges among its eighteen members. Feminist scholars point out that not only are few women involved in the formal international legal system, but also the categories and concepts of international law do not accommodate the realities of most women's lives.[26]

Feminist analysis has pointed to the way that the exclusion of women's lives has affected the development of international law. For example, why are migratory species of sea life regulated by treaty when the use of breast milk substitutes, which is a major health issue for women in Africa, remains subject to voluntary World Health Organization codes? Why is extra-territorial jurisdiction,

---

[24] The distinction between sex and gender on the basis of biological characteristics has been criticised by some feminist scholars: see Margaret Davies, 'Taking the Inside Out: Sex and Gender in the Legal Subject' in Ngaire Naffine and Rosemary Owens (eds.), *Sexing the Subject of Law* (Sydney: Law Book Company, 1997).

[25] Marysia Zalewski, 'Well, What is the Feminist Perspective on Bosnia?' *International Affairs*, 71/2: 339-56 (1995). See also Cynthia Enloe, *The Curious Feminist: Searching for Women in a New Age of Empire* (Berkeley: University of California Press, 2004).

[26] See generally Hilary Charlesworth and Christine Chinkin, *The Boundaries of International Law: A Feminist Analysis* (Manchester: Manchester University Press, 2000); Doris Buss and Ambreena Manji (eds.), *International Law: Modern Feminist Approaches* (Oxford and Portland: Hart Publishing, 2005).

traditionally invoked against violations of monopoly and competition law, only rarely used in cases of trafficking of women and children?[27]

What work is gender doing in international law? Feminists have argued that the language and imagery of the law draw on gendered categories: international law lays claim to rationality, objectiveness and abstraction, characteristics traditionally associated with Western masculinity, and it is defined in contrast to emotion, subjectivity, and contextualised thinking. The power of international legal discourse rests on a series of binary oppositions: order/chaos, logic/emotion, legal/political, and binding/non-binding. Feminist scholars have pointed to the gendered coding of these dichotomies, with the stronger term associated with masculinity and the less preferable one with femininity.

There has also been considerable debate *within* international legal feminist scholarship. For example, Ratna Kapur has criticised what she terms the 'victimisation' rhetoric used by the international human rights movement when discussing the situation of Third World women, particularly in relation to violence and trafficking. Kapur argues that the assumption of a common international women's victimhood operates to keep women in their place by presenting them as both vulnerable and ignorant.[28] She has rejected a focus on the sexual as the locus of women's oppression and has urged a more complex understanding of women's lives through considering factors such as race, wealth, class and religion. Anne Orford has also tracked the relationship between feminism and imperialism, cautioning against an approach that simply moves women from the private to public domain. She has drawn attention to the way that intervention narratives depend upon the construction of a gendered and racialised 'other' which makes intervention appear the only acceptable response to atrocities.[29]

Critical work on feminism in international law, then, has asked questions about the location of women in its structures and investigated the role that gender plays in its formation. At the same time international law has also been invoked in feminist struggles as a source of transformation and empowerment. This has created a certain tension within feminist international legal scholarship, and sometimes a fractured politics.[30]

---

[27] Charlesworth and Chinkin, *The Boundaries of International Law*, chapter 1.

[28] Ratna Kapur, 'The Tragedy of Victimization Rhetoric: Resurrecting the "Native" Subject in International/Post-Colonial Feminist Legal Politics' *Harvard Human Rights Law Journal*, 15/1, 1-37 (2002).

[29] Anne Orford, *Reading Humanitarian Intervention: Human Rights and the Use of Force in International Law* (Cambridge: Cambridge University Press, 2003), pp. 56-71.

[30] Marysia Zalewski has described a parallel debate within feminist international relations scholarship: 'Do We Understand Each Other Yet? Troubling Feminist Encounters With(in)

A central concern of feminism is the location of power within a society; scholars have emphasised the dispersal of power and the fact that it does not 'reside only and always in a centre' leaving women on its periphery.[31] For this reason, as Sneja Gunew has pointed out, '[feminism] is not simply a question of storming a series of male citadels and occupying the controls.' Feminist inquiry involves attention to the way that power produces knowledge and ideas. If power is understood as a network, operating in complex and inconsistent ways, the possibilities of resisting it in different contexts increase.[32]

Because of the considerable scholarly literature in this area over the last two decades, some feminist ideas have now been absorbed into the rhetoric of international law and its institutions.[33] International women's groups have taken up feminist critiques of the international legal order and concepts such as 'gender mainstreaming' have been embraced in national, regional and international systems. In many areas, however, progress has been limited. Feminist issues have been either corralled in the margins of international law or rendered so bland that they have no transformative bite.[34]

Feminist analysis of the responsibility to protect principle

What feminist questions are raised by the responsibility to protect principle? On one level, the concept appears hospitable to feminist agendas. Its emphasis on a conditional, limited form of sovereignty departs from the traditional paradigm of sovereignty as autonomy and impermeability, which feminist scholars have linked to the male body.[35] So too the language of responsibility resonates with research on the nature of female reasoning. For example, Carol

International Relations', *British Journal of Politics and International Relations* 9/2: 302-12 (2007).

[31] Sneja Gunew, 'Feminist Knowledge: Critique and Construct' in Sneja Gunew (ed.), *Feminist Knowledge: Critique and Construct* (New York: Routledge, 1990), p. 23.

[32] Ibid.

[33] See Alice Edwards, 'Violence against Women as Sex Discrimination: Judging the Jurisprudence of the United Nations Human Rights Treaty Bodies', *Texas Journal of Women & the Law*, 18: 1-44 (2008).

[34] Hilary Charlesworth, 'Not Waving but Drowning: Gender Mainstreaming and Human Rights', *Harvard Human Rights Journal*, 18, 1-18 (2005).

[35] See Hilary Charlesworth, 'The Sex of the State in International Law' in Ngaire Naffine and Rosemary Owens (eds.), *Sexing the Subject of Law* (Sydney: Law Book Company, 1997); Christine Sylvester, 'Feminists and Realists View Autonomy and Obligation in International Relations' in V. Spike Peterson (ed.), *Gendered States: Feminist (Re)Visions of International Relations Theory* (Boulder, Colorado, Lynne Rienner Press, 1992) p. 157.

Gilligan's path-breaking work on modes of moral decision-making and problem-solving by girls and boys showed differences between them. Girls tended to reason on the basis of values such as caring and connection, while boys' decisions were influenced more by abstract logic. Responsibility for individuals and the community and the preservation of relationships figured more largely in decisions taken by girls.[36] Gilligan observed that the psychological literature generally rated the masculine pattern of reasoning as more mature and developed.[37] Her concern was the privileging of one perspective and the marginalising of alternative modes of reasoning. It might be argued that the responsibility to protect doctrine in this sense breaks away from the standard masculine forms of rationality endorsed in international law and international relations and allows an analysis based on a broader range of factors. By factoring in the needs of a population and downplaying the values of an abstract sovereignty, the doctrine can get around some of the inhumane aspects of realism and legalism.

Another aspect of the responsibility to protect doctrine that apparently responds to feminist critiques of the international security system is the prominence it gives to prevention of mass atrocities ('overwhelmingly the most important [responsibility] to pursue')[38] and its emphasis on non-military modes of intervention. Gareth Evans reports that an impetus for the doctrine in the ICISS was precisely 'to sideline the humanitarian intervention terminology … [which] had become irretrievably linked to the use of military force, and *only* military force, as a way to respond to actual or impending mass atrocities.'[39]

A closer look at the concept of the responsibility to protect suggests however that it remains susceptible to feminist critique. Its design has been influenced by men's lives and the dominance of masculine modes of reasoning.

Where are the women?

Women have been largely absent from the development of the responsibility to protect principle. The ICISS had a single woman member, Gisele Côté-Harper, and eleven men. The High Level Panel had four women members (Gro Harlem Brundtland, Mary Hesse, Sadako Ogata and Nafis Sadik) and

36 Carol Gilligan, *In a Different Voice: Psychological Theory and Women's Development* (Cambridge: Harvard University Press, 1982).

37 Ibid., pp. 9-18.

38 Evans, *The Responsibility to Protect*, p. 43.

39 Ibid., p. 40.

twelve men. These are unexceptional figures in the international arena, but they underline the routine under-representation of women in the development of international law, despite widely-ratified treaty provisions that require the elimination of discrimination against women in political and public life.[40]

Would the participation of more women in the development of international norms affect the content of the norms? The evidence is uncertain as there are so few cases of norm-generation where equal numbers of women and men are involved. The sex of the architects of a principle does not necessarily determine the reach or significance of the concept, although it may affect the way that it is presented. But it is at least clear that the realities of women's lives do not contribute in any significant way to the shaping of international principles. Karen Knop has suggested that women's under-representation of women in international decision-making could be characterised as impinging on their 'collective autonomy'.[41] She has argued that 'women should be able to decide at least certain international issues not because they will decide them better than or even differently from men, but because they as a group … should be able to make the decisions that affect their lives'.[42]

The representation of women's interests by men is complex. Anne Phillips points out that 'if women's interests were transparently obvious to any intelligent observer, there might be no particular case … for insisting on representatives who also happen to be women.' If, on the contrary, women's interests are 'varied, unstable, perhaps still in the process of formation', the separation of the representative from what is to be represented is more difficult.[43] In the international arena, the category of 'women's interests' is inevitably diverse; differences in culture, social and economic circumstances loom large in this context. For this reason, men's representation of women's interests is unlikely to be adequate. The imbalance in men's representation in decision-making structures at the international level allows male life experiences to be seen as a general, rather than a specific, category.

Proponents of the responsibility to protect principle assert its universal reach, a prerequisite for international legal status. However, there has been little study of the way that the principle might affect women's lives, or its

---

[40] For example, Convention on the Elimination of All Forms of Discrimination Against Women 1979, articles 7 and 8.

[41] Karen Knop 'Re/statements: Feminism and State Sovereignty in International Law', *Transnational Law and Contemporary Problems*, 3: 293-344 (1993), p. 306.

[42] Ibid., pp. 306-7.

[43] Anne Phillips, *Engendering Democracy* (Cambridge: Polity Press, 1991), p. 15.

relationship to Security Council Resolution 1325, adopted in 2000, which urged increased participation of women in national and international institutions and mechanisms dealing with the prevention, management and resolution of conflict.[44] The lives of women appear peripheral to the development of the responsibility to protect principle, except for occasional references to the need to protect women from mass rape.[45] The principle focuses on the public realm of the state and the government as the source of injury,[46] but for most women, danger comes from the 'private' realm of the family or community as much as from the state. Violence against women is at epidemic levels around the world, with two-thirds of women experiencing violence during their lives, mainly at the hands of men in their family.[47] Discrimination against women in areas such as inheritance and family law is justified by custom or religion.

Gareth Evans' book length study of the responsibility to protect makes several references to women. Women appear as particular victims of mass atrocities, especially in the case of sexual crimes.[48] Evans refers to the 'special needs' of women caught up in conflict, although he does not elaborate on what they are;[49] and he remarks on the problems women face under traditional justice mechanisms in places like Pakistan.[50] Evans also presents women as the backbone of peace initiatives. He writes that women 'are often the key not only to preventing the re-emergence of violence and resolving ongoing conflict, but to rebuilding societies once the guns go silent.'[51] This is because women 'tend to adopt a more inclusive approach toward security and address key social and economic issues that would otherwise be ignored.'[52] He supports the appointment of women as Special Representatives of the UN Secretary-General[53] and as UN police (especially because this will be useful in detecting sexual violence).[54] Evans also deplores the failure to give teeth to Security Council Resolution 1325.[55] His brief depictions of women present them as either

[44] One exception is Marilou McPhedran, Laurel Sherret and Jennifer Bond, 'R2P Missing Women – Canada's Responsibility to Perceive', discussion paper for Fragile States Conference, 27 November 2005.

[45] For example, ICISS, *The Responsibility to Protect*, paras. 2.29, 4.20.

[46] Evans, *The Responsibility to Protect*, pp. 74-75.

[47] Ban Ki-moon, Speech on International Women's Day, 8 March 2010.

[48] Evans, *The Responsibility to Protect*, p. 40.

[49] Ibid., p. 156.

[50] Ibid., p. 168.

[51] Ibid., p. 171. See also p. 156.

[52] Ibid., p. 171.

[53] Ibid., p. 203.

[54] Ibid., pp. 212-3.

[55] Ibid., p. 203.

victims of public crimes such as mass rape or as inclusive peacebuilders, both popular UN stereotypes.[56] One implication of such images is that violence and conflict are the province of men; in Jean Bethke Elshtain's words, they allow 'the collective projection' of a pure and peaceful Other against which a violent male is constructed'. She refers to a 'nasty historic bargain' which allows women to remain removed from the fray while 'boys will be boys'. In other words, presenting women as integral to peace 'winds up endorsing – indeed requiring—that which they would oppose'.[57]

Descriptions of the responsibility to protect doctrine make clear that it is designed to apply only in exceptional ('few and far between') circumstances.[58] This is a pragmatic feature to shore up the legitimacy of the concept by reassuring states that it will only allow intervention in extreme cases, and to preserve its value as a 'rallying cry'.[59] Gareth Evans emphasises this by stating that the principle will not apply in 'common … cases of conflict or human rights concerns',[60] for example the spread of HIV/AIDS. The types of conduct that will trigger the responsibility to protect – genocide, war crimes, ethnic cleansing and crimes against humanity – are a very limited subset of inhuman behaviour. The principle thus excludes structural forms of discrimination and violence against women in both public and private areas from its purview, factors that account for greater, systemic, harms to women's lives than the four categories of international crimes it mentions. In this sense, the principle's dependence on international military intervention as the final guarantee against mass atrocities skews its coverage from large-scale forms of harm and violence that appear routine to occasional outbreaks of particular forms of public violence. Some feminist scholars have argued for an international legal principle that would allow military intervention to protect women's rights.[61] The major problem with such a proposal is that it uses a volatile and risky technique to support women's equality, one that is easily misused and indeed capable of exacerbating violence against women.[62]

---

[56] See Hilary Charlesworth, 'Are Women Peaceful? Reflections on the Role of Women in Peace-Building', *Feminist Legal Studies*, 16: 347-61 (2008).

[57] Jean Bethke Elshtain, *Women and War* (Chicago: Chicago University Press, 1995), p. 265.

[58] Evans, *The Responsibility to Protect*, p. 75.

[59] Ibid., p. 69.

[60] Ibid., p. 75; see also ibid., pp. 68-9.

[61] For example, Catharine MacKinnon, *Are Women Human?* (Cambridge: Harvard University Press, 2007), pp. 271-72.

[62] See Karen Engle, '"Calling in the Troops": The Uneasy Relationship among Women's Rights, Human Rights, and Humanitarian Intervention', *Harvard Human Rights Journal*, 20: 189-226 (2007).

The responsibility to protect, whether in its prevention, reaction or rebuilding phases, requires the importation of expertise; it involves top-down intervention, with little emphasis on empowering local people, particularly women.[63] Although some iterations of the principle support the inclusion of women in the public realm, they do not address discrimination against women in the private sphere where traditional or religious practices can perpetuate women's inferiority to men.

Another way that the responsibility to protect principle marginalises women's experiences is through the prominence it accords to ex-combatants in the context of peace-making and rebuilding after conflict. There is an assumption that brokering peace should primarily involve those who had engaged in armed conflict, most commonly men. Despite the effects of conflict on women, they are regarded as inappropriate participants in ending the fighting.[64] The focus of rebuilding is on disarmament, demobilisation and reintegration of armed forces,[65] and little attention is paid to the way that women are regularly excluded from the rebuilding process. In Angola, for example, women were marginalised in the peace process because of their emphasis on social welfare as opposed to military power, and because they had neither the power nor interest in threatening to disrupt the talks with violence.[66] Women's rights are indeed often traded for the support of political factions in post-conflict situations; for example in 2009 Hamid Karzai's government in Afghanistan shored up its popularity with Shia leaders by adopting a law that imposed extraordinary restrictions upon Shia women, including the requirement that a woman must obtain a male relative's permission to seek employment, granting custody of children to fathers and grandfathers only, and allowing a man to withhold food from his wife if she did not accede to his sexual demands.[67] Through its focus on ex-combatants, then, the responsibility to protect principle does not offer any impetus for states to improve the position of women as part of rebuilding projects.

---

[63] Evans discusses the importance of local ownership using the example of East Timor (at pp. 162-63), but he does not address the problem of women being marginalised in local decision-making, as has occurred in that country.

[64] Ban Ki-moon, *Women and Peace and Security*, S/2009/465, 16 September 2009, para. 71.

[65] E.g. Evans, *The Responsibility to Protect*, pp. 154-56.

[66] J. Zoe Wilson, 'State Making, Peacemaking, and the Inscription of Gendered Politics into Peace: Lessons from Angola' in Dyan Mazurana, Angela Raven-Roberts and Jane Parpart (eds.), *Gender, Conflict, and Peacekeeping* (Boulder, Colorado: Rowman and Littlefield, 2005), p. 252.

[67] See Human Rights Watch, 'Afghanistan: Law Curbing Women's Human Rights Takes Effect', 13 August 2009, http://www.hrw.org/en/news/2009/08/13/afghanistan-law-curbing-women-s-rights-takes-effect, accessed 10 March 2010.

While Security Council Resolution 1325 can be criticised for being rather limited in the roles it imagines for women in peace-making and peacebuilding,[68] the UN and its members have failed to take its modest prescriptions seriously. References to the need to include women in peace processes have become ritualistic in international institutions, but result in little change. For example, a UNIFEM study in 2009 found that only 2.4 per cent of signatories to peace agreements since 1992 had been women and that no woman had ever been designated as a 'chief mediator'.[69]

What work is gender doing?

Investigating gender can be 'a conceptual tool to make us see things at work that we would rather not see.'[70] I use the term 'gender' here to mean the socially constructed categories of masculinity and femininity. This is distinct from the characteristics of particular men and women. The content of the categories of masculinity and femininity alters across time and cultures, but these concepts are typically defined in contrast to one other.[71] Thus the essence of being masculine is to be *not feminine*. Another feature of gender is that what is deemed masculine is typically assigned a greater value than what is defined as feminine.[72] Images of gender frame our political life; leadership is understood as requiring decisiveness, objectivity and rationality, detachment from the messiness of ordinary life. The vocabulary of objectivity, logic and order positions a person as being manly, which immediately gives their words a higher value. The use of subjective, emotional or 'disordered' discourse is coded as feminine and thus devalues a statement or argument.[73]

Gender informs the responsibility to protect doctrine in a number of ways. For example, Gareth Evans' account of his identification of and campaigning for the principle emphasises the role of the bold, fearless, decisive hero

---

[68] See Charlesworth, 'Are Women Peaceful?'.

[69] Cited in Ban Ki-moon, *Women and Peace and Security*, S/2009/465, 16 September 2009, para. 21.

[70] Cynthia Enloe, cited in Angela Raven-Roberts, 'Gender Mainstreaming in United Nations Peacekeeping Operations' in Dyan Mazurana, Angela Raven-Roberts and Jane Parpart (eds.), *Gender, Conflict, and Peacekeeping* (Boulder, Colorado: Rowman and Littlefield, 2005), p. 43.

[71] Joan Scott, 'Gender: A Useful Category of Analysis', *American Historical Review*, 91: 1053-75 (1986).

[72] Zalewski, 'Well, What is the Feminist Perspective on Bosnia?'.

[73] Carol Cohn, 'War, Wimps, and Women: Talking Gender and Thinking War' in Miriam Cooke and Angela Woollacott (eds.), *Gendering War Talk* (Princeton: Princeton University Press, 1993), p. 397.

overcoming resistance and scepticism to produce a formula that will change international politics. Evans credits 'a fairly unquenchable sense of optimism' as the source of his energy in shepherding the responsibility to protect principle through international institutions. He is also sustained by 'a belief that even the most horrible and intractable problems are soluble; that rational solutions for which there are good, principled arguments do eventually prevail; and that good people, good governments, and good governance will eventually prevail over bad.'[74] The principle is described as one that can, properly applied, solve the problem of mass atrocities 'once and for all'; it is the single solution to the problem.[75] There are close shaves and lucky breaks on the journey, but the principle of responsibility to protect, once identified, must remain pure and undiluted.[76]

Evans presents the principle as a basis for action in a programmatic, objective, quasi-scientific way, although its major components are all indeterminate and open to contestation. His account of the responsibility to protect depicts the use of force as a last resort,[77] but it is also a vital guarantee of effectiveness for him. 'When is it right to fight?' Evans asks, as he reasons 'if there is one thing as bad as using military force when we should not, it is *not* using military force when we *should*.'[78] Evans proposes five criteria for the legitimate use of force as part of the responsibility to protect, drawn from just war theories.[79] The description of the scope and implementation of the principle is built on a series of contrasts that draw their power from gendered images: for example humanitarian action as opposed to inaction; force as opposed to passivity; order as opposed to disorder and chaos; practicality as opposed to theory; optimism as opposed to pessimism. In this version of 'muscular humanitarianism'[80] action, force, order, practicality and optimism are associated with masculine behaviour and their contrasts appear weak and feminine.

This account of the responsibility to protect does not pay adequate attention to the effects of intervention; indeed intervention prompted by just motives is assumed to be a positive force, whereas, as Anne Orford has noted, 'when we join our voices to the call for military intervention in a particular situation, we may find ourselves part of a different narrative.'[81] One of Evans'

[74] Evans, *The Responsibility to Protect*, p. 7.
[75] Ibid., p. 11.
[76] Ibid., pp. 64-5.
[77] Ibid., p. 213.
[78] Ibid., p. 128 (emphasis in the original).
[79] These criteria were originally formulated in the ICISS report: ibid. pp. 140-47.
[80] Orford, *Reading Humanitarian Intervention*, p. 7.
[81] Ibid., p. 37.

criteria of legitimate force is consideration of the balance of consequences of military action, but the inquiry into consequences is framed narrowly as 'halting or averting the atrocities or suffering that triggered the intervention in the first place.'[82] Catastrophes that attract intervention are rarely discrete and susceptible to a neat resolution; they are better understood as protracted crises of security, financing, power and legitimacy, engineered by political elites, invariably dominated by men.[83] The politics of masculinity and femininity are deeply implicated in these chronic situations yet international interventions do not take them into account. For example, there is now considerable evidence pointing to the unintended consequences of intervention, such as its contributions to the sex trade and to violent war economies.[84] Dyan Mazurana observes that women and gender are seen as 'soft' or peripheral issues in conflict and post-conflict situations and are thus easily postponed to be dealt with after the 'hard' problems of establishing new governmental or economic structures are resolved.[85] In this sense, interventions regularly reinforce the unequal and oppressive political and social systems that have caused and sustained the immediate conflict. The increasing fusion of humanitarian and military goals in international interventions thus pushes questions of social justice off the agenda.

Gendered images frame the rationale for the responsibility to protect principle. A major catalyst for the concept was the international inaction during the Rwanda genocide in 1994.[86] Nesam McMillan has shown how the discourse of the 'horrors' of the failure of the international community to rescue the Tutsis has created an image of Western responsibility for global order in the face of the brutal, atrocious behaviour of non-Western peoples.[87] This image is both masculinised and racialised, in that it

> produce[s] a mode of thinking about the response [to the Rwandan genocide] that both figures the West as *the* global actor and calls upon this global actor to have the will to intervene in non-Western countries around the world on the basis of its relative superiority.[88]

---

[82] Evans, *The Responsibility to Protect*, p. 145.

[83] Dyan Mazurana, 'Gender and the Causes and Consequences of Armed Conflict' in Dyan Mazurana, Angela Raven-Roberts and Jane Parpart (eds.), *Gender, Conflict, and Peacekeeping* (Boulder, Colorado: Rowman and Littlefield, 2005), pp. 30-1.

[84] Mazurana, 'Gender and the Causes and Consequences of Armed Conflict', pp. 34-6.

[85] Ibid., p. 40.

[86] For example, Evans, *The Responsibility to Protect*, pp. 66, 105.

[87] Nesam McMillan, '"Our" Shame: International Responsibility for the Rwandan Genocide', *Australian Feminist Law Journal*, 28: 3-28 (2008).

[88] Ibid., p. 20.

The deployment of gendered images in the responsibility to protect doctrine makes it appear a logical, strong and appropriate response to violence. The international community is positioned as the ultimate guarantor of stability and peace. The principle however does not deal with the complexities of the situation of groups who do not wield public power. It does not address the widespread subordination of women or the way that violence shapes women's lives. Military force is presented as a last resort to enforce the principle, but this carries with it the possibility of exacerbating women's inequality and oppression. It also has the effect, as Karen Engle has argued, of forcing those who want to redress a major problem of presenting it 'in terms of a crisis that only immediate military intervention can resolve'.[89] This can in turn obscure how both military and non-military interventions have themselves contributed to the crisis, and how international intervention is typically followed by a period of international administration that creates new forms of dependence, powerlessness and exploitation.[90]

Conclusion

For international lawyers, the development of the responsibility to protect doctrine has been a striking feature of the first decade of the twenty-first century, reconceptualising understandings of the duties of states and the international community when faced with potential or actual atrocities. It has shown not only the significance of norm-entrepreneurs in identifying and publicising new ideas, but also the resilience of the traditional concept of sovereignty. The designers of the responsibility to protect are animated by the hope of ending mass atrocities 'once and for all'; while they see themselves as breaking new ground by placing the interests of vulnerable populations first, some states regard them as the vanguard of neo-colonialism.

Given the resistance the doctrine has encountered politically, its international legal status is uncertain. It may be that it is not capacious enough to embrace all the contradictory interests at stake, unlike concepts such as 'sustainable development', or 'proportionality' and 'reasonableness' in the laws of war, which, as Koskenniemi points out, is the essence of international law.[91]

---

[89] Engle, "Calling in the Troops", p. 190.

[90] Orford, *Reading Humanitarian Intervention*, pp. 28-31.

[91] Martti Koskenniemi, 'International Law in the World of Ideas' in James Crawford and Martti Koskenniemi (eds.), *Cambridge Companion to International Law* (Cambridge: Cambridge University Press, 2011) (forthcoming).

Feminist scholars have an ambivalent attitude to international law, sometimes working to extend its coverage and sometimes worrying that invoking it may legitimate oppressive state structures. I think it worth engaging with concepts such as the responsibility to protect because they can unsettle the standard boundaries of the discipline and increase the possibility of its transformation. As the history of Security Council Resolution 1325 shows, international developments can also inspire and support local action to promote women's equality.[92] However, I have argued that, from a feminist perspective, the responsibility to protect doctrine has been devised within a very limited context. It has paid desultory attention to women's lives and has reinforced gendered and racialised accounts of peace and conflict and the capacity of intervention to defuse violence. For the doctrine to offer support for women's equality, it would need to take into account a broader set of factors that impinge on women's lives, including women's economic marginalisation, the effect of militarisation and systemic discrimination against women. It would need to engage with the private subordination of women and the widespread violence against them outside the formal structures of the state. It would need to problematise the idea of intervention, recognising that it can exacerbate injustices by reinforcing particular forms of world order.[93] The responsibility to protect principle would also need to be framed more modestly, not as a single solution to atrocities, but as one strand of a complex response that draws inspiration and ideas from everyone affected by violence.[94]

---

[92] Dianne Otto, 'The Security Council's Alliance of Gender Legitimacy: The Symbolic Capital of Resolution 1325' in Hilary Charlesworth and Jean-Marc Coicaud (eds.), *Faultlines of International Legitimacy* (Cambridge: Cambridge University Press, 2010), pp. 263-65.

[93] See generally Orford, *Reading Humanitarian Intervention*.

[94] An idea suggested by John Braithwaite's account of international law: John Braithwaite, 'Conclusion: Hope and Humility for Weavers with International Law' in Brett Bowden, Hilary Charlesworth and Jeremy Farrall (eds.), *The Role of International Law in Rebuilding Societies after Conflict: Great Expectations* (Cambridge: Cambridge University Press, 2009).

Responsibility to Protect: A Framework for Prevention

*Sheri Rosenberg**

Abstract

Most agree that prevention is the most important aspect of the Responsibility to Protect. The best way, after all, to protect populations from mass atrocities is to ensure that they do not occur in the first instance. Nonetheless, since the adoption of the R2P Doctrine at the World Summit, academic and policy debates concerning the legal and normative content of R2P continue to neglect its preventative dimension. This paper seeks to fill that gap in scholarship by examining the relationship between developing international human rights law on protection/ prevention and the developing norm of R2P, with two specific objectives. The first objective is to bring a much needed focus to the law on prevention. The second objective is to mediate the debate between those who claim R2P is a major departure from existing law and those who claim it adds nothing new to the existing body of international law. The paper concludes with two propositions: First, resting upon international human rights principles, R2P provides, under certain circumstances, for an obligation of 'due diligence' requiring states to take such reasonable measures of prevention as could be expected of states in a similar position; and second, one of the R2P doctrine's greatest strengths is that it harnesses the disparate body of law on the duty to prevent and provides a modicum of conceptual clarity and discipline to its application to mass atrocities.

Keywords

prevention, 2005 World Summit Outcome Document, international human rights, duty to protect/prevent, due diligence, positive obligations in international human rights law, international law, Bosnia v. Serbia judgment

* This article was originally presented at the R2P: The Responsibility to Protect: A Framework for Confronting Identity-based Atrocities Conference, presented by The Program in Holocaust and Human Rights Studies, Benjamin N. Cardozo School of Law and The Department of Political Science, Yeshiva University, 10-11 March 2008. The author is grateful to Professor Bryan Daves and Chris Chapman for their helpful comments and suggestions and Kyra Hild for her superior research assistance.

Introduction

The Responsibility to Protect (R2P) is a doctrine of prevention.[1] It commits states to take action to prevent genocide, war crimes, crimes against humanity, and ethnic cleansing (hereinafter 'Atrocity Crimes')[2] when they know or should know that populations are at grave risk. Although R2P is understood by some as another name for humanitarian intervention, R2P takes a broader view which, as a last resort allows for the possibility of humanitarian intervention.[3] It provides for a much larger set of policy tools to forestall the need for such intervention in recognition that prevention is the best form of protection.[4]

This paper is concerned with the often neglected legal aspect of the prevention dimension of R2P. It seeks to examine the relationship between developing international human rights law on prevention and the developing norm of R2P with two objectives. The first objective is to bring a much needed focus to the law on prevention, and the second objective is to advance the debate between those who claim R2P is major departure from international law and those who claim that it adds nothing new to the existing body of human rights law. In the process, the paper indicates where R2P affirms existing law on prevention, where it innovates, and where it signals the progressive development of international law.

The R2P doctrine as expressed by the International Commission on Intervention and State Sovereignty (ICISS) in its Report, and as adopted at the 2005 World Summit, lays bare that responding to mass atrocities, like a Rwanda or a Srebrenica, is not a false choice either between putting boots on

---

[1] Though the doctrine includes the responsibility to prevent, to react and to rebuild the UN Secretary General and others consistently affirm that the emphasis should be on prevention.

[2] David Scheffer, 'Genocide and Atrocity Crimes', *Genocide Studies and Prevention*, 1/3: 229-250 (2006) (arguing for a single term 'atrocity crimes' to capture genocide, war crimes, crimes against humanity and ethnic cleansing); Madeleine K. Albright and William S. Cohen, *Preventing Genocide: A Blueprint for U.S. Policymakers*, Genocide Prevention Task Force, 2008, addressing genocide and mass atrocities, pp. xxi-xxii, http://www.ushmm.org/genocide/taskforce/pdf/report.pdf, accessed 22 June 2009,.

[3] Gareth Evans, *The Responsibility to Protect: Ending Mass Atrocity Crimes Once and For All* (Washington D.C.: The Brookings Institution, 2008), p. 56. (Endorsing the view that R2P and classical conceptions of humanitarian intervention are 'very different concepts'); Susan E. Rice, 'Remarks on the UN Security Council and the Responsibility to Protect', at the International Peace Institute Vienna Seminar, 15 June 2009 available at http://www.usunnewyork.usmission.gov/press_releases/20090615_126.html

[4] Ban Ki-Moon, *Implementing the Responsibility to Protect*, A/63/677, 12 January 2009.

the ground or doing nothing; it is not a zero-sum game.[5] Rather, its significant achievement lies in identifying a continuum of actions ranging from preventing atrocities, to protecting populations should they occur, to rebuilding in the aftermath. The ICISS report provides that 'prevention is the single most important dimension of the responsibility to protect'[6] stating that 'it is high time for the international community to be doing more to close the gap between rhetorical support for prevention and tangible commitment.'[7]

The most authoritative statement on and formulation of R2P was made by the General Assembly (GA) at the September 2005 High-level plenary meeting of the United Nations General Assembly where world leaders adopted the Summit Outcome Document (Outcome Document), which embraced the concept of R2P.[8] In Paragraphs 138 and 139 of the Outcome Document, heads of state unanimously affirmed that each individual state has the responsibility to protect its populations from genocide, war crimes, crimes against humanity, and ethnic cleansing, including the prevention of such crimes. They further agreed that states should assist others states in exercising their respective responsibility.

Moreover, they affirmed that the international community has the responsibility to take actions using peaceful means to protect populations; and should a state 'manifestly fail' to protect its population from atrocity crimes, 'we are prepared to take collective action, in a timely and decisive manner, through the Security Council, in accordance with the Charter'.[9] Prevention was perceived as the cornerstone obligation undertaken by the international community.[10]

Since the World Summit, the R2P framework and the language it employs infiltrate most policy discussions of humanitarian crises. Significantly, the UN Security Council has endorsed R2P three times in resolutions concerning the protection of civilians in armed conflicts in general and in reference to the situations in Darfur, Sudan and Somalia in particular.[11] In 2009, the Secretary

---

[5] International Commission on Intervention and State Sovereignty (ICISS), *The Responsibility to Protect* (Ottawa: IDRC, 2001), p. 16 para. 2.28. The ICISS found that the expression 'humanitarian intervention' and past debates over the 'right to intervene' were not helpful and did not help to 'carry the debate forward.'

[6] *Ibid.* p. XI.

[7] *Ibid.* p.19.

[8] '2005 World Summit Outcome', UNGA Res. 60/1, 16 September 2005.

[9] *Ibid.*, Para. 139.

[10] Ban Ki-Moon, *Implementing the Responsibility to Protect*, A/63/677, 12 January 2009.

[11] S/RES/1674, 28 April 2006, p. 2; S/RES/1706, 31 August 2006, p. 1; S/RES/1814, 15 May 2008, p. 5.

General produced a report summarising and setting forth a three-pillared strategy for implementing R2P. Pillar one addresses the responsibility of the state to protect its population; pillar two addresses the international community's duty to assist states to fulfill their responsibility to prevent and protect; and pillar three addresses the international community's responsibility to take timely and decisive responses through peaceful means, and should that fail through other more forceful means, in a manner consistent with international law. Pillars one and two constitute crucial elements in the effective prevention of mass atrocity crimes, again placing the emphasis on prevention.[12]

Since the adoption of R2P by the GA in its 2005 resolution, academic and policy debates continue over whether R2P has legal content, whether it should have legal content and whether identifying legal content matters.[13] Relevant actors continue to debate the principle's status in international law and policy. Some say it is a tool of 'moral suasion',[14] others a combination of legal and political norms,[15] and yet others state that it is firmly grounded in international law.[16]

Broadly, most commentators would likely accept that Paragraphs 138 and 139 of the Outcome Document are in themselves a convoluted compromise of political and legal statements and considerations.[17] Moreover, most would likely agree that while a number of the constituent parts of R2P are unquestionably grounded in international law, R2P as a whole does not presently

---

[12] Ban Ki-Moon, *Implementing the Responsibility to Protect*, A/63/677, 12 January 2009, p. 2. The three Pillar typology will be used throughout the paper.

[13] Jose E. Alvarez, 'The Schizophrenias of R2P', Panel Presentation at the 2007 Hague Joint Conference on Contemporary Issues International Criminal Law: Criminal Jurisdiction 100 Years After the 1907 Hague Peace Conference, 30 June 2007, http://www.asil.org/pdfs/r2pPanel.pdf, accessed 24 June 2009. (highlighting the risks of R2P as a legal concept).

[14] Albright and Cohen, *Preventing Genocide, p.* 89, 'R2P is best understood as an important tool for moral suasion'.

[15] Carsten Stahn, 'Responsibility to Protect: Political Rhetoric or Emerging Legal Norm', *American Journal of International Law*, 101/1: 99-120 (2007) (arguing that the R2P concept encompasses different normative prescriptions that vary widely in their degree of legal foundations). After the adoption of the Outcome Document, Paul Martin, Prime Minister of Canada referred to R2P as a 'powerful norm of international behaviour', Italy referred to it as a principle. Statements, 16 September 2005, http://www.un.org/webcast/summit2005/statements.html, accessed 23 June 2009.

[16] Ban Ki-Moon, *Implementing the Responsibility to Protect*, A/63/677, 12 January 2009, p. 4, para. 2.

[17] Stahn, 'Responsibility to Protect', p. 67; Ekkehard Strauss, 'A Bird in the Hand is Worth Two in the Bush – On the Assumed Legal Nature of the Responsibility to Protect', in this volume.

constitute a legal norm. A GA resolution (Paragraphs 138 and 139 of the Outcome Document) coupled with follow up statements[18] and affirmations[19] by the Security Council, are not generally considered to establish the existence of customary international law.[20] That, is not to say, however, that states did not interpret, reinforce, and, in fact, clarify existing legal obligations in the various 'responsibilities' of R2P.[21]

Where one locates R2P on the spectrum from politics to law matters. If the content of R2P is political or moral then the failure to discharge the obligation there under results in different types of repercussions, depending upon the socio-political circumstances surrounding the situation. If however, the obligation rests upon international law then with the failure to discharge that duty comes a host of potential remedies, including the legal liability of the wrongful actor. Some argue that politics and institutional arrangements for prevention are important, but they need a relationship with legal norms that give weight and clarity to political aspirations.[22] As Louise Arbour, the former High Commissioner for Human Rights has stated, a lesson learned from Srebrenica

---

[18] For a discussion of the General Assembly's statements on R2P see, Ekkehard Strauss, *The Emperor's New Clothes?: The United Nations and the Implementation of the Responsibility to Protect* (Nomos Publishers 2009).

[19] S/RES/1674, 28 April 2006, p. 2; S/RES/1706, 31 August 2006, p. 1; S/RES/1814, 15 May 2008, p. 5.

[20] International custom is a source of international law established by state practice accompanied by a sense of legal obligation – *opinio juris*. See generally, Weissbrodt, Fitzpatrick and Newman (eds.), *International Human Rights: Law, Policy and Process* (Anderson Publishing 2001 3rd edition), pp. 22-23. General Assembly resolutions can provide evidence for the existence of a certain rule or *opinio juris*. They are not however, conclusive of customary international law. See, *Legality of the Threat or Use of Nuclear Weapons*, Advisory Opinion, ICJ Rep, 8 July 1996, p. 254. Juan Mendez, the first Special Advisor to the Secretary General for the Prevention of Genocide, has argued that a norm does not need to be respected in all cases for it to be considered a norm. The *opinion juris* in respect of R2P, in his opinion "is that no one says that we can let thousands of people die or that we condone genocide, crimes against humanity, war crimes, and ethnic cleansing. See, 'Meeting Summary, Reflections on the UN General Assembly debate on the Responsibility to Protect', International Coalition for the Responsibility to Protect, 26 October 2009, p. 3, available at http://globalr2p.org/media/pdf/Meeting%20Summary%20Reflections%20on%20the%20UN%20General%20Assembly%20debate%20on%20R2P.pdf

[21] General Assembly resolutions may assist in the determination and interpretation of international law. See, Stahn, 'Responsibility to Protect'.

[22] Over the past decade there has been a burgeoning of institutional mechanisms established to facilitate the prevention of mass atrocities. For example, in 2004 the UN established the Special Advisor's Office for the Prevention of Genocide, the Constitutive Act of the African Union granted African heads of state a collective right to intervene, and the United States created a task force on genocide prevention, which recently issued a key report: Albright and Cohen, *Preventing Genocide*.

and Rwanda is that we need a compulsory legal framework for action – 'a framework that would trigger not just a political or moral responsibility to act, but a legal one that carries legal consequences.'[23]

This paper suggests that the prevention obligation of the R2P doctrine, insofar as it requires states to take action in the face of genocide, crimes against humanity, war crimes and ethnic cleansing, short of military intervention, rests upon established norms of international human rights law. The scope and content of these obligations are disaggregated in two ways: the first based upon the particular instrument under which the obligation is established, and second based upon the role of the actor committing the infringements, the place where the infringements are occurring, and the relationship between the perpetrator and the victim.

The first part of the paper examines the duty to prevent in human rights laws corresponding to pillar one of R2P. The second part of the paper focuses on the *Bosnia and Herzegovina v. Serbia and Montenegro* decision rendered by the International Court of Justice (ICJ) in 2007[24] in order to explore the separate question of a state's obligations under international law to protect human rights outside of its territory, corresponding to pillar two of R2P. The third part of the paper examines the relationship between the duty to prevent in human rights law and R2P and disaggregates the ways in which each works to define the content and scope of the other.

Protect Rights /Prevent Violations

Preliminary Issues – Clarification of Terminology and Concepts

As a threshold matter certain concepts and terminology must be clarified. First, the ICISS developed R2P as a guiding principle for the international community of states that rests upon a range of legal obligations and political responsibilities.[25] In fact, the negotiating history of the Outcome Document reveals that R2P were considered to rest on existing

---

[23] Louise Arbour, 'Preventing Mass Atrocities', transcript from lecture at the Council on Foreign Relations, 12 June 2007, p. 12. http://www.cfr.org/publication/13580/preventing_mass_atrocities_rush_transcript_federal_news_service.html?breadcrumb=%2Fmedia%2Ftranscripts, accessed 24 June 2009.

[24] *Case concerning the Application of the Convention on the Prevention and Punishment of the Crime of Genocide* (*Bosnia and Herzegovina v. Serbia and Montenegro*), Judgment, ICJ Rep, 26 February 2007.

[25] ICISS, *The Responsibility to Protect*, p. XI.

international law.[26] In his 2009 report Secretary General Ban Ki-Moon underscored that the provisions of 138 and 139 of the Summit Outcome are 'firmly anchored in well-established principles of international law. Under conventional and customary international law, States have obligations to prevent and punish genocide, war crimes, and crimes against humanity.'[27]

These 'firm anchors' as alluded to by the Secretary General are found throughout international law ranging from state responsibility as articulated under the International Law Commission's Articles of State Responsibility to principles of international criminal and human rights law. In fact, some commentators criticise the concept for being overly broad in its scope and redundant as to content, because it does not add anything new to states' existing obligations under international law.[28] This critique however, overlooks the potential strength of R2P. Certainly, the endeavour of exploring the rights of individuals and corresponding duties of states encompassed under the R2P framework is theoretically, doctrinally, and politically difficult, but this does not delegitimize the category or unit of analysis. While R2P in some aspects may reinforce or reiterate existing law, its strength lies in the framework it establishes – unearthing, interpreting, and crystallising the obligation to act in the face of mass atrocity crimes.

Given the scope of obligations undertaken under R2P, it is necessary to disaggregate the legal bases for the varying sets of obligations. Since R2P primarily requires states to act to ensure that atrocities do not occur in the first place, it is necessary to identify the legal standards that will determine if and when a state may be held responsible for failing to take action to prevent.

Additionally, the 'responsibility to protect' is a term now commonly associated with the concept first articulated by the ICISS report as adopted in the Outcome Document. The '*duty* to protect', a separate yet related term of art, is a well known concept in international human rights law. The 'duty to protect' provides, generally, that states have a positive obligation in certain circumstances to take measures to prevent private actors from infringing on the rights of other individuals.[29] In essence it requires states to prevent infringements of

---

[26] Strauss, 'A Bird in the Hand is Worth Two in the Bush', p. 14.

[27] Ban Ki-Moon, *Implementing the Responsibility to Protect*, A/63/677, 12 January 2009, para. 3.

[28] Hurst Hannum, remarks at the 'The Responsibility to Protect: A Framework for Confronting Identity-based Atrocities, Benjamin N. Cardozo School of Law, March 10-11, 2008 (on file with the author).

[29] Thomas Buergenthal, 'To Respect and to Ensure: State Obligations and Permissible Derogations' in Louis Henkin (ed.) *The International Bill of Rights: The Covenant on Civil and*

international human rights, including through punishing, investigating and redressing human rights violations. For the purpose of this paper, the term 'duty to protect' as understood in international human rights law, will be used synonymously with the duty to prevent, since in essence it is a duty of prevention.

Finally, R2P entails collective obligations of the international community and national obligations of individual states. While these obligations are autonomous, there is a symbiotic relationship between the two sets of obligations. R2P relies heavily on the concept of peaceful 'coordinated actions' to be taken by the international community as a whole, and, should peaceful means prove inadequate, more coercive collective measures through the Security Council. The notion of collective responsibility resembles the tentative positive duty of cooperation found in Articles 40 and 41(1) of the International Law Commission's Articles of State Responsibility.[30] These Articles provide that certain breaches of international law may be so grave as to trigger not only a right but an obligation (a positive duty) of cooperation among states to foster compliance with the law. This principle is limited to a certain category of violations designated as 'serious breaches'. Serious breaches are defined 'as a gross or systematic failure by the responsible state' to perform 'an obligation arising under a peremptory norm of general international law.'[31] Such breaches would result in a positive obligation of states to cooperate to bring the serious breach to an end by lawful means through coordinated action. It should be noted, that the Commission is skeptical about whether general

Political Rights (New York: Columbia University Press, 1981), pp. 72, 77-78. For an exploration of positive obligations in international human rights law, see, generally, Sandra Fredman, *Human Rights Transformed: Positive Rights and Positive Duties* (Oxford University Press, 2008).

[30] Draft Articles on Responsibility of States for Internationally Wrongful Acts, in Report of the International Law Commission on the Work of Its Fifty-third Session, UN GAOR, 56th Sess., Supp. No. 10, UN Doc A/56/10 (2001), *reprinted* in James Crawford, *The International Law Commission's Articles on State Responsibility: Introduction, Text and Commentaries* (Cambridge University Press:, 2002). (hereafter Articles on State Responsibility). The International Law Commission was established by the UN in 1948 to assist in the development and codification of international law. The Draft Articles on State Responsibility are an authoritative statement on the law, which have been referred to, but not yet adopted by the GA.

[31] Articles on State Responsibility, Article 40. A peremptory norm of international law (otherwise known as a *jus cogens* norm) is one which is accepted and recognised by the international community from which no derogation is permitted. See, Article 53 of the Vienna Convention on the Law of Treaties. Commentators have suggested that prohibitions against aggression, slavery, apartheid, genocide, racial discrimination and 'international crimes' have acquired *jus cogens* status. Crawford, *The International Law Commission's Articles on State Responsibility*, p. 246, Note 4 to Article 40, see also, Restatement of the Law (Third) The Foreign Relations Law of the United States at 102 reporters note 6 (1987).

international law at present prescribes an obligation of cooperation stating in that respect that Article 41 (1) 'may reflect the progressive development of international law.'[32]

R2P also places autonomous, positive obligations upon UN member states to take steps to ensure that they do not contribute to mass atrocities outside of their borders. At the World Summit, states committed themselves to 'encourage and help' other states exercise *their* responsibility to prevent and to assist states 'as necessary and appropriate' in building their capacity to protect populations – such assistance being a crucial component of prevention. At a minimum, this suggests that individual states should refrain from exacerbating atrocity crimes committed by other states. Moreover, the collective obligation of the international community to take coordinated action to assist states to protect populations from atrocity crimes implies individual state responsibility to take reasonable steps to prevent the acts it seeks to prohibit. It would be incongruous, though of course not implausible, to suggest that states committed themselves to cooperate to bring atrocity crimes to an end, while omitting each state's individual commitment to do their best not to contribute to such crimes.

The Duty to Protect: States' Positive Obligations to Prevent

Under international human rights law, states have a duty to protect individuals from human rights violations. These duties are defined in specific international treaties in different contexts, with different purposes. The scope and content of these obligations are disaggregated based upon the role of the actor committing the act, the place where the interference occurs, and the relationship between the alleged perpetrator and victim. In order to appreciate the specific legal obligations to prevent affirmed in Paragraphs 138 and 139 of the Outcome Document, one needs to parse through these separate obligations.

International human rights law is focused primarily on the conduct of states. It is grounded in a concept of human dignity, which provides that individuals have inherent attributes that cannot be legitimately restricted by governmental power. On this view, human rights law gives rise to 'negative duties' upon a state not to interfere with an individual, rather than positive duties which would require the state to take positive action to effectuate human rights protections. At a minimum, human rights law requires states to respect

[32] Crawford, *The International Law Commission's Articles on State Responsibility*, p. 249, Commentary, para. 3.

human rights. That is to say state actors may not infringe upon individuals' human rights.

This obligation is firmly rooted in international law. Since Nuremberg and the birth of the Universal Declaration of Human Rights, how a sovereign treats its population has become a legitimate subject of international concern and of international law.[33] The Universal Declaration of Human Rights, along with the International Covenant on Civil and Political Rights (ICCPR) and the International Covenant on Economic, Social and Cultural Rights (ICESCR)[34] form the core of international human rights law. Since their adoption, a multitude of other human rights treaties have been promulgated.[35] By the 1980s, human rights had been firmly established as a cornerstone of international law.

By the 1990s, there was a significant movement to pursue *individual* accountability for mass atrocities with the creation of the *ad hoc* tribunals and, ultimately, the adoption of the Rome Statute of the International Criminal Court (ICC) which entered into force in 2002.[36] While international criminal law does not implicate state responsibility for the underlying crime, because it seeks to hold individuals accountable for crimes rather than the state, it is another source of protection for victims and places a responsibility on states to hold perpetrators of mass atrocities accountable.[37]

---

[33] Sheri Rosenberg, 'What's Law Got to do with it?: The *Bosnia v. Serbia* Decision's Impact on Reconciliation', *Rutgers Law Review*, 61/1: 131-159 (2008), pp. 131-132.

[34] The International Covenant on Civil and Political Rights, G.A. Res. 2200A, U.N. GAOR, 21st Sess., U.N. Doc. A/Res/2200 [Dec. 16, 1966], 999 U.N.T.S. 172 (ICCPR) [entered into force 23 March 1976]; the International Covenant on Economic, Social, and Cultural Rights G.A. Res. 2200A art. 2, U.S. GAOR, 21st Sess., UN Doc. A/6316, [Dec. 16, 1966] 993 U.N.T.S. 3.(ICESCR)[entered into force 3 Jan. 1976].

[35] For example, the International Convention on the Elimination of All Forms of Racial Discrimination, Jan. 4 1969, 660 U.N.T.S. 195 (CERD) [entered into force 4 January 1969]; Convention on the Elimination of All Forms of Discrimination against Women, G.A. Res. 34.180, U.N. GAOR Supp., 46th Sess., U.N. A/34/180 (CEDAW), [entered into force 3 Sept. 1981]; Convention against torture and Other Cruel, Inhuman or Degrading Treatment or Punishment, G.A. Res. 39/46, U.N. GAOR, 51st Sess., U.N. Doc. A/39/51 (CAT), [entered into force 26 June1987].

[36] Rome Statute of the International Criminal Court, 17 July, 1998, 2187 U.N.T.S. 90 [entered into force on 1 July 2002][hereinafter Rome Statute].

[37] In fact an examination of the approaches of the International Criminal Court (as provided for in the Rome Statute) and the Responsibility to Protect (as provided for in the World Summit Outcome Document) illustrates a striking similarity in that both focus explicitly on the *primary* responsibility of the State to punish perpetrators or protect its people and giving the international community an active, as opposed to supportive, role in these matters *only* if the relevant State is 'unable or unwilling' (in the case of the ICC, Article 17) or there is a 'manifest failure' (regarding the Responsibility to Protect, para 139).

The highly developed body of international human rights and international criminal law provides states with clear indications of the content and scope of the complex set of violations to bodily integrity that make up the majority of atrocity crimes.[38] Indeed, the right to life is considered a fundamental right provided for in most international human rights and criminal law treaties and is a peremptory norm of international law. Thus, the legal obligation upon *states* not to commit mass atrocities against its own populations is straight forward.

In today's world, however, many of the atrocity crimes that we experience around the globe are committed surreptitiously at the hands of *non-state* actors, with varying degrees of relationship with the state. For instance, in Darfur, Sudan, many of the atrocity crimes are being committed by the Janjaweed, an organised group that has a complex relationship with the Sudanese government. During the Balkan wars from 1990-1994, many of the crimes were committed by the Bosnian Serbs, who themselves were non-state actors acting under a certain level of influence from Serbia. The question then becomes what obligations, under existing international human rights law,[39] do states have to prevent private individuals from committing human rights abuses, in particular, human rights abuses involving violations of the right to life, like atrocity crimes. Likewise, what international human rights obligations do states have in respect of mass atrocity crimes committed outside their own boarders – including aiding and abetting other states or non-state actors?

As will be examined below, there is an evolving trend in international human rights law to delimit and define states' positive obligations to protect individuals from interferences with the right to bodily integrity committed by private individuals inter and intra-state. Essentially, positive obligations require states to take specific affirmative steps under certain circumstances to prevent the human rights violation in the first place. This is obligation is commonly known as the 'duty to protect'.

---

[38] These include, *inter-alia*, the ICCPR Arts. 6, 7, 9; the ICESCR Arts. 11-12; Rome Statute; European Convention for the Protection of Human Rights and Fundamental Freedoms, Nov. 4 1950, 213 U.N.T.S 222 (ECHR), Arts. 2-5; African Charter on Human and Peoples' Rights, Organization of African Unity, June 27, 1981, O.A.U. Doc. CAB/LEG/67/3rev5 (African Charter) Arts. 4-6; the American Convention on Human Rights, Organization of American States, Nov. 22, 1969, O.A.S.T.S. No. 36, 1144 U.N.T.S. 123 (American Convention) Arts. 4-7.

[39] While international criminal law principles are certainly implicated under R2P and bear on specific questions of accountability, as will be seen below, this paper focuses on state responsibility.

Because international human rights law traditionally focused on state conduct the two core international human rights treaties, the ICCPR and the ICESCR, do not set forth specific provisions requiring the state to take steps to protect the rights of individuals from interferences by non-state actors. Likewise, the principal regional human rights treaties – the American Convention on Human Rights (ACHR) and the European Convention on Human Rights (ECHR) – are also silent on this point. Each, however, contains ambiguous phrasing that leaves room for interpretive devices to establish just such obligations.[40]

While there are no express provisions in international law requiring a state to protect individuals from human rights violations committed by private individuals, it is now generally accepted that states have positive obligations under international human rights treaties to prevent such violations, including by punishing, investigating, and redressing human rights violations in areas ranging from the right to life, to respect for private and family life, to the prohibition on discrimination.[41] In other words states must not only take steps to ensure all governmental actors refrain from committing violations but must also take active steps to prevent private individuals from committing human rights violations within their jurisdiction.[42]

The positive obligation to protect is based upon the idea that rights protected under international human rights instruments must be practical and effective, not theoretical or illusory.[43] Under this theory, for certain rights to be realised the state may be under a duty to take particular actions to ensure

---

[40] ICCPR Art. 2; ICESCR Art. 8; ECHR Art. 1; ACHR Art. 1.

[41] It is outside the scope of this paper to examine the range of positive obligations under international human rights. For an exploration of positive obligations in the European system see Mastair Mowbray, *The Development of Positive Obligations under the European Convention Human Rights by the European Court of Human Rights* (Oxford: Hart, 2004); J.G. Merrills, *The Development of International Law by the European Court of Human Rights* (Manchester University Press, 1994); Andrew Byrnes, 'Women, Feminism and International Human Rights Law - Methodological Myopia, Fundamental Flaws or Meaningful Marginalisation?: Some Current Issues', *Australian Yearbook of International Law*, 12 (1988), p. 205.

[42] G.J.H van Hoof, 'The Legal Nature of Economic, Social and Cultural Rights: a Rebuttal of Some Traditional Views', in P. Alston and K. Tomaševski (eds.), *The Right to Food* (Martinus Nijhoff Publishers, 1984), p. 97. Positive obligations of conduct are extant in other areas of international law. See for example, *Case Concerning United States Diplomatic and Consular Staff in Tehran* (*United States of America v. Iran*), Judgment, ICJ Rep, 24 May 1980, (the Court held that Iran was responsible for failing to take any steps to protect the U.S. embassy from the attack that took place in 1979), *United States v. Canada (Trail Smelter)* preliminary decision, 3 Int. Arb. Awards 1911 (1938), final decision, 3 Int. Arb. Awards 1938 (1941) (holding Canada responsible for trans-boundary damage caused by air pollution into the United States).

[43] *Golder v United Kingdom*, App. 4451/70, Judgment, Eur. Ct. H.R., 21 February 1975.

the right. By deconstructing a right into its related state duties, a clearer notion of the 'content or proposed content of the right itself'[44] is provided. Building on this conceptual foundation, in essence, positive obligations have evolved to require, under some circumstances, that states not stand idly by while private individuals infringe upon the rights of others. For example, the right to life requires that state actors do not kill, but it also requires that states take action to prevent the taking of life by non-state actors, in so far as possible. Of course, a state cannot anticipate every infringement committed by private actors, but it must take positive steps to stop the infringement through its laws and administrative processes, and to offer redress for the victim should a violation occur.

Due Diligence –A Duty to Act

The positive obligation to prevent violations by non-state actors has developed as a standard of due diligence, a concept known in the national law of torts.[45] Due diligence requires such reasonable measures of prevention as could be expected from governments under similar circumstances. It is an obligation of conduct, not of result. This means that if the state took all reasonable measures within its power to prevent the interference, it will not be held responsible should the violation nonetheless occur. For example, if a state authority is aware that individual x harbours the intent to cause bodily harm to individual y, and the public authority takes measures to protect y, such as enforcing a restraining order or providing physical protection to person y, yet person x, nonetheless causes harm to person y, the state will not be liable for its failure to prevent the harm. Seen as a due diligence obligation, prevention is the mirror image of protection. From the perspective of the state it has failed in its obligation to protect the victim. From the perspective of the victim, the state has failed to prevent the violation.[46]

---

[44] Henry L. Steiner and Philip Alston, *International Human Rights in Context*, 2nd Edition (Oxford: Oxford University Press, 2000), pp. 180-181.

[45] See Restatement (Third) Torts: Liability for Harm at paras. 37, 39-40 (preliminary draft No. 4) (Sept. 5, 2003). In tort, duties arise most frequently from relationships of influence or care.

[46] In its application to the ICJ in 1993, the government of Bosnia, among other things, asked the Court to declare that Bosnia had the right to defend itself and its people, and therefore construe Security Council Resolution 713 placing an arms embargo on the whole of the former Yugoslavia in such a way as to provide Bosnia with the right to self-defense. The jurisdictional basis for this claim was Article 1 of the Genocide Convention, because the obligation to prevent should also be read as an obligation to protect the Bosnian people.

The Human Rights Committee has coherently articulated this standard in its General Comment on Article 2 of the ICCPR. Article 2(1) of the ICCPR demands that state parties '*ensure* to all individuals within its territory and subject to its jurisdiction the rights recognised in the present Covenant, without distinction of any kind…[emphasis added]'[47] More specifically, Articles 2(2-3(c)) require States Parties to adopt legislation and remedies necessary to give effect to the rights recognised by the Covenant.[48]

General Comment 31 on the ICCPR provides that the failure to *ensure* Convention rights found in Article 2, in certain circumstances, may 'give rise to violations by States Parties of those rights, as a result of a State Parties'… failing to exercise *due diligence* to prevent, punish, investigate or redress the harm caused by such acts by private persons or entities.'[49] The positive obligations that follow from the requirement in Article 2, that states 'ensure' protection of Covenant rights, entail a particular set of measures for each right that is protected. For example, the right to be free from torture in Article 7 also implies that States Parties have to take positive measures to ensure that private persons or entities do not inflict torture or cruel, inhuman or degrading treatment or punishment on others within their power.[50]

While the positive obligation to ensure rights attaches to all Convention rights, this paper focuses on the right to bodily integrity for two reasons. First, the obligations under R2P are primarily focused on preventing mass interferences with the right to life. Second, in practice, the Human Rights Committee

[47] ICCPR, Art. 2 para. 1.

[48] ICCPR, Art. 2 para. 2.

[49] ICCPR General Comment No. 31: Nature of the General Legal Obligation Imposed on States Parties to the Covenant, CCPR/C/21/Rev.1/Add.13(2004) para. 8. General Comment 31 states that the legal obligation under Article 2(1) is 'both positive and negative in nature'. It further provides that Article 2's positive obligations on States Parties to ensure Covenant rights requires the State to protect individuals not just from state action, but from private actors as well. *Ibid.* para. 8. Paragraph 8 further explicates the positive obligation of States Parties to address the actions of private parties: '[T]he privacy-related guarantees of article 17 must be protected by law…' *Ibid.* Additionally, according to General Comment 24, States Parties may not make reservations regarding Article 2's positive obligation requirement such reservations would contravene the objects and purposes of the Covenant. ICCPR General Comment 24(9). General Comment 6 observes that Article 7's right to bodily integrity 'cannot properly be understood in a restrictive manner,' and therefore the protection of that right 'requires that States adopt positive measures'. ICCPR General Comment 6, para. 5.

[50] ICCPR General Comment No. 31: Nature of the General Legal Obligation Imposed on States Parties to the Covenant, para. 8. See generally, Rhonda Copelon, 'The Indivisible Framework of International Human Rights: A Source of Social Justice in the U.S.', *New York City Law Review*, 3/: 59 (1998), p. 66.

and the regional bodies have attached this positive obligation most often in the context of interferences with bodily integrity.[51]

The seminal judgment setting forth the due diligence standard is *Velásquez–Rodriguez* where the Inter-American Court of Human Rights examined a case involving disappearances in Honduras. The Court determined that the Honduran government could be held liable under the American Convention if it failed to take appropriate steps to prevent or punish private individuals who caused others to disappear. In the Court's words,

> [I]n principle, any violation of rights recognized by the Convention carried out by an act of public authority or by persons who use their position of authority is imputable to the States. However, this does not define all the circumstances in which a State is obligated to prevent, investigate and punish human rights violations, nor all the cases in which the State might be found responsible for an infringement of those rights. An illegal act which violates human rights and which is initially not directly imputable to a State (for example, because it is the act of a private person or because the person responsible has not been identified) can lead to international responsibility for the State, not because of the act itself, but because of the lack of *due diligence* to prevent violation or to respond to it as required by the Convention.[52]

The Inter-American Court's case-law reflects this principle, repeatedly holding States responsible on account of their lack of due diligence to prevent human rights violations.[53]

---

[51] Minorities have been regarded as especially vulnerable therefore requiring protective measures to safeguard them from violations. *Case of D.H. and Others v. The Czech Republic*, App. 57325/00, Judgment, Grand Chamber, Eur. Ct. H.R., 13 November 2007, para. 115; *Case of Timishev v. Russia*, Apps. 55762/00 and 55974/00, Judgment, Eur. Ct. H.R., 13 December 2005, paras 55-56. Similarly, treaties geared to the protection of identifiable groups such as children, women and racial minorities explicitly articulate the positive duty to protect. CEDAW art. 2e, General Recommendation 19 clarifying that states are responsible for otherwise private acts if they fail to fulfill their positive duty to prevent and punish such acts, CERD art. 1 & 2(1)(d)-(1)(e). These developments mirror the concerns addressed by the R2P framework, since minorities and other vulnerable groups are most often the victims of mass atrocities.

[52] *Velásquez-Rodríguez v. Honduras* Case, Judgment, Inter-Am.Ct.H.R. (Ser. C) No. 4, Judgment of July 29 1988, para. 172. (finding the state of Honduras responsible for the involuntary disappearance of Angel Manfredo Velasquez Rodriguez because it failed to take appropriate steps to prevent or punish private individuals who caused Mr. Rodriguez to disappear.) (emphasis added).

[53] Inter-American Court of Human Rights: *Godínez-Cruz v. Honduras*, Judgment of 21 January, 1989; *Case of Fairén-Garbi and Solís-Corrales v. Honduras*, Judgment of 15 March, 1989 (on the issue of the disappearances in Honduras); (*Villagran Morales et al. v. Guatemala*, Judgment of November 19 1999(finding that Guatemalan government failed to protect the street children from death and torture).

The European Court of Human Rights has developed the most extensive case law over the past decade establishing significant positive obligations upon states parties to the European Convention, in areas ranging from the right to life, to respect for private and family life, and to the prohibition on discrimination.[54]

In the context of the right to life provided under Article 2 of the European Convention states are obligated under certain circumstances, to take preventative operational measures to safeguard individuals known to be at 'immediate risk to life' from the actions of others. In the seminal case of *Osman v. U.K.* the Court examined the applicants' complaint that the police had failed to protect the lives of Mr. Osman and Ahmet as required under the right to life provided for under Article 2 of the Convention. Mr. Osman had been shot dead and Ahmet wounded by a former teacher of Ahmet who had developed a fatal obsession with him. Prior to the killing the police had been informed of the teacher's attachment, but they had decided that the matter should be dealt with by the school.

The Court held that Article 2 requires states to take appropriate steps to safeguard the lives of those within its jurisdiction. Such steps include the establishment of state apparatus for the prevention of such acts by private individuals.[55] Specifically, the Court established that where there is an allegation that the state authorities have failed in their positive duty to protect the right to life from the criminal acts of an individual,

> it must be established to its satisfaction that the authorities knew or *ought to have known* at the time of the existence of a real and *immediate risk* to the life of an identified individual or individuals from criminal acts of a third party and that they *failed to take measures* within the scope of their powers which, judged *reasonably*, might have been expected to avoid that risk.[56] [emphasis added]

[54] The growing importance of the notion of positive obligations in European law is well-stated by Judge Evrigenis of the European Court of Human Rights: '[t]he growing complexity of the social fabric is obliging the State to take positive action to protect rights and freedoms which, in the traditional view, only required protection against interference by public authorities. Modern human rights legislation increasingly relies on the concept of a "State conferring benefits". Human Rights have become an area in which the State finds itself confronted with a subtle, shifting synthesis between prohibited interference and compulsory intervention. 'Dimitries Evrigenis, 'Recent Case Law of the European Court of Human Rights under Article 8 and 10 of the ECHR', *Human Rights Law Journal*, 3 : 121(1982), p. 136.

[55] *Osman v. The United Kingdom*, App. 87/1997/871/1083, Judgment, Eur. Ct. H.R., 28 October 1998, para. 116. (a significant majority of the Court concluded that the state had not failed in its obligation to prevent under the articulated standard, since they were unable to identify any stage prior to the shootings, where the police knew or should have known that the Osman family was at risk).

[56] *Ibid.*

In *Paul and Audrey Edwards v. United Kingdom*[57] the Court found that the public authorities failed in their positive obligation to protect the life of an inmate, such obligation arising out of a duty of care owed to detainees. In *Mahmut Kaya v. Turkey* the Court found a duty to protect arising in the context of Turkey's well known crackdown on members of the Kurdistan Workers Party (PKK). The applicant, the brother of the deceased, alleged that the Turkish authorities had failed to protect Hasan (the deceased) from contra-guerilla activities operating in the region.[58] Noting the strong indications of illicit links between officials and nationalistic death squads, the Court was satisfied 'that Hasan Kaya as a doctor suspected of aiding and abetting the PKK was at this time at particular risk of falling victim to an unlawful attack. Moreover, this risk could in the circumstances be regarded as real and immediate.'[59]

As the case law establishes, positive obligations require that under certain circumstances states must exercise due diligence, meaning they must take all reasonable measures under the circumstances, to prevent private individuals from infringing upon another's right to life, in circumstances where they know or should know there is a risk. The duty arises when the state has significant influence over the actor committing the infringement or is under a duty of care in relation to the victim.

What remains vague under the jurisprudence is the precise action required to prevent. In *Valásquez*, the Court remarked that '[t]his duty to prevent includes all those means of a legal, political administrative and cultural nature that promote the protection of human rights and ensure that any violations are considered and treated as illegal acts, which, as such, may lead to the punishment of those responsible and the obligation to indemnify the victims

---

[57] *Case of Paul and Audrey Edwards v. The United Kingdom,* App. 46477/99, Judgment, Eur. Ct. H.R., 14 March 2002. (The applicants' 30 year old son, who had a history of mental illness, had been remanded to custody for making inappropriate comments to women in the street. He was put in a cell with an inmate who had schizophrenia. A few hours later the applicants' son was killed by the second inmate).

[58] *Case of Mahmut Kaya v. Turkey*, App. 22535/93, Judgment, Eur. Ct. H.R., 28 March 2000. (In *Kaya*, a medical doctor Hasan and a friend had secretly treated a member of the PKK and three days later Hasan and his friend were found dead.). Similar breach of this positive obligation was found in *Case of Akkoc v. Turkey*, Apps. 22947/93 and 22948/93, Judgment, Eur. Ct. H.R., 10 October 2000, paras. 81-82 (finding that the Turkish government failed in its positive obligation to protect the life of Zubeyir Akkoc, a Kurdish teacher, being satisfied that she was at a real and immediate risk of falling victim to an unlawful attack and that the authorities must be regarded as being aware of this risk).

[59] *Ibid.* p. 89.

for damages.'[60] It is clear from *Valásquez* that punishment is an aspect of prevention, but it is not all that is required of the state to satisfy the obligation to prevent.[61] *Valásquez* failed, however, to set forth any objective criterion for determining specific prevention actions beyond requiring a general rights-protective regime.

It is outside the scope of this paper definitively to assess what concrete measure must be taken to prevent in respect of each circumscribed right related to the right to bodily integrity. The content and the scope of the right to bodily integrity varies from one treaty to another, according to the wording of the relevant provisions, and depending on the nature of the act to be prevented, each requiring its own set of measures. Generally, states are not required to anticipate and avert other-actor interferences before they occur. Rather, the duty to protect arises when the state owes a duty of care to the victim, such as to inmates who have lost the ability to protect themselves,[62] when the state has a significantly close relationship with the other-actor teetering on direct influence over the act,[63] and with regard to 'vulnerable' groups such as minorities and women.[64] Moreover, that international practice is evolving toward a standard of compulsory intervention is evidenced by the specific prohibitions on private interferences with human rights set forth in the more recently adopted international human rights treaties.[65]

R2P internalises and builds on the duty to protect as developed in international human rights law, by explicitly providing that the duty upon a state to protect its population from mass atrocity crimes includes the obligation to

---

[60] *Velásquez-Rodríguez v. Honduras* Case, Judgment, Inter-Am.Ct.H.R. (Ser. C) No. 4, Judgment of July 29 1988, para 175.

[61] The idea that punishment does not equal prevention is picked up by the ICJ in the *Bosnia v. Serbia* decision discussed below.

[62] *Case of Paul and Audrey Edwards v. The United Kingdom.*

[63] *Case of Mahmut Kaya v. Turkey*; *Rodriguez-Valezquez v. Honduras*; *Godínez-Cruz v. Honduras*; *Fairén-Garbi and Solís-Corrales v. Honduras.*

[64] *Case of Opuz v. Turkey*, App. 33401/02, Judgment, Eur. Ct. H.R., 9 June 2009, (finding that the government in breach of its obligations under Articles 2 (right to life) and 3 (torture) because its legal system did not sufficiently safeguard victims of domestic violence in general, and in particular, the government failed in this specific case to take reasonable measures under the circumstances to prevent the foreseeable injuries to bodily integrity and life of the applicant and her mother).

[65] See, the Convention on the Elimination of All Forms of Discrimination against Women, G.A. Res. 34.180, U.N. GAOR Supp., 46th Sess., U.N. A/34/180 (CEDAW) art 2(e),[entered into force 3 Sept. 1981]; Convention against torture and Other Cruel, Inhuman or Degrading Treatment or Punishment, G.A. Res. 39/46, U.N. GAOR, 51st Sess., U.N. Doc. A/39/51 (CAT), art.2, [entered into force 26 June1987].

prevent the act in the first place.[66] In this way, R2P could be seen as harnessing the disparate and sometimes discursive body of international human rights law on protection to provide a simple directive to act in the face of mass atrocities. At the same time, international human rights law develops and explains the parameters of the obligation that the international community has to prevent under R2P. As explored below, the Genocide Convention as interpreted by the International Court of Justice utilizing, in part, an international human rights framework, provides a further legal basis for this obligation, at least in respect of genocide.

Extraterritorial Obligations – The Bosnia v. Serbia Decision

As established above, the obligation to protect individuals from human rights violations to bodily integrity, by private actors, in a state's own territory is relatively well settled. The question of what obligations, if any, states have under international law to protect populations from human rights abuses extraterritorially is less so.

International human rights treaties contain 'jurisdiction' clauses, which provide that states must respect or secure to everyone *within their jurisdiction* the rights provided therein.[67] The wording varies from instrument to instrument, but the prescription is the same. States, except under exceptional circumstances, have no treaty obligations to secure human rights if they do not have jurisdiction.[68] This means that generally international human rights law does not constrain state action outside of its territory. Exceptionally, a state's obligations under international human rights treaties apply extraterritorially, when the state is deemed to have 'effective or overall control' over a territory or over the actions of non-state actors.[69]

---

[66] '2005 World Summit Outcome', UNGA Res. 60/1, 16 September 2005. Para. 138.

[67] See for example; ICCPR, Article 2.1: Each State Party to the present Covenant undertakes to respect and to ensure to all individuals within its territory and subject to its jurisdiction the rights recognised in the present Covenant…; ICESCR, Article 2; CAT, Article 2; Convention on the Rights of the Child, Article 2; American Convention on Human Rights, Article 1. See also, Ralph Wilde, 'Triggering State Obligations Extraterritorially: The Spatial Test in Certain Human Rights Treaties', *Israel Law Review*, 40/7: 503-526 (2007).

[68] *Legal Consequences of the Construction of a Wall in the Occupied Palestinian Territory*, Advisory Opinion, ICJ Rep 36, 9 July 2004, para 109: 'jurisdiction of states is primarily territorial'.

[69] *Case concerning Military and Paramilitary Activities in and against Nicaragua* (*Nicaragua v USA*), Merits, ICJ Rep 14, 27 June 1986; *The Prosecutor v Dusko Tadic*, Judgment, IT-94-1-A (AC), 15 July 1999; *The Prosecutor v Predrag Banovic*, IT-02-65/1-S (TC), 28 October 2003.

The territoriality concept is affirmed by the International Law Commission in its authoritative statement on the Articles of State Responsibility. During the process of developing an overarching methodology of state responsibility, the International Law Commission, separated the unit of analysis into two parts – primary rules and secondary rules. The primary rules determine the content of state obligations under substantive international law, for example that torture is forbidden or that states must punish individuals that commit crimes against humanity. The secondary rules concern state attribution – whose actions can be considered the actions of the state for the purpose of holding it responsible.

The secondary rules provide for instances where state responsibility may result from conduct occurring extraterritorially or in other words for the conduct that occurs in another state. But in order for the extraterritorial state to be held responsible, it must have contributed to that conduct in some way. Under certain circumstances a state may be held responsible for the conduct occurring in another state if it directs, controls, coerces, or assists in the commission of the wrongful act.[70] There, the liability results from the extraterritorial states own wrongful act under the primary rules. But first one must establish the primary (or substantive) rule of international law that provides for the wrongful conduct in the first instance. The acts concerning R2P are found in the primary rules of international law prohibiting the commission of genocide, war crimes, and crimes against humanity, as codified in the Rome Statute. Ethnic cleansing lacks an independent legal foundation, but is generally found to be a subset of the other crimes.

For the purpose of our inquiry, however, the question is whether there is an existing substantive (or primary) rule of international law that requires a state to *take positive action to prevent* another state from committing genocide, crimes against humanity, ethnic cleansing or war crimes, as required by the Responsibility to Protect? Here the law is more ambiguous.[71] The most clearly

---

[70] Articles on State Responsibility, Articles 16-18.

[71] In two cases involving interferences by the local Turkish Cypriot administration (TRNC) in Northern Cyprus, the Court found Turkey responsible for violations of the ECHR. The Court's decisions however are ambiguous on whether Turkey is responsible because the TRNC's conduct is attributable to it or because it failed in its obligation to protect. *Cyprus v. Turkey*, App. 25781/94, Judgment, Eur. Ct. H.R., 10 May 2001, paras. 77-81; *Loizidou v. Turkey*, App. 15318/89, Judgment- merits, Eur. Ct. H.R., 18 December 1996, paras. 52-56. See Marko Milanovic, 'From Compromise to Principle: Clarifying the Concept of State Jurisdiction in Human Rights Treaties', *Human Rights Law Review* 8/3: 411-448 (2008), p. 411, pp. 441-446.

articulated legal obligation to take steps to prevent mass atrocities outside of ones own borders, is the duty to prevent genocide established in the 1948 Convention on the Prevention and Punishment of the Crime of Genocide (Genocide Convention).[72]

Punishment Does Not Equal Protection

In the recent *Bosnia v. Serbia* decision, the ICJ articulated a standard for assessing the parameters of a state's obligation to act to prevent genocide from occurring in another state. It began by explicitly affirming that the obligation to prevent and the obligation to punish are related, yet, autonomous legal obligations.[73] It then set forth a reasonable, practical, context-driven standard drawing from national and international law standards on due diligence, and the law on state attribution to define its content. While the Court strained to confine its ruling to the duty to prevent under the Genocide Convention, the legal standard articulated and methodology applied by the Court bear on state responsibility with respect to other mass atrocity crimes.

Article I of the Genocide Convention provides that genocide is a crime under international law that states undertake to *prevent* and punish.[74] The operative Article VIII of the Convention provides that states may call upon the competent organs of the UN to take such action under the Charter as they consider appropriate for the prevention and suppression of acts of genocide. Article IX provides the jurisdictional basis for bringing contracting states before the ICJ, the UN international court established to hear inter-state disputes. Article I and Article IX are the only provisions related to prevention. Much stronger provisions in the Convention relate to individual criminal responsibility as found in Articles III through V, which place upon states the obligations to criminalise genocide and provide for individual punishment.

Until the 2007 judgment rendered by the ICJ in the *Bosnia v. Serbia* case, international law concerning the crime of genocide only addressed individual criminal responsibility. It had not addressed the issue of state responsibility. Since the Nuremberg Trials, and the adoption of the Genocide Convention, individual criminal responsibility for genocide has been generally recognised. Importantly, since the establishment of UN *ad hoc* tribunals for the Balkans

[72] Convention on the Prevention and Punishment of the Crime of Genocide, Dec. 9, 1948, 102 Stat. 3045, 78 U.N.T.S. 277.

[73] *Bosnia and Herzegovina v. Serbia and Montenegro*, Judgment 2007, para. 427.

[74] Convention on the Prevention and Punishment of the Crime of Genocide, 78 UNTS 277, 9 December 1948. Hereinafter, Genocide Convention.

and Rwanda, the scope, content and status of individual criminal responsibility for genocide, war crimes and crimes against humanity has rapidly evolved. These crimes are now codified in the 2002 Rome Statute of the International Criminal Court.[75] States, however, may not be brought before these criminal tribunals, as the tribunals' jurisdiction is limited to individuals. This focus on individual criminal accountability reflects what had been the prevailing understanding that states prevent genocide by punishing *genocidaires*.

Academics and policy makers focus on international criminal law as the vital legal source underpinning R2P. This is natural, given that the Outcome Document uses international criminal law categories to define R2P's scope and content. Punishment, however, so far has not established itself as a successful prevention tool. While the war and impending genocide was occurring in Bosnia, the international community, paralysed into inaction, managed to agree to create the ICTY, by Security Council resolution 827 in 1993. The genocide in Srebrenica occurred in July of 1995. Not one case had been heard by then. The threat of prosecution had not deterred individuals from committing acts of genocide.

In the wake of the swift one hundred day genocide in Rwanda, of which the UN Rwanda peace keeping commander - Romeo Dallaire - had warned the UN Department of Peacekeeping Operations explicitly,[76] the Security Council created the ICTR. The major response to the ongoing atrocities in Darfur has been to refer the situation to the ICC. Despite the referral in March 2005 atrocities continue in Darfur more than four years later. On 4 March 2009, the ICC issued an arrest warrant for President Omar Bashir. As a result, thirteen humanitarian aid agencies (60% of all humanitarian assistance in Darfur) were promptly expelled from the Darfur region of Sudan, leading to a significant risk of further civilian deaths.[77] Sudanese leaders have not been deterred.

In all of these situations the international community equivocates – then establishes a tribunal or makes a referral to the ICC. With the establishment of the ICC in 2002 war criminals can no longer count on impunity. This is a significant step forward. Further, these threats of criminal prosecution may serve to deter would-be *genocadaires*, once an established track record demonstrates that there will, in fact, be no impunity.

---

[75] Rome Statute, 17 July, 1998, 2187 U.N.T.S. 90, Article 5: Crimes within the jurisdiction of the Court; Article 6: Genocide; Article 7: Crimes against humanity; Article 8: War Crimes.

[76] Philip Gourevitch, *We Wish to Inform You That Tomorrow We Will Be Killed With Our Families: Stories From Rwanda* (New York: Farrar, Straus and Giroux, 1998), pp.104-107.

[77] Julie Flint, 'Justice and Hunger', SSRC Blog; Making Sense of Darfur, 6 March 2009, http://www.ssrc.org/blogs/darfur/2009/03/06/justice-and-hunger/, accessed 22 June 2009.

But, the jubilant celebration of international criminal law observed among colleagues has obscured the fact that little to no prevention efforts have taken place.[78] In this respect, R2P, with its explicit focus on the responsibility to prevent the kinds of mass atrocities that international criminal law can only punish, has an important contribution to make toward the normative shift away from 'punishment equals prevention' toward prevention as a set of positive obligations to take action.[79]

Until the *Bosnia v. Serbia* judgment the duty to prevent genocide under the Convention had been vague to non-existent. In its judgment, the ICJ finally identified state obligations to prevent genocide and confirmed that *states* may in fact be responsible for committing genocide. The Court gave a tempered, yet wide, reading to the state obligation to prevent under Article 1 of the Convention. Bringing together existing international human rights concepts of positive obligations requiring due diligence and general international law concepts of state attribution based upon the nature and extent of the relationship between states and non-state actors, the Court provides significant guidance for the emerging obligation of a state's responsibility to prevent mass atrocities extraterritorially.

Use Your Influence Wisely

On March 20, 1993, during the height of the Balkan wars of the 1990s, Bosnia sued the Federal Yugoslav Republic (subsequently Serbia and Montenegro, subsequently Serbia) on the basis of Article IX of the Genocide Convention. Bosnia alleged violations of the Genocide Convention, asking the ICJ for relief in connection with Serbia's actions during the conflict and for reparations for civilian casualties. Specifically, Bosnia asked the ICJ to find that Serbia had committed genocide under Article II of the Genocide Convention. In addition, Bosnia asserted that Serbia violated its obligations under Articles I and III of the Convention by failing to prevent and punish genocide, being complicit in genocide, and for conspiring to commit and incite genocide.[80] Finally, Bosnia requested provisional measures requiring

---

[78] Michael Reisman, 'Before Victims Become Victims: Preventing Genocide and Mass Murder', Webcast -Klatsky Seminar in Human Rights, 15 January 2008, Case Western Reserve University School of Law, http://law.case.edu/lectures/index.asp?yr=2007-2008, accessed 24 June 2009.

[79] Some suggest that R2P has already exerted an influence on the international community prompting it to act to prevent a full scale conflagration in Kenya. See, Donald Steinberg, 'Responsibility to Protect: Coming of Age?' *Global Responsibility to Protect,* 1/4: 432-41(2009).

[80] *Bosnia and Herzegovina v. Serbia and Montenegro,* Judgment 2007, p. 20.

Serbia to cease its actions in the conflict. For its part, Serbia claimed that the Genocide Convention only applied to individual accountability – not state responsibility. Moreover, it claimed that the acts complained of by the applicant were not committed.

In April 1993, the Court ordered provisional measures requiring that Serbia immediately 'take all measures within its power to prevent the commission of the crime of genocide'[81] and in particular 'to do all in their power to prevent the commission of any such acts in the future.'[82] Yugoslavia 'should in particular' ensure that any military or paramilitary organisation under its control or influence, or supported by it,

> do[es] not commit any acts of genocide, of conspiracy to commit genocide, of direct and public incitement to commit genocide, or of complicity in genocide, whether directed against the Muslim population of Bosnia and Herzegovina or against any other national, ethnical, racial or religious group.[83]

In September of that year, the Court reaffirmed the provisional measures indicated in April, finding that 'the present perilous situation [as now exists in Bosnia Herzegovina] demands ... immediate and effective implementation of those measures.'[84] The final decision in the case was not rendered until February 26, 2007, long after the conflict had ended and the hard line regime in Belgrade was gone.[85]

In its one-hundred and seventy-one page decision, which includes over ten separate opinions, the Court made several important rulings: 1) states may be responsible for committing genocide, thus confirming that individual criminal responsibility under the Convention does not supplant state responsibility; 2) the court confirmed that genocide had occurred in Srebrenica, confirming the decision of the International Criminal Tribunal for Yugoslavia in *Krstic*;[86] 3) the Court established that while Serbia is *not* responsible for committing genocide, Serbia *is* responsible for failing to prevent and to punish

---

[81] *Bosnia and Herzegovina v. Serbia and Montenegro*, Request for the Indication of Provisional Measures, Order, ICJ Rep, 8 April 1993, para. 52.

[82] *Ibid*, para. 45.

[83] *Ibid*, para. 52.

[84] *Bosnia and Herzegovina v. Serbia and Montenegro*, Further Requests for the Indication of Provisional Measures, Order, ICJ Rep, 13 September 2003, para. 59.

[85] In fairness to the Court the delay was in some part due to unusual procedural maneuvers, including one in 1999 where the Bosnian co-agent – of Serb ethnicity – without knowledge or support of the agent of the state withdrew the case before the ICJ – as Vojin Dimitrijevic notes 'injecting a whiff of the Balkans into the halls of the Peace Palace'. See, Vojin Dimitrijevic and Marko Milanovic, 'The Strange Story of the Bosnian Genocide Case', *Leiden Journal of International Law*, 21: 65-94 (2008), p. 74.

[86] *The Prosecutor v. Kristic*, Judgment, IT-98-33-A (AC), 19 April 2004.

genocide in Srebrenica, thus making clear that states may be responsible for actions outside its boarders (i.e., there is no territorial limitation on the responsibility to prevent and punish); and 4) the failure to prevent and to punish is not a criminal act, but a breach of an international obligation. The Court distinguished between the criminal act, which is committed by individuals, attracting individual accountability, and the obligation of the state under international law not to commit genocide and to take action prevent and punish genocide.

The Court's determination on Serbia's responsibility to prevent and punish forms the core of the decision, these being the only obligations Serbia was found to have breached. The Court begins by establishing that the obligation to prevent is autonomous and not merged with the responsibility to punish.[87] Moreover, the duty to prevent extends beyond Article VIII, which provides for submission to the competent UN organs to take such action as appropriate to prevent genocide. Drawing on the legal concepts of due diligence and the relationship between states and non-state actors it defines the scope of the responsibility to prevent genocide found in Article 1 of the Genocide Convention.

The Court held that the specific obligation to prevent requires that a state party to the Genocide Convention employ *all* means *reasonably* available to it, so as to prevent genocide so far as possible. It is an obligation of conduct, not of result; an obligation of due diligence. In the Court's words,

> [a] State does not incur responsibility simply because the desired result was not achieved; responsibility is however incurred if the State manifestly failed to take all measures to prevent genocide which were in its power, and which might have contributed to preventing genocide.[88]

Moreover, the obligation to prevent and the corresponding duty to act arises

> the instant that the State learns of, or should normally have learned of, the existence of a *serious risk* that genocide will be committed. From that moment onwards, if the State has available to it means likely to have a deterrent effect on those suspected of preparing genocide, or reasonably suspected of harbouring specific intent (*dolus specialis*), it is under a duty to make such use of those means as the circumstances permit.[89]

---

[87] That punishment and prevention are two separate though related endeavours was also recognised recently by the ICC in its appointment of Juan E. Mendez as a Special Advisor on Crime Prevention. See ICC Press Release, 19.06.2009 available at http?www.icc-cpi.int/Menus/ICC/Press%20and%20Media/Press%20Releases/News%20a [last accessed 26 June 2009].

[88] *Bosnia and Herzegovina v. Serbia and Montenegro*, Judgment 2007, para. 430.

[89] *Ibid* at para. 431. (emphasis added).

The Court used an objective standard of knowledge to gauge when the state's duty is triggered. The obligation to prevent does not require the State to know that a genocide is occurring or is about to be perpetrated; it is sufficient for the relevant state to be aware of the serious risk of genocide.[90] In the Court's opinion

> [A] state may be found to have violated its obligation to prevent even though it had no certainty, at the time when it should have acted, but failed to do so, that genocide was about to be committed or was under way; for it to incur responsibility on this basis it is enough that the State was aware, or should normally have been aware, of the serious danger that acts of genocide would be committed.

This objective standard is consistent with the Court's construction of the content of the obligations of states under Article I. Article I obliges contracting states to exercise due diligence – take any possible measures – to forestall acts of genocide – so far as possible. It follows that they must do so, even when there is only the high risk that private individuals or state agents may engage in genocide.[91]

Having established that states have a responsibility to take reasonable measures to prevent genocide even outside their own borders, when it knows or should know of a serious risk of genocide, the Court then set forth parameters for identifying when the responsibility to take such measures arises. It can not be the case that each time genocide occurs every state is responsible because each state individually and collectively failed to prevent it. There must be a limiting principle. If all states are always under some vague obligation to prevent genocide wherever it occurs, than no one state is ever under any specific obligation to prevent genocide in a particular instance. Such a conclusion would be a recipe for inaction.

Essentially, the Court had to determine the basis upon which the actions of the Bosnian Serbs might be attributed to the state of Serbia under international law. This question took the Court into the murky area of extraterritorial

---

[90] In respect of complicity in genocide, the ICJ held that the relevant state must possess full knowledge of the facts of the crime committed or to be committed by the perpetrator. *Ibid* at para. 432.

[91] Former High Commissioner for Human Rights Louise Arbour describes the Court's approach to constructive knowledge as analogous to the common laws' analysis of the duty of care in torts: 'What the Court posits is, at heart, an internationalized form of duty of care, as between States, already well known in domestic legal systems as between private litigants.' Louise Arbour, 'The Responsibility to Protect as a Duty of Care in International Law and Practice', *Review of International Studies*, 34/3: 445-458 (2008), p. 452.

responsibility for the commission/omission of human rights violations committed by actors other than the state.[92]

In this regard, the Court first established that the notion of 'due diligence' calls for an assessment *in concreto*.[93] Hence, the determination is heavily fact-dependent. Having described the obligations, it then sets forth 'various parameters' to assess whether a state has discharged its obligations. The first parameter is an assessment of whether the relevant state has the 'capacity to influence effectively the action of persons likely to commit, or already, committing, genocide.'[94] This capacity depends upon several elements including geographic distance, the strength of political links, and all other relevant links between the state and the relevant actors. The second parameter provides that a state's capacity must also be assessed by legal criteria, since 'every State may only act within the limits permitted by international law'.[95] This necessarily limits the use of military force in accordance with the UN Charter. Finally, a state may only be held responsible for breaching its obligation if genocide is actually committed.[96] Essentially, a state may be held responsible for failing to prevent genocide if the court finds that a state had the means and influence actually to affect the outcome of events and that it manifestly refrained from using them.

After noting that Serbia had been enjoined by the Court, in two Orders on provisional measures issued in 1993 to ensure that no genocide be committed, including by persons under its influence (reinforced duty to prevent), the Court goes on to state that FRY 'was in a position of influence, over the Bosnian Serbs who devised and implemented the genocide in Srebrenica, unlike that of any other States parties to the Genocide Convention owing to the strength of the political, military and financial links between the FRY on the one hand the Republika Srpska and the VRS [*Vojska Republike Srpska* – Bosnian Serb Army] on the other'.[97]

Using a lesser standard of proof than that required for complicity to commit genocide, that of a 'high level of certainty' (rather than proof beyond all doubt)[98], the Court determined that Serbia had significant influence over the

---

[92] The failure to act can constitute an omission giving rise to a violation. For a general discussion of omissions in international criminal law, see Gerhard Werle, *Principles of International Criminal Law* (Asser Press, 2005), pp. 170-172.

[93] *Bosnia and Herzegovina v. Serbia and Montenegro*, Judgment 2007, para. 430.

[94] *Ibid.*

[95] *Ibid.*

[96] Articles on State Responsibility, Article 14.

[97] *Bosnia and Herzegovina v. Serbia and Montenegro*, Judgment 2007, para. 434.

[98] *Ibid.* at para. 210.

Bosnian Serbs. Serbia therefore was under a positive, substantive obligation to take action. Nonetheless, Serbia took no initiative to prevent the atrocities in Srebrenica, and therefore was in violation of Article 1 of the Genocide Convention. It found Serbia responsible for its own wrongful act of failing to exercise due diligence so as to prevent violations by third parties.

The obligation to prevent arises and is established based upon the level of *influence* a state has to change the course of action, determined by its political, economic and all other links to the actors in question. Two dissenting opinions from Justices Tomka and Skotnikov raise concerns about the Court's standard of influence. They believe that the recognised legal standard for constraining state action outside of its territory should be one of 'control'.[99]

These concerns, however, are misplaced. Attachment to the 'control' standard presumes that the control standard is determinate. It is not. It is indeterminate and hotly contested.[100] 'Control' in the sense of state attribution or in the sense of extraterritorial obligations is elastic. While international practice often speaks in terms of 'control' to determine the application of human rights obligations outside the state, the word does not have an autonomous meaning. Moreover, notions of control exist on a continuum from complete control,[101] effective control,[102] overall control,[103] and even influence.[104] The usage is heavily dependent on the facts of the case and the nature and content of the specific obligation at issue.

The influence standard articulated by the Court fits well with its construction of the positive obligation to prevent, and is a useful move. It draws a clear distinction between the standard for attributing the wrongful act of genocide or conspiracy to commit genocide (effective control) to Serbia and the standard for attributing responsibility to Serbia for *its failure* to discharge its obligation to take reasonable steps to prevent genocide. It establishes that to the extent the state has a significant level of influence over the actors committing genocide such that it is highly likely it can change the course of events, then it must use that influence wisely.

---

99 *Bosnia and Herzegovina v. Serbia and Montenegro*, Judgment 2007, Skotnikov Declaration pp. 9-10, Tomka Declaration pp. 28-29.

100 Milanovic, 'From Compromise to Principle: Clarifying the Concept of State Jurisdiction in Human Rights Treaties'; Wilde, 'Triggering State Obligations Extraterritorially'.

101 *Nicaragua v. United States*, para. 109-110 (description of case).

102 *Ibid.* at para. 115.

103 *Loizidou v. Turkey*; *The Prosecutor v. Dusko Tadic* (AC), 15 July 1999, paras. 83-89; *Ilascu v. Moldova and Russia*, App. 48787/99, Judgment, Eur. Ct. H.R., 8 July 2004, para. 316.

104 *Ilascu v. Moldova and Russia*, para. 392. (holding Russia responsible for acts committed by a separatist movement in Moldova because of Russia's 'decisive influence' over the separatist group).

It is difficult to ascertain precisely the distinction between the low end of the control standard (overall control) and influence. After all, in its decision the Court makes clear that it is cognisant of the central role that Serbia played in the actions and policies of Bosnian Serb forces. For instance, after hearing evidence that Serbia provided up to 90 percent of the material needs of the Republika Srpska, that Serbia was paying a substantial portion of the Serb paramilitary forces, and that the economies of Republika Srpska and Serbia were almost completely integrated, it found that had Serbia withdrawn this support, the Republika Srpska's options would have been greatly constrained.[105] Given this level of influence, the bar remains very high for establishing the sufficient level of influence necessary for the legal duty to prevent to arise. Moreover, the Court gives no clear indication of what preventative measures Serbia should have taken. Instead it found Serbia responsible for failing to take *any* action. This is less than helpful in setting objective criterion for action. Nonetheless, the shadowy obligation to prevent genocide receives a much needed modicum of substance with this decision.

The Relationship between the duty to protect and R2P

While the Outcome Document is the most authoritative statement on R2P, it is certainly not its only articulation.[106] R2P is a dynamic norm which has and will continue to develop. UN member states specifically agreed to keep R2P on the General Assembly's agenda with a commitment to continue considering 'the responsibility to protect populations from genocide, war crimes, ethnic cleansing and crimes against humanity and its implications, bearing in mind … *international law*.'[107]

How then can one relate developing international human rights law on the positive obligation of states to prevent human rights violations with the

[105] *Bosnia and Herzegovina v. Serbia and Montenegro*, Judgment 2007, paras. 240-241.

[106] Ban Ki-Moon, *Implementing the Responsibility to Protect*, A/63/677, 12 January 2009, para. 10, drawing on earlier articulations of R2P in preparing his report. See for example: High-Level Panel on Threats, Challenges and Change, *A more Secure World: Our Shared Responsibility*, A/59/565, 2 December 2004; Kofi Annan, *In Larger Freedom: Towards Development, Security and Human Rights for All*, A/59/2005, 21 March 2005, paras. 16-22.

[107] '2005 World Summit Outcome', UNGA Res. 60/1, 16 September 2005, para.139 (emphasis added). It should be noted that there are concerns that further deliberations by the GA may claw back some of the commitments made at that 2005 World Summit Outcome. In July of 2009, the General Assembly once again took up the subject of R2P, and states, for the most part, reaffirmed their commitment to the principle and agreed to continue its consideration,, UNGA Res 63/308, 7 October 2009.

developing norm of R2P? As established above, the responsibility to protect rests upon the articulation of positive obligations under international human rights law to prevent state and non-state actors from infringing on another person's human rights. This obligation requires states to take reasonable measures to prevent the violation from occurring in the first instance. It is based upon the notion of due diligence, which has now been expressly incorporated into the responsibility to prevent genocide by non-state actors, within and outside of a state's borders.[108] The evolving trend toward requiring states to take action to prevent human rights violations generally, and in relation to mass human rights atrocities in particular, has manifold implications for understanding the current legal content of R2P and its potential for future development of which this paper addresses three.

First, reading the responsibility to protect through the lens of the duty to protect expressed in human rights law highlights and clarifies the preventative thrust of R2P. The duty to protect, like the first pillar of R2P, is an obligation upon states to prevent human rights violations by state actors and private individuals. Like R2P, human rights 'protection' obligations exist on a continuum. First, protection requires setting up an effective rights regime, which should act to stave off human rights violations; second it entails the obligation to investigate infringements; third it requires punishment; and fourth it requires redress.

R2P builds on these obligations and innovates when it makes the link between a state's obligation to protect its population and the responsibility of states to assist other states with their obligations. Delimiting the scope of R2P in this way, may help to mediate the persistent debates over whether R2P applies to a particular situation where atrocity crimes are occurring. R2P 'applies' to all situations where mass atrocities are occurring, based upon existing human rights law, and innovates where it calls upon states to assist. The question is not *whether* states have an obligation under R2P in the face of mass atrocities, but rather *what* are states obligations in the face of these mass atrocities? While R2P provides the framework for action, the underlying human rights principles upon which it rests fill in the content.[109]

Moreover, this approach underscores the dynamic relationship between the development of R2P and the development of international law. As explored above, R2P is consistent with international human rights law in providing for

---

[108] *Bosnia and Herzegovina v. Serbia and Montenegro*, Judgment 2007, para. 430.

[109] Alex Bellamy, 'The Conflict in Sri Lanka and the Responsibility to Protect', 1 May 2009, http://www.e-ir.info/?p=1053&print=1.accessed 24 June 2009 (providing that the first pillar points to a universal and enduring R2P).

an obligation upon states to take certain steps to prevent the acts it seeks to prohibit. R2P as articulated by the GA in the Outcome Document assists in the interpretation of international human rights law on positive obligations and gives a modicum of conceptual clarity and discipline to its application to mass atrocities. In this respect it is of consequence to note that the representatives of Bosnia in the Bosnia v. Serbia case specifically invoked R2P in its argumentation regarding Serbia's obligation to prevent genocide under the Convention.[110]

Second, the obligation of states to protect populations from mass atrocities is one of collective and national responsibility. These separate obligations, however, should be read together for the obligation to prevent to be practical and effective, not theoretical or illusory. The collective component of R2P provides that when a state manifestly fails to protect, the *international community* will take action through cooperative action. Likewise, the international community as a whole committed itself to 'encourage and help' states prevent mass atrocities and assist other states 'as necessary and appropriate' to build capacity to protect their populations from atrocity crimes. While, the concept of collective cooperation is not unknown in international law, the International Law Commission is ambivalent about whether general international law prescribes a duty of cooperation, providing that such a duty may reflect the progressive development of international law.' This second pillar of R2P, therefore, does not presently appear to rest upon firm legal ground. Though, the reiteration of a duty of collective cooperation by the GA in R2P itself exerts an influence upon the law's development.

More interestingly, is the fact that the collective obligation undertaken by the international community to take coordinated action to assist states to prevent atrocity crimes implies individual state responsibility to take reasonable steps to prevent the acts its seeks to prohibit. In this respect, an emerging legal obligation exists and is most developed when one state has an extensive amount of influence over another state or non-state actors, such that the state may be in a real position to influence the course of events. The due diligence standard that is developing in international human rights law, from the jurisprudence of the *Valázquez* and *Osman* cases as articulated in modified form in the *BiH v. Serbia* judgment gives, guidance, albeit limited, to states about what is expected of them in this regard.[111]

[110] Transcript of the oral argument of Mr. Condorelli before the ICJ on 7 March 2006 CR 2006/11 available at http://www.icj-cij.org/docket/files/91/10606.pdf [accessed 8 July, 2009].

[111] See for example, Andrea Gattini, 'Breach of the Obligation to Prevent and Reparation thereof in the ICJ's Genocide Judgment', *European Journal of International Law*, 18/4: 695-713

Three examples clarify this second point. If the United States precipitously pulls out of Iraq and genocide occurs could there be a viable claim that the United States violated its responsibility to prevent? Under the *BiH v. Serbia* test, there is a strong argument that the United State has significant influence over Iraq, economically, militarily, and politically giving rise to a duty to use all means reasonably available to it, which might contribute to preventing genocide. Given that the ICJ did not set forth objective standards for determining when a state has sufficient capacity or influence to prevent genocide, aside from emphasising the nature of the close relationship between Serbia and the Bosnian Serbs, it is unclear what level of influence would be sufficient. Moreover, it would have to be established that the United States could have been expected to foresee a serious risk of genocide.

A second example can be found in the Rwandan context. Rwanda has hinted at the possibility of future legal action against France for its alleged material support in 1994 to the radical Hutu regime found responsible for the genocide. Over the past few years, journalists and scholars have explored the relationship between the French government and the Hutu government during the 1990s.[112] Generally, these reports suggest that France provided military and political support to the Hutu government and assisted alleged perpetrators to escape. In a 2008 report, the Rwandan Government accused the French of active assistance to the Hutu *genocadaires*, and an international panel has concluded that France had both the knowledge and the influence to stop the genocide.[113] If a case was brought to the ICJ, the Court would seek to determine the extent of Frances influence over the actions of the *genocadaires* and whether it should have known that genocide was likely to occur.[114]

The final example concerns the continuing crisis in Darfur, Sudan. It is well known that China more than any other state has contributed diplomatically,

(2007), p. 698 (remarking that the Court missed the opportunity to give much needed guidance 'on the highly debated question of the existence and scope, *de lege lata* or *ferenda*, of the duty or responsibility to protect').

[112] See Gourevitch, *We Wish to Inform You That Tomorrow We Will Be Killed With Our Families*; Gerarard Prunier, *The Rwanda Crisis: History of a Genocide* (C. Hurst & Co. Publishers, 1995).

[113] Andre Wallis, *Silent Accomplice: The Untold Story of France's Role in the Rwandan Genocide* at 84 (2006) citing International Panel of Eminent Personalities, Rwanda: The Preventable Genocide (July 2007). The panel was composed of representatives from Botswana, Mali, India, Algeria, Liberia, Canada and Sweden.

[114] For an extensive analysis of the application of the *Bosnia v. Serbia* decision on Rwanda see, Paul Schmitt, 'The Future of Genocide Suits at the International Court of Justice: France's Role in Rwanda and Implications of the Bosnia v. Serbia Decision', *Georgetown Journal of International Law*, 40/2:585-623 (2009).

economically, and, militarily to sustaining the mass atrocities in Darfur.[115] Some have suggested that it may be possible to establish that China has the relevant influence over Sudan, and it has already been established that at a minimum, there is most certainly a grave risk of genocide occurring in Darfur.[116] Moreover, as described above, under general international human rights principles, depending upon the extent of China's influence or control over the relevant actors or territory, China could be under a positive obligation to take steps to prevent crimes against humanity from being committed. Though, this claim would be more difficult to establish under current international law practice.[117]

Third, the due diligence concept adopted by the ICJ in the *Bosnia v. Serbia* judgment establishes that governments do not face the same definitional challenge when determining whether they are under an obligation to act to prevent genocide that a prosecutor does to secure a genocide conviction. The ICJ does not require the state to have knowledge that genocide is occurring or is about to occur. It is enough if the relevant state was aware or should normally have been aware of the serious *risk* of genocide. Former U.S. Secretary of State Colin Powell articulated this concept to the U.S. Senate Foreign Relations Committee in 2004 when he testified that Sudan bears some responsibility for the genocide in Darfur in part *because* 'despite having been put on notice multiple times, Khartoum has failed to stop the violence.'[118]

The articulation of a standard for prevention based upon a duty to act when a state has objective knowledge of a 'serious risk', can guide the international community when it seeks to determine the evidentiary threshold for the application of R2P in respect of extraterritorial obligations. Over the past decade governments and institutions have painstakingly sought to determine whether

[115] Eric Reeves, 'Beijings's Propaganda Campaign Can't Obscure Complicity in Darfur Genocide', 5 March 2008, http://www.sudanreeves.org/Article207.html, accessed 23 June 2009.

[116] *The Prosecutor v. Omar Hassan Ahmad Al Bashir*, Application of the Prosecutor for a warrant of arrest warrant 14 July 2008. For a discussion of the application of the Bosnia v. Serbia decision to the situation in Sudan, see Ademola Abass, *Proving State Responsibility for Genocide: The ICJ in Bosnia v. Serbia and the International Commission of Inquiry for Darfur*, 31 Fordham Int'l L. J. 871 (2008).

[117] As noted above, it is unclear whether states have an obligation to protect against human rights violations, even mass atrocities, outside its jurisdiction. See generally, Milanovic, 'From Compromise to Principle'.

[118] Remarks of Secretary of State Colin L. Powell on the Crisis in Darfur before the Senate Foreign Relations Committee, 9 September 2004, Washington, D.C., http://www.voanews.com/english/archive/2004-09/a-2004-09-09-8-Text.cfm?moddate=2004-09-09, accessed 22 June 2009.

a situation rose to the level of genocide before deciding whether it had to take action. Similar questions are now presenting themselves in the context of R2P where governments and institutions have sought to determine whether R2P applies in terms of states' extraterritorial obligation.

Since R2P is explicitly a doctrine of prevention, it is logical to suggest that the international community apply a similar evidentiary standard as that applied by the ICJ in the *Bosnia v. Serbia* judgment when determining R2P's relevance to a certain situation. The 'objective knowledge of a serious risk' standard provides a conceptual jumping off point for lawyers, policy makers, and academics. Utilising this standard the international community should be analysing whether there is a serious risk of genocide in Darfur (for example) such that certain individual state obligations, as well as a collective obligation to prevent, are being triggered. It gives us a conceptual framework within which to deal with genocide prevention, rather than *post hoc* genocide punishment. In fact, as will be addressed in the final point, R2P signals a move, albeit tentative, toward the extension of the responsibilities on states to include the prevention of war crimes, crimes against humanity, and ethnic cleansing in addition to genocide.

Finally, the obligation to prevent genocide as a peremptory norm of international law raises the specter of an obligation upon States to prevent the commission of certain other peremptory norms of international law.[119] The object and purpose of the Genocide Convention and R2P support this suggestion. The Genocide Convention grew out of the horrors of the Holocaust and is intended to prevent genocide. R2P grew out of the mass atrocities committed during the 1990s and is intended to prevent genocide and mass atrocities. In this sense, R2P is the progeny of the Genocide Convention reflecting the complex social fabric that now makes up today's gruesome tales of crimes that 'shock the conscience' of the world.

Generally, the popular understanding of genocide is broader than the legal understanding. Often, what the ever growing anti-genocide movement is really complaining against are most likely crimes against humanity. But the point is that members of the movement are outraged by certain mass atrocities that have completely offended their sense of decency. Like genocide, the codification of crimes against humanity grew out of the conception that some crimes 'shock the conscience of mankind'.[120] As Geoffrey Robertson explains, perpetrators of these crimes are conceived as enemies of the world because 'the

---

[119] See, William Schabas, *Genocide in International Law* (Cambridge: Cambridge University Press, 2000), p. 500.

[120] Genocide Convention, Preamble; Rome Statute, Preamble.

very fact that a fellow human could conceive and commit them diminishes every member of the human race.'[121]

In this way, that sense of moral urgency that led to the Genocide Convention and its prevention obligation applies equally to crimes against humanity. The author suggests that the urgent sense that it is necessary to react to crimes against humanity and war crimes in addition to genocide, has led a growing number of policymakers, academics and activists to utilise the term – mass atrocities - rather than specific legal categories of genocide, war crimes, crimes against humanity.[122]

There appear to be several other reasons for this conflation of terms as well. First, legalistic arguments about whether a situation is or is not genocide have impeded fast and appropriate action.[123] Second, this semantic twist evidences, perhaps even unconsciously, that measures required to prevent and punish mass atrocities are in the eyes of the world the same for all mass atrocities. Indeed, the same methodological principles that the ICJ applied in delimiting the duty to prevent genocide in the *Bosnia v. Serbia* judgment would apply, at least in theory, to state responsibility for other mass atrocity crimes.[124] Thus, the underlying principle and methodology grounding the obligation to prevent genocide may apply with equal force to certain types of crimes against humanity. In other words, mass crimes against humanity and genocide may require similar responses, even though they are legally different crimes.

In a strict legal sense, however, the non-applicability of the Genocide Convention to crimes against humanity means that currently international law does not place upon states a positive obligation to prevent mass atrocity crimes that do not rise to the level of genocide. In fact, even in respect of genocide, it is unclear how far the *Bosnia v. Serbia* judgment will extend given Serbia's unique and intimate relationship with the Bosnian Serbs. But, we can see an emerging trend toward the possible acceptance of such an obligation in limited circumstances. In accepting the responsibility to protect in the Outcome Document, states affirmed that they are committed to preventing mass atrocity crimes, including crimes against humanity. That this

---

[121] Geoffrey Robertson, *Crimes Against Humanity: The Struggle for Global Justice* (New York: The New Press, 2000), p. 236.

[122] For example, Albright and Cohen, *Preventing Genocide*. See also, Scheffer, 'Genocide and Atrocity Crimes'.

[123] Scheffer, 'Genocide and Atrocity Crimes', p. 230, Albright and Cohen, *Preventing Genocide*, pp. xxi-xxii.

[124] The ICJ however does not have jurisdiction generally over crimes against humanity. It has jurisdiction over acts of genocide only by virtue of the explicit jurisdictional provision in Article IX of the Genocide Convention. So, even if states were found to have breached a hypothetical obligation to prevent crimes against humanity, the question of legal adjudication remains.

commitment may eventually solidify into a legal norm is cumulatively supported by the Rome Statute's codification of crimes against humanity, Article 41 of the Articles of State Responsibility, which provides that where the responsible state commits a serious breach of a peremptory norm of international law, other states have an obligation to cooperate to bring an end to that serious breach through lawful means, the *Bosnia v. Serbia* decision, and the development of positive obligations under international human rights law. This legal practice reflects the progressive development – *de lege frenda* – of the acceptance of a legal norm to prevent, not only genocide, but atrocity crimes.[125]

Conclusion

The responsibility to prevent mass atrocities articulated in R2P is firmly rooted in international human rights law, with respect to the duty that states have to protect individuals within their own territory. In fact, the 'duty to protect' developing in international human rights law is functionally a duty of prevention. States are obligated to respect human rights and to take reasonable steps to ensure that non-state actors do not infringe upon the fundamental rights others. Thus, pillar one of R2P represents a continuing obligation upon states at all times to prevent atrocity crimes within their boarders.

R2P further builds on these internal obligations establishing states' responsibility to assist other states with their obligations. The interstate obligation to prevent mass atrocities is, however, not as clear under international law. Nor was it *expressly* agreed to by the member states in the Summit Outcome Document, having only committed to assist states with *their obligations* to protect. The due diligence standard – to take reasonable measures to prevent violations in so far as possible – in international practice, especially as articulated in the *Bosnia v. Serbia* judgment, however, reflects a nascent, yet developing trend in international law toward the acceptance of a positive interstate obligation to prevent mass atrocities under certain circumstances.

R2P itself is an important part of this developing trend, harnessing the general duty to protect/prevent and crystallising its application to the prevention of mass atrocities. It is another step in the development of the bedrock principle underlying the Genocide Convention, namely that states may no longer stand idly by when faced with crimes that shock the conscience of the mankind.

---

[125] See, Marko Milanovic, 'State Responsibility for Genocide', *European Journal of International Law,* 17/3: 553-604 (2006), p. 601.

Stopping the Killing: The International Criminal Court and Juridical Determination of the Responsibility to Protect

Michael Contarino and Selena Lucent

Abstract

This paper argues that an enhanced role for the International Criminal Court in determining when a government has failed in its Responsibility to Protect (R2P) could help develop a faster, more effective, more predictable, and more impartial R2P enforcement mechanism. We outline how a juridical R2P determination process by the ICC could be actualised, and we argue that such juridical R2P determination could facilitate timely and legal multilateral actions to stop violence. We also argue that juridical R2P determination by the ICC could dissuade opportunistic and unilateral violations of national sovereignty made in the name of R2P enforcement, and reduce the concerns of R2P critics that the principle may be misused. Finally, we maintain that an enhanced R2P role for the ICC could strengthen the credibility of the United Nations Security Council, and could be politically appealing to its five permanent member states.

Keywords

crimes against humanity, genocide, humanitarian intervention, international criminal court, international legal reform, responsibility to protect, war crimes

Introduction

The Responsibility to Protect (R2P) principle, enunciated in the 2001 International Commission on Intervention and State Sovereignty (ICISS) report, 'The Responsibility to Protect,'[1] and then adopted by the UN General Assembly in a 2005 World Summit Outcome Document,[2] has generated

---

[1] The International Commission on Intervention and State Sovereignty, 'The Responsibility to Protect', http://www.iciss.ca/pdf/, accessed 31 July 2009.

[2] '2005 World Summit Outcome', UNGA Res. 60/1, 16 September 2005. It has been observed, sometimes with concern, that the 2005 World Outcome Document narrowed the earlier ICISS interpretation of R2P, by limiting it to genocide, war crimes, crimes against humanity and ethnic cleansing. See, for example, Alex Bellamy, *Responsibility to Protect: The Global*

considerable controversy. Proponents of R2P, such as Gareth Evans and Mohamed Sahnoun,[3] Ramesh Thakur,[4] and W. Andy Knight,[5] argue that adoption of the principle by the UN General Assembly was a vital step toward a global norm that could protect vulnerable populations from gross human rights violations. Some supporters of R2P have claimed that the principle already has had a positive impact, citing, for example, former UN Secretary General Kofi Annan's invocation of R2P in his successful 2008 effort to broker a peace in Kenya after that nation's disputed December 2007 election.[6]

Critics of R2P, by contrast, such as Mary Ellen O'Connell,[7] have expressed the view that R2P is at best a distraction, and indeed potentially an encouragement to international lawlessness, as it could, in their view, undermine the norm of peace and encourage armed violations of sovereign nations. Some critics have even portrayed R2P as a Trojan horse for neo-colonialist military interventionism.[8] Critics of R2P cite the Bush administration's attempt to justify the 2003 invasion of Iraq at least partially as a 'humanitarian

---

Effort to Stop Mass Atrocities (Cambridge: Polity Press 2009). See also, Thomas G. Weiss, 'R2P After 9/11 and the World Summit', *Wisconsin International Law Journal*, 24/3: 741-760 (2006). However, some of the strongest and earliest proponents of R2P have argued that it is appropriate that R2P apply only to the four crimes listed in the World Outcome Document, as attempts to broaden its application would erode the fledgling norm. See, for example, Ramesh Thakur, 'Should the UN Invoke the Responsibility to Protect?' *The Globe and Mail*, 8 May 2008.

[3] A seminal piece in the development of R2P is Gareth Evans and Mohamed Sahnoun, 'The Responsibility to Protect', *Foreign Affairs*, 81/6: 99-110 (2002).

[4] Ramesh Thakur, *The United Nations, Peace and Security: From Collective Security to the Responsibility to Protect.* (Cambridge: Cambridge University Press, 2005).

[5] W. Andy Knight, 'The Responsibility to Protect as an Evolving International Norm', Notes for Canadian Peacebuilding Coordinating Committee Meeting, 22 September 2003, Ottawa Conference Centre http://www.worldfederalistscanada.org/R2P/Knight.pdf, accessed 31 July 2009.

[6] See http://www.responsibilitytoprotect.org/index.php/component/content/article/129-africa/2259-kofi-annanopening-remarks-to-the-opening-plenary-sessionkenya-national-dialogue-one-year-later, accessed 31 July 2009.

[7] Mary Ellen O'Connell, 'Taking *Opinio Juris* Seriously', *International Customary Law on the Use of Force*, 9/13 (2005), p.28-29. See also O'Connell's debate with Thakur in, Ramesh Thakur and Mary Ellen O'Connell, 'The R2P Controversy' http://www.globalpolicy.org/component/content/article/154/26068.html, accessed 3 August 2009.

[8] Noam Chomsky, 'Humanitarian Imperialism: The New Doctrine of Imperial Right', *Monthly Review*, September 2008. UNGA President Miguel D'Escoto Brockmann has championed this critique recently at the UNGA, and several governments have expressed concern that R2P can be used as a cover for opportunistic interventions by powerful states. See, for example, http://blogs.reuters.com/global/2009/07/24/saviors-or-conquerors-un-mulls-responsibility-to-protect/, accessed 3 August 2009; See also http://www.nytimes.com/2009/07/23/world/23nation.html?_r=1&scp=2&sq=United%20Nations&st=cse, accessed 31 July 2009.

intervention', and Russia's attempt to invoke R2P to justify its 2008 incursion into Georgia, as examples of how military aggression can be facilitated by the notion that states may intervene in the affairs of other sovereign states to protect populations.

Both the aspirations of those who seek a strong R2P norm, and the apprehensions of those who fear abuse of R2P deserve to be taken seriously. We believe, however, that the concerns of both R2P supporters and of R2P critics ultimately result not from the principle of R2P *per se*, but rather from the weakness and arbitrariness of the existing R2P enforcement mechanism, which is based upon the willingness and capacity of the UN Security Council (UNSC) to make politically-difficult decisions (and to do so without incurring a veto by any of the permanent Five UNSC members). A weak or inconsistently-enforced R2P principle both fails to meet the hopes of proponents and potentially invites the sort of abuses feared by critics. This paper explores a possible way to create a faster and more effective, predictable and impartial R2P enforcement mechanism.

Enforcement of the responsibility to protect necessarily entails two components: first, it must be *determined* that a government has failed or is failing to protect a population, and then appropriate *actions*[9] must follow to stop the abuses. Such actions may include a variety of measures, such as advice, mediation, diplomatic pressure, international assistance and capacity-building, economic sanctions, or, when all else fails, the use of force. The UN Security Council currently is responsible for both the determination function and the action function, and it has not performed either very well. Rather, as we will discuss below, the Security Council has not always been willing or able to determine in a timely manner that a violation has occurred, and even when it has identified an R2P breach, it has failed to mobilise swift and effective action. In both cases, it has been the political character of the Security Council, in which any of the permanent five members can slow down and impede action, which has caused these failures.

We argue in this paper that a *juridical* process to determine when an R2P violation has occurred could strengthen not only the determination function, but also the action function. Were a juridical process, rather than a

[9] The ICISS report identified three components of R2P: *the responsibility to prevent* atrocities from occurring, *the responsibility to react* once atrocities occur, and *the responsibility to rebuild* after the atrocities have ceased to occur. Implicit in this concept is that some body (currently UNSC) must first determine that atrocities have occurred or are likely to occur, so that appropriate actions may be taken.

political process, to determine when the R2P norm has been violated, swifter determination might well be possible. Over time, juridical R2P determination could produce a body of R2P jurisprudence that would clarify the bases for legal international interventions, and thereby facilitate effective, legal enforcement actions. Such jurisprudence, by clearly defining legal options, also would render the illegal military interventions feared by R2P critics more difficult to justify. Accordingly, a juridical R2P determination mechanism might well prove better able than the present system both to protect vulnerable populations *and* to discourage violations of the norm of peace by nations using R2P opportunistically and/or unilaterally taking R2P into their own hands. We believe that the International Criminal Court (ICC) has the potential to provide such a juridical R2P determination mechanism.

The Responsibility to Protect, the UN Security Council, and the International Criminal Court

The R2P principle essentially suggests that sovereignty is not an absolute right of national governments, but is rather an *earned* right, based upon fulfilment of government's responsibility to protect its people from violence. In a significant challenge to traditional Westphalian conceptions of national sovereignty, R2P says that governments that fail to protect their inhabitants from genocide, war crimes, ethnic cleansing, and crimes against humanity forfeit the sovereign right to a monopoly of the legitimate use of force within their national boundaries. Under such circumstances, R2P says the international community has both the right and the responsibility to intervene to stop the killing.

The belief that preventing atrocity crimes is a responsibility of both national governments and the international community also underlay the establishment of the International Criminal Court. The 1998 Rome Statute, which led to the creation of the ICC, affirms that those (including government officials) who commit genocide, crimes against humanity or war crimes must be held accountable. If national courts fail to prosecute in good faith those guilty of such crimes, the ICC will prosecute them.[10] The common moral commitments

[10] Article 5 of the Rome Statute lists the following as crimes within the jurisdiction of the Court: Genocide, Crimes against humanity; War Crimes, the Crime of Aggression. This latter, however, has not yet been defined. Rome Statute of the International Criminal Court, A/CONF.183/9, Article 5 (1), p. 8.

of R2P and the ICC are clear: R2P obligates governments to protect people from gross human rights abuses, and the ICC obligates them to prosecute individuals who commit such abuses. Both R2P and the International Criminal Court also affirm that when governments fail to protect people, the responsibility to do so befalls the international community.[11]

However, under current law, the ICC has no role in determining when a violation of the R2P principle has taken place. The Rome Statute, as currently written, limits the court to prosecution and punishment of those responsible for human rights violations. Determination that the R2P principle has been violated is specifically assigned by the 2005 Outcome Document not to the ICC, but rather to the UN Security Council.

The earlier 2001 ICISS report also had maintained that The United Nations Security Council should be the international body responsible for identifying, preventing and stopping violations of the R2P norm – in other words, for determining when a government has failed to protect its citizens, and for mobilising international action to protect suffering populations. While R2P enforcement can take many forms, such as negotiations, capacity-building, economic sanctions, peacekeeping, coercive diplomacy, and armed action, the ICISS report clearly states that, should armed intervention be needed, 'there is no better or more appropriate body than the United Nations Security Council to authorize military intervention for human protection purposes'.[12]

To those who may have doubted the appropriateness of assigning this responsibility to a political body like the UNSC, the report was clear: 'The task is not to find alternatives to the Security Council as a source of authority, but to make the Security Council work better than it has'.[13] The report urged the five permanent Security Council members 'not to apply their veto power in matters where their vital state interests are not involved, to obstruct the passage of resolutions authorizing military intervention for human protection purposes for which there is otherwise majority support'.[14] Aware that failure of the Security Council to perform its role effectively could damage the UN

[11] The common moral foundations of the ICC and R2P have been discussed elsewhere. See, for example, *The Responsibility to Protect and the International Criminal Court: America's New Priorities*, Conference Report, Center for International Human Rights at Northwestern University, December 2007. http://www.cfr.org/publication/15802/northwestern_university_school_of_law.html, accessed 3 August 2009.

[12] The International Commission on Intervention and State Sovereignty, *The Responsibility To Protect*, December 2009, p. XII.

[13] Ibid.

[14] Ibid., p. XIII.

itself, the Commission cautioned that if the UNSC failed to respond in a timely manner to discharge its responsibility, 'concerned states may not rule out other means to meet the gravity and urgency of the situation to the detriment of the stature and credibility of the United Nations'.[15]

The 2005 World Summit Outcome Document also specifically says that UNSC shall be the organ responsible for R2P enforcement. After noting in paragraph 138 that 'each individual State has the responsibility to protect its populations from genocide, war crimes, ethnic cleansing and crimes against humanity,' the document notes in paragraph 139 that:

> The international community, through the United Nations, also has the responsibility to use appropriate diplomatic, humanitarian and other peaceful means, in accordance with Chapters VI and VIII of the Charter, to help protect populations from genocide, war crimes, ethnic cleansing and crimes against humanity. In this context, we are prepared to take collective action, in a timely and decisive manner, through the Security Council, in accordance with the Charter, including Chapter VII, on a case-by-case basis and in cooperation with relevant regional organizations as appropriate, should peaceful means be inadequate and national authorities manifestly fail to protect their populations from genocide, war crimes, ethnic cleansing and crimes against humanity.[16]

In the four years since R2P was adopted by the General Assembly, unfortunately, the UNSC has not lived up to the hopes expressed in the ICISS report, or to the responsibilities assigned to the Council in the 2005 Outcome Document: indeed, the Security Council has failed repeatedly to prevent violence of precisely the sort cited in both the 2001 report and the 2005 UNGA Outcome Document.[17] As has been the case for decades with situations of territorial aggression by nation-states,[18] the UNSC generally has failed to find the

---

[15] Ibid.

[16] '2005 World Summit Outcome', UNGA Res. 60/1, 16 September 2005.

[17] For example, massive organised killings in the Democratic Republic of Congo, where combatants have raided villages, looted homes, raped women, and abducted children and forced them to become child soldiers. Well over one million people have been displaced in this conflict. In Zimbabwe, government-backed militias have been implicated in numerous killings and the torture of over thousands of people since May 2008. See www.hrw.org for more information on these and other ongoing human rights violations of precisely the sort referenced in the 2005 World Outcome Document.

[18] Examples of armed interventions since 1945 not authorised by the Security Council are numerous. Some, such as the US invasion of Iraq, the Soviet invasion of Afghanistan, and the Chinese invasion of Tibet, have been widely criticised. The 1999 Kosovo intervention by NATO, however, has been criticised by some, but applauded by others. It has been seen by many as 'not legal but legitimate' because it was a multilateral action taken in the context of clear human rights crimes which UNSC had failed to find the political consensus to address. The frequency

needed consensus among its member states to enforce international law in a timely and effective way.

The Security Council has not taken sufficiently decisive and strong action even regarding Darfur, where an egregious situation of mass murder, which the US government in 2004 defined as 'genocide',[19] has persisted for several years. While the Security Council condemned the violence in Darfur, sent limited forces, and referred the case to the ICC in 2004,[20] its member governments have not found the political will to pursue sufficiently robust economic sanctions or other actions to end the violence. Despite sustained demands for decisive action from international, and especially western, public opinion, the Council has failed to successfully force a change in Sudan's behaviour, or failing that, to mobilise a robust multilateral intervention to stop the killing in Darfur. And by recognising its responsibility to enforce R2P, but then failing to enforce its words with adequate measures, the Security Council arguably may have precluded more effective intervention by other international organisations or multilateral coalitions.

The record to date suggests that if determination of R2P remains the sole prerogative of the UN Security Council, R2P may be little more than an ideal respected primarily in the breach. In the absence of (highly improbable) reform of the veto held by its five permanent members, we should expect the Council to remain as blocked in the future as it has been in the past. Accordingly, for R2P to develop into an enforced international norm, some alternative, or at least additional, mechanism for its determination and enforcement is needed.

The International Criminal Court came into being only seven years ago, in 2002. Like any new court, its role and its powers will be defined in part by the powers other political actors assign to it, and in part by its own assertions of

---

of illegal interventions suggests that, in the absence of UNSC leadership, other coalitions will sometimes fill the gap. In the case of Kosovo, with the failure of the Rambouillet Accords, and in the context of Security Council inaction, NATO intervened militarily. Secretary General Kofi Annan summed up the situation in a 1999 press release, saying: 'Normally the use of the force in the past for these operations has required Security Council approval. The Council has not discussed this issue fully. There are expectations that there may be difficulties in the Council, one of two members may have difficulties embracing the use of force. But they have not really either vetoed it or not'. See UN Press Release SG/SM/6875.

[19] Colin Powell, Testimony Before US Senate Foreign Relations Committee, 9 September 2004, http://geneva.usmission.gov/press2004/0910CrisisinDarfur.htm, accessed 3 August 2009.

[20] UNSC Res. 1564, 18 September 2004. UN Security Council Resolution 1564 referred the situation in Darfur to the ICC in 2004. In March 2009, five years later, ICC issued a warrant for the arrest of Sudanese president al-Bashir.

authority. The ICC is the first standing global human rights court, but efforts to establish such a court go back decades. On 9 December 1948, after the Holocaust and the Nuremberg trials, the United Nations General Assembly adopted The Convention on the Prevention and Punishment of the Crime of Genocide, which called for the prosecution of those guilty of genocide by an international tribunal. UNGA also asked the International Law Commission (ILC)[21] to study the possibility of developing a permanent international criminal court to enforce human rights law. On 10 December 1948, UNGA also adopted the Universal Declaration of Human Rights, and between 1949 and 1954, the ILC drafted several statutes for an international criminal court. Cold War tensions ultimately undermined these efforts: the Security Council was permanently divided, and even the General Assembly was unable to agree on a definition of 'acts of aggression'.[22] In 1989, however, as the Cold War ended, efforts began anew to establish an international criminal court: in June of that year, UNGA requested that the ILC prepare a new ICC statute. The following five years, of course, saw horrendous acts of ethnic cleansing and genocide in the former Yugoslavia and Rwanda, as well as the establishment of two *ad hoc* international tribunals to address these atrocities. In 1994, the ILC presented a draft ICC statute to the UNGA, which after further review led to the 1998 meeting in Rome, where 160 countries negotiated the Rome Statute, establishing the International Criminal Court. By 2002, the required 60 ratifications had been gathered, and on 1 July 2002, the treaty entered into force. As of September 2009, 109 UN member states will have joined the ICC. Almost all European, Latin American and sub-Saharan nations are ICC members, as are Australia, Canada, Japan, and several other states. Some major powers, however (USA, Russia, China, and India) have not yet joined the court.

A Proposal for Reform

The failure of the UN Security Council to deal decisively and swiftly with R2P violations has impeded the emergence of a functional and robust international

[21] UNSC Res.174, 21 November 1947. The International Law Commission is composed of legal experts appointed by the UN General Assembly. The commission is responsible for the promotion of the progressive development of international law and its codification.

[22] Disagreements over the 'Crime of Aggression' also impeded definition of that crime when the Rome Statute was negotiated, and remain a concern for many countries that still have not signed the statute.

regime[23] which clearly defines when R2P violations exist – and when they do not exist – and which assures that timely, legal, and effective multilateral action will take place to stop abuses. Such a regime also could dissuade opportunistic invasions or other armed actions defended in the language of liberation and humanitarian concern, as the lack of a mechanism to remove all legal ambiguity as to whether or not international human rights standards are being violated facilitates unauthorised military interventions. Governments may cite respect for national sovereignty to justify *not* intervening to save lives, but they generally have been less circumspect when their own national priorities, rather than the lives of victims of violence, are at stake.

Determining when a government has failed to protect its citizens need not be the sole responsibility of the UN Security Council. Rather, a few revisions of the Rome Statute, which established the International Criminal Court, could empower the ICC to examine any situation of suspected R2P violation, and to issue a formal ruling as to whether or not a violation has occurred. Such revisions could be undertaken in the Rome treaty revision conference which is to be held in 2010,[24] and could be negotiated to assure that they were acceptable to all the major powers, including the UNSC permanent Five.

The reforms we suggest would empower the ICC to consider any situation of possible R2P violation, and to issue a formal ruling declaring whether or not a violation has occurred. Such a ruling, it should be emphasised, would only determine the existence of the violation, and would not prescribe any specific response or remedy. It would supplement, but not supplant, the UN Security Council: ultimate authority over R2P would remain with the UNSC, which would still be able to stop ICC prosecutions.[25] But should UNSC

---

[23] The literature on international regimes is extensive. The seminal contributions are in Stephen D. Krasner, *International Regimes* (Ithaca: Cornell University Press, 1983). For an excellent short overview of the literature, see Eric Brahm, 'International Regimes' in Guy Burgess and Heidi Burgess (eds.), *Beyond Intractability* (Boulder: Conflict Research Consortium, 2005).

[24] Article 121 of the Rome Statute states that, seven years after entry into force date, any state party to the treaty may propose revisions. Such proposed revisions would be submitted to the UN Secretary General, who then would distribute the proposed reform to the states. Three months later, the Assembly of State Parties would determine whether or not to adopt the proposals. This conference, which is to be held in the first semester of 2010 in Kenya, will provide a strong incentive for non-member states, above all USA, Russia and China, to join the ICC so that they can influence treaty revisions. Rome Statute of the International Criminal Court, A/CONF.183/9, Article 121 (1) (2) p. 79.

[25] The Security Council has the power, under Article 16 of the Rome Statute, to defer prosecution for a period of 12 months. This deferment is indefinitely renewable. Rome Statute of the International Criminal Court, A/CONF.183/9, Article 16, p. 17. Further guarantees of ultimate UNSC authority over R2P could be negotiated in the context of the reform.

choose to remain silent, the ICC could rule autonomously, thereby providing an alternative, less politicised mechanism to determine that an R2P violation has occurred.

The extension of such R2P determination authority to the ICC could be negotiated and agreed in the ICC treaty Review Conference, and technically would not require UNSC approval. In practice, however, reform would require the assent of the five permanent members of the UN Security Council, since the Council can block ICC prosecutions. Each of the Five would have to conclude that the benefits of a bigger role for the ICC would exceed the costs. The politics of reform will be discussed in the following section of this essay.

The Rome Statute gives the International Criminal Court the authority to issue an arrest warrant and try an alleged human rights criminal either because a situation is referred to the court by the UN Security Council,[26] or *proprio motu* in the case of ICC member states. But the current treaty does not give the court worldwide jurisdiction (except by referral from the UNSC), and it does not empower the court to formally rule that a state is failing in its responsibility to protect its people. The following revisions to the ICC Statute (which could be accomplished at the Review Conference) would enable the court to make formal R2P rulings with global scope.

The first change which the Review Conference could make would be to give the ICC Prosecutor the power to investigate alleged R2P violations even in non-party states *proprio motu* (i.e. without a Security Council referral). This reform would require the revision of Article 15, Section 1 of The Rome Statute, and would enable the court to make a determination even when the Security Council is blocked. It would provide an alternative to UNSC determination, but it would not undermine the UNSC's ultimate authority: the Prosecutor would be able to act more quickly and in a less politicised manner than the Council to determine that the R2P principle had been violated, but ICC still would not be able to issue arrest warrants for or to prosecute non-member state individuals without UNSC authorisation, and UNSC still would be able to interrupt any ICC prosecution. Clearly, negotiating this reform will be politically delicate, as it would reduce the *de facto* immunity from ICC scrutiny which USA, China and Russia (as non-ICC members) currently enjoy. It is unlikely that these nations would submit to even this limited measure of

[26] The Rome Statute of the International Criminal Court, A/CONF.183/9, Article 13 (b), p. 16. This is the reason why the Security Council referred Sudan (over the situation in Darfur) to the ICC, as Sudan is not a member of the Court.

ICC jurisdiction prior to actually joining the court. Accordingly, the politics of getting Russia, China and USA to support reform will be linked to the politics of getting them to join ICC. We return to this point below.

Article 15, Section 2 of the Rome Statute requires that the ICC Prosecutor submit evidence to a Pre-Trial Chamber of ICC judges,[27] in order to gain approval to investigate individuals, and it gives the Prosecutor direct access to the governments, UN organs, other intergovernmental organisations, and NGOs that are capable of documenting human rights violations. In order to proceed with a prosecution, the Prosecutor first must gather enough information to prove that massive human rights violations are occurring in the territory in question. A Pre-Trial judge then considers those violations that constitute the jurisdiction of the ICC, as listed under Articles 6-8 of the Rome Statute: genocide, crimes against humanity and war crimes.[28] The Pre-Trial Chamber then determines whether there is enough evidence to merit further investigation.

In other words, while the ICC does not presently have the *authority* to rule that a government has failed in its responsibility to protect, the current ICC mandate and its investigative procedures already effectively provide the court with the *expertise and capability* to do so. When the ICC Pre-trial Chamber decides that a situation is sufficiently grave to warrant an investigation, it essentially has determined that a government has failed in its responsibility to protect. This determination could be released as an official ICC ruling that massive human rights violations are occurring, and, consequently, that the R2P norm has been violated.

For the ICC to make such a ruling would be beyond the current function of the Pre-Trial Chamber, but the chamber's function could be expanded by clarifying Article 25, Section Four, which states: 'No provision of this Statute

[27] The processes of nomination and election of ICC judges, Prosecutors and Deputy Prosecutors are described in Article 36 and 42 of The Rome Statute. Article 36, Section 3 (a) states that 'The judges shall be chosen from among persons of high moral character, impartiality and integrity who possess the qualifications required in their respective States for appointment to highest judicial offices'. Article 36, Section 6 (a) states that 'the judges are elected by secret ballot at a special session of the Assembly of States Parties'. Article 36, Section 7 states: 'No two judges may be nationals of the same state'. Article 42, Section 4 states: 'The Prosecutor and the Deputy Prosecutors shall be elected by secret ballot by an absolute majority of the members of the Assembly of State Parties'. The Rome Statute of the International Criminal Court, A/CONF.183/9, Articles 36 and 42 pp. 26-30.

[28] The Rome Statute of the International Criminal Court, A/CONF.183/9, Article 15 (1), p 12. For more information on the Rome Statute negotiations see Roy S. Lee, *The International Criminal Court: The Making of the Rome Statute–Issues, Negotiations, Results* (Martinus Nijhoff Publishers, 1999).

relating to individual criminal responsibility shall affect the responsibility of States under international law'. This essentially states that the ICC focuses its investigations on individuals, not states themselves. With this revision, the ICC still would not prosecute states, but it would be able to make a legal determination regarding that state's failure to protect its citizens.

Essentially the Pre-Trial Chamber would rule that a specific violation had occurred, without however issuing an arrest warrant for any individuals for the violation. Unless its actions were blocked by the UNSC, the Chamber would thereby assume responsibility for legally determining that a violation was taking place in a specific state. Such a ruling would not preclude any similar statement by the Security Council, but rather would provide a less politicised and possibly more expeditious mechanism for making an R2P determination.

Empowering the ICC to so rule, of course, would not create any enforcement mechanism to stop the violence, nor would it either obligate or prohibit the UNSC from taking any steps it chose to take. Should the Security Council remain silent, however, it would provide multilateral coalitions willing to act with the legal justification to do so. Equally important, should this juridical process achieve widespread international credibility as being fair and functional, the absence of such a ruling likely would make it difficult for states to justify unauthorised interventions.

Over time, juridical R2P determination by the International Criminal Court might be expected to produce norms and standards, supported by a body of international jurisprudence, that defined precisely both the content of R2P[29] and appropriate and legal multilateral measures to enforce it. ICC jurisprudence could, among other things, clarify the content of the paragraph 138 crimes listed in the 2005 World Outcome Document (genocide, war crimes, ethnic cleansing, and crimes against humanity), and might reasonably also come to coordinate the language of that document with that of the Rome Statute. As it investigated and ruled on possible violations, the court would be able to develop criteria for future cases. Such criteria might eventually achieve

---

[29] At present, there is some ambiguity regarding the definition of R2P. The ICISS Report defined it broadly as 'the idea that sovereign states have a responsibility to protect their own citizens from avoidable catastrophe—from mass murder and rape, from starvation—but when they are unwilling or unable to do so, that responsibility must be borne by the broader community of states'. ICISS Report, p. VII. The 2005 World Outcome document refers specifically to 'genocide, war crimes, ethnic cleansing and crimes against humanity'. 2005 World Summit Outcome Document, p. 30. The 1998 Rome Statute defined in detail only 'genocide, crimes against humanity and war crimes'. The Rome Statute of the International Criminal Court, A/CONF.183/9, pp. 8-15.

a similar moral salience to that of Just War Theory.[30] According to Just War Theory, for example, war should be waged only for just cause, with right intention and with proportional means and only after all non-violent alternatives have been exhausted. Over time, similar criteria regarding R2P and R2P enforcement measures could develop. For example, ICC jurisprudence might establish rules for armed intervention, such as multilateralism, disinterestedness of the intervening parties, and prior exhaustion of all diplomatic options.[31]

The Politics of Reform

The reform we outline in the previous section would be based upon explicit intergovernmental negotiation and agreement, and accordingly could produce a strong political and legal basis for ICC jurisprudence. However, such a strong reform is not the only conceivable path to an enhanced role for ICC in R2P determination. A softer version of reform, which also could emerge from negotiations, might amend the Rome Statute merely to allow the ICC to issue non-binding legal *recommendations* to the UNSC. Such non-binding recommendations might over time come to define a body of respected legal opinion defining norms of governmental conduct, both regarding the substance of R2P and appropriate forms of international intervention. It is also possible that enhancement of the ICC role might follow a less intergovernmental, more 'functionalist' path, in which the court gradually came to enhance its own capacity to define the R2P norm simply by making such determinations, even in the absence of explicit political agreement to empower the court to do so.[32]

---

30 Just War Theory, rooted Roman and Catholic philosophy, provides guidelines for when and how a war may be justly waged. See, for example, Brian M Kane, *Just War and the Common Good: Jus Ad Bellum Principles in Twentieth Century Papal Thought* (San Francisco: Catholic Scholars Press, 1997).

31 In its rulings, the court also could express its views on appropriate and inappropriate types of intervention, and cite precedents as it developed an R2P jurisprudence (e.g. the court could note similarities and/or differences with previous situations, could state that only non-military means might be appropriate in a specific case, or even suggest that a specific type of multilateral action might be preferable).

32 The landmark 1803 US Supreme Court case of *Marbury v. Madison*, in which the court asserted its right to judicial review, is an excellent example of how a judicial body can help define and enhance its own powers. Nowhere in the US Constitution is it stated that the Supreme Court may nullify a law passed by Congress, but two centuries later the authority that the court asserted in *Marbury* still stands. See, for example, Gustavus Myers, *History of the Supreme Court of the United States*, (C.H.Kerr Publishers, 1912). See also Cliff Sloan, David McKean, *The Great*

In our judgement, however, there is a significant possibility that a strong, negotiated reform empowering ICC as outlined in the preceding section could indeed occur through deliberate intergovernmental agreement, as it would take a difficult and often politically costly responsibility away from UNSC, without however taking away its final authority. A reform that lessened the UNSC's political responsibility without lessening its power might indeed appeal to the permanent Five. In this section, we explore this possibility, showing why having power but not full political responsibility could be attractive to each of the Five, and we also examine some key concerns which each of the Five would need to see addressed. While national interests often prevent the UNSC Five from acting effectively themselves in the Council, national interests might well favour delegation to the ICC of greater responsibility over R2P determination, so long as they retained the power to block rulings and to prevent their own prosecution by the court. Furthermore, if juridical determination of R2P actually worked to strengthen the norm, it would enhance the credibility of the UNSC itself, to the benefit of the five permanent members who dominate that institution. In short, a reform which de-politicises R2P determination could be both good news for victims of violence, and good politics for the Five.

The ICC Review Conference will provide an opportunity for governments to amend the ICC Statue to enhance the court's role over R2P, in a manner consistent with their respective national concerns. The details of any Rome Statute reform would be the result of considerable negotiation, and we cannot predict the specific content of reform language. However, we may be able to outline the issues that most likely would need to be resolved in order to satisfy the concerns of each of the five permanent UNSC member states. We argue below that reform would require, first and foremost, that the USA make a strategic commitment to join the International Criminal Court, and then to engage the other permanent members in a reform effort. Were the USA to do this, we believe it is likely that the other two democratic permanent members (UK and France) – who already are ICC members and strong supporters of the court – would support reform. The real question would be whether Russia and China – two nations with poor human rights records and a history of hostility toward ICC – could be persuaded. For these two governments to agree to empower ICC to rule on R2P likely would require important shifts in their respective strategies toward the court, as well as significant agreed

Decision: Jefferson, Adams, Marshall and the Battle for the Supreme Court (New York: Public Affairs, 2009).

safeguards to insure that they would not become objects of ICC prosecution. Accordingly, we need to consider what factors might push Russia and China to shift their strategies toward the ICC, and what safeguards they would require for them to see more benefits than costs to taking such a new course. Broadly, we argue below that there are good reasons to expect the Obama administration to join the ICC, and were USA to do so and embrace reform, that this would put considerable pressure upon Russia and China to do the same. Furthermore, we argue that both Russia and China value the benefits of being permanent members of a credible UN Security Council, and neither is indifferent to the soft power[33] costs of being seen as a defender of atrocity criminals. China, as we will discuss below, may be especially eager to be relieved of responsibility in this area, as it seeks to improve its international image.[34]

France and UK

Of the five permanent members of the Security Council, France and the UK are the most likely to support juridical R2P determination by the ICC. Both nations have demonstrated consistent strong support for the ICC. Both are already ICC members, and therefore are already subject to its jurisdiction, even in the absence of UNSC action. France and UK also are two of the three top financial supporters of the ICC, having contributed together nearly 18 million dollars in 2008.[35]

Both France and UK have long records of leadership in building the EU, and in supporting a rules-based international order more generally. Both have good human rights records, and both are members of The European Court of Human Rights, and are therefore already under the jurisdiction of a regional

[33] We use the term soft power as it was originally coined by Joseph Nye, to refer to a nation's ability to get others to want what it wants through cooption and attraction. Joseph Nye, *Bound to Lead: The Changing Nature of American Power* (New York: Basic Books, 1991).

[34] The Chinese government has shown considerable appreciation of the importance of soft power in recent years, and Chinese leaders have repeatedly shown concern that China's rise be perceived by others as non-threatening. Indeed, Chinese President Hu Jintao's 2007 address to the 17th Communist Party Congress stressed the central importance to China of soft power. A good analysis of the value to contemporary China of soft power as it pursues its foreign policy objectives today is Neal M. Rosendorf, 'Popaganda: What Hollywood Can Do for (and to) China' *The American Interest*, 4/4 (2009).

[35] In 2008, the United Kingdom contributed nearly 9 million dollars to the ICC and France contributed 8.5 million. See *The ICC Report of the Committee on Budget and Finance* 2008, http://www.icc-cpi.int/library/asp/ICC-ASP-7-3_English.pdf, accessed 3 August 2009.

human rights court. Both have ratified the Convention on the Rights of the Child, a treaty that many states have not signed.

Public opinion in both countries is and always has been very favourable to both the ICC and to international human rights actions in general. Public opinion polls in France indicate that 87% of the French public would like to see France play a greater roll in protecting human rights worldwide.[36] UK public opinion polls show strong support for anti-torture legislation[37] as well as advocacy for international women's rights.[38]

France has a strong record of cooperation with the ICC. It was the twelfth state to sign the Rome Statute, after a unanimous vote in Parliament, and France even modified its constitution to allow entry into the Statute. France is also one of the first States to have authorised the ratification of the agreement on the privileges and immunities of the International Criminal Court. Currently a bill is under consideration that would adapt France's criminal code, bringing it further in line with the ICC's Principle of Complementarity. France also offers technical advice to states considering joining the ICC.

The United Kingdom has an equally strong record of support for the International Criminal Court. Despite the 'special relationship' between UK and USA, the UK Mission to the UN clearly distanced itself from the anti-ICC positions of the USA during the Bush presidency, stating: 'We recognize that not all states support the ICC. Some, most notably the US, are concerned that their citizens could be subjected to politically motivated "nuisance" cases. We understand these concerns but we do not share them. We are satisfied that the safeguards in the ICC Statute will prevent the court from pursuing such cases'.[39] The United Kingdom Foreign and Commonwealth Office also states that the UK energetically supports advancing the R2P principle by, for example, using its influence at the UN to advocate the use of R2P in UN Outcome Documents and in Security Council Resolutions.[40] And UK led the effort to get a unanimous UNSC vote for the deployment of peacekeeping troops to Darfur.

---

[36] Opinion Way Poll (2007), results released by Human Rights Watch. See http://www.hrw.org/en/news/2007/10/07/france-public-backs-strong-human-rights-policy, accessed 3 August 2009.

[37] http://www.worldpublicopinion.org/pipa/articles/btjusticehuman_rightsra/261.php?lb=bthr&pnt=261&nid=&id=, accessed 3 August 2009.

[38] http://www.worldpublicopinion.org/pipa/articles/btjusticehuman_rightsra/453.php?lb=bthr&pnt=453&nid=&id=, accessed 3 August 2009.

[39] http://ukun.fco.gov.uk/en/uk-at-un/un-bodies/international-criminal-court, accessed 3 August 2009.

[40] The United Kingdom Foreign and Commonwealth Office Annual Human Rights Report (March 2007). http://www.fco.gov.uk/resources/en/pdf/human-rights-report-2007, accessed 3 August 2009.

USA

The linchpin for achieving juridical R2P likely will be the USA, which under George W. Bush rejected the court, and indeed denounced it and sought to weaken it. The Bush administration's ideological orientation and policies, notably the invasion of Iraq without a UNSC authorisation, as well as human rights abuses at Guantanamo and elsewhere, put it squarely at odds with ICC and indeed with the very notion of international legal constraints on USA actions. However, indications from the first months of the Obama administration suggest a profound change in USA policy is taking place. Barack Obama has repeatedly expressed appreciation for the ICC,[41] as well as the intention to break sharply with Bush administration human rights policies.[42] In his first days and weeks in office, he took several important steps in this direction, including a clear rejection of torture, including water boarding, and a pledge to close Guantanamo Bay prison. Furthermore, Obama's appointment of Susan Rice, an R2P supporter and an outspoken advocate for both human rights and of the ICC, to the now cabinet-level position of US Ambassador to the UN, suggests that human rights will be priorities of the administration.[43] Other outspoken human rights advocates, such as Samantha Power, also have strongly supported R2P and may be expected to support ICC membership, as will Secretary of State Clinton and Vice President Biden. While much of the Republican Party remains hostile to international organisations in general and to the International Criminal Court in particular, and may be expected to vociferously voice opposition to the ICC, the Democrats who now dominate both the executive and the legislative branches have a clear

---

[41] For example, in response to a question asked by The United Nations Association of the United States of America (UNAUSA) regarding his stance on the ICC, candidate Obama said, 'Now that it is operational, we are learning more and more about how the ICC functions. The Court has pursued charges only in cases of the most serious and systemic crimes and it is in America's interests that these most heinous of criminals, like the perpetrators of the genocide in Darfur, are held accountable. These actions are a credit to the cause of justice and deserve full American support and cooperation. Yet the Court is still young, many questions remain unanswered about the ultimate scope of its activities, and it is premature to commit the U.S. to any course of action at this time. However, we should be exploring ways to cooperate with the Court in its investigative work on the African crisis situations in which it is now involved'. See http://www.unausa.org/Page.aspx?pid=892, accessed 3 August 2009.

[42] Barack Obama, 'Renewing American Leadership' *Foreign Affairs*, 86/4: 1-16 July/August 2007.

[43] Ambassador Rice's words on R2P have indeed been quite strong. See, for example, http://www.responsibilitytoprotect.org/index.php/crises/37-the-crisis-in-darfur/2109-us-ambassador-to-the-un-susan-rice-voices-us-support-for-rtop, accessed 3 August 2009.

mandate for change – and US public opinion surveys show very strong support for the promotion of human rights internationally.[44] The Obama administration has made important gestures toward both China and Russia, indicating a desire for improved relations, which could facilitate negotiations on the ICC.

Of particular importance to the USA (and, as we will see below, also for Russia and China) is the fact that the ICC Review Conference will seek to define 'Crimes of Aggression'.[45] This will force the USA to make a fundamental strategic decision about its relationship with the ICC: either the USA will join the court and engage negotiations to make sure that this contentious issue is resolved in a way that is acceptable to USA interests (Article 121 of the Rome Statute points out that a state must be an ICC member in order to propose revisions to the treaty) or the Obama administration will need to reject the court, as did the Bush administration.[46] Such a rejection would undermine the message that Obama has been seeking to send about US willingness to engage, listen and lead in global affairs, and it would antagonise much of Obama's liberal base in the Democratic Party.

It should be noted that Bush administration claims that ICC membership would subject USA troops and officials to prosecution, simply is not supported by the language of the Rome Statute. The 'Principle of Complimentarity' clearly states that ICC does not prosecute individuals unless their governments have shown an inability or unwillingness to investigate or prosecute within their own court system.[47] The Principle of Complimentarity also respects pre-existing treaties regarding criminal jurisdiction, and as Frank and Yuhan observe in 'The United States and The International Criminal Court:

---

[44] A February, 2005 Gallup Poll, for example, indicated that 86% of Americans rated 'promote human rights in other countries' as an important foreign policy goal. http://americans-world.org/digest/global_issues/human_rights/PromotingHR.cfm, accessed 3 August 2009.

[45] Article 5, Section 2 of the Rome Statute states, 'The Court shall exercise jurisdiction over the crime of aggression once a provision is adopted in accordance with articles 121 and 123 defining the crime and setting out the conditions under which the Court shall exercise jurisdiction with respect to this crime. Such a provision shall be consistent with the relevant provisions of the Charter of the United Nations'. The Rome Statute of the International Criminal Court, A/CONF.183/9, Article 5 (2).

[46] See David Scheffer, Richard Cooper and Juliette Voinov Kohler, 'The End of Exceptionalism in War Crimes: The International Criminal Court and America's Credibility in the World', *Harvard International Review* (November 2007). http://www.harvardir.org/index.php?page=article&id=1647&p=, accessed on 3 August 2009.

[47] Many experts consider Bush administration arguments against USA membership to be specious. See, for example, John Burroughs, 'US Opposition to the International Criminal Court,' (Santa Barbara: Nuclear Age Peace Foundation, 2003).

Unilateralism Rampant', Status of Force Agreements in host countries where USA forces are stationed cover most US troops abroad.[48] ICC Prosecutor Louis Moreno Ocampo's 2006 decision not to prosecute the United States for alleged human rights violations in Iraq also strongly suggests that the USA will be able to negotiate an entry into the ICC which is compatible with USA global interests and commitments, and which protects American officials from prosecution for past practices.

The Bush administration's opposition to the ICC contrasted sharply with the more open attitude of the Clinton administration, whose ambassador, David Scheffer, was deeply engaged in negotiating a Rome Treaty that would suit USA interests. When President Clinton signed the Rome Statute, he expressed concern over possible prosecution of USA military personnel, but he signed the treaty, saying that it was important for the United States to be part of the ICC's development.[49] And even the Bush Administration, which nullified the USA signature to the Rome Statute and threatened to veto future UN peacekeeping operations in Bosnia, found itself drawn into dealing with the ICC: When Secretary of State Colin Powell proclaimed the killings in Darfur 'genocide', the USA referred the matter to the ICC. It is likely that the Obama administration will return to positions closer to those of President Clinton, and will pick up where Clinton left off in USA-ICC negotiations. This will happen just in time for the scheduled 2010 Rome Statute Review Conference.

---

[48] SOFAs are agreements between the United States and host governments that determine civil and criminal jurisdiction regarding USA forces. According to Franck and Yuhan, 'The empirical data regarding the deployment of U.S. personnel overseas indicates that the overwhelming majority of U.S. nationals (1) are protected by bilateral SOFAs, (2) are stationed in jurisdictions where the host government is under no obligation to participate in ICC proceedings, or (3) are stationed in Kosovo and Bosnia, and are therefore—irrespective of the existence of the ICC—subject to the jurisdiction of the International Criminal Tribunal for the former Yugoslavia (ICTY)'. Thomas M. Franck, Stephen H. Yuhan, 'The United States and The International Criminal Court: Unilateralism Rampant', *New York University Journal of International Law and Politics*, 35:3: 519-558 (2002), p.536. Participants in a December 2007 conference on 'The Responsibility to Protect and the International Criminal Court', argued in their conference report that, 'Critics must also realize that under international law, military officials can already be prosecuted by any country, wherever they are captured (unless a Status of Forces Agreement requires or permits US enforcement); thus, the jurisdictional reach of the ICC should appear less foreboding and equally omnipotent'. The report also suggested that a theoretical risk already exists that the ICC might prosecute a US national, even though the US is not a member state. *The Responsibility to Protect and the International Criminal Court: America's New Priorities*, Conference Report, Center for International Human Rights at Northwestern University, December 2007 (pp.17-18). http://www.cfr.org/publication/15802/northwestern_university_school_of_law.html, accessed 3 August 2009.

[49] http://www.unwire.org/unwire/20010102/12349_story.asp, accessed 3 August 2009.

China and Russia

China and Russia, two non-ICC members with poor human rights records, are the least likely of the UNSC Five to join ICC or to support juridical determination of R2P. Beijing is a serial human rights violator and has repeatedly demonstrated that it considers state sovereignty as absolute within its territory.[50] The nationalistic and authoritarian tendencies of the Russian government, and its tendency to privilege hard over soft power in its recent dealing with its neighbours, also would not appear to auger well for Russian support of juridical R2P through ICC reform.

It is reasonable to expect that Russia and China will resist any empowerment of the ICC that might subject their own human rights actions to scrutiny. In order to support juridical R2P determination, they likely would extract safeguards to insure that the jurisdiction of the ICC be clearly-focused to exclude human rights abuses which they regularly engage in themselves. Were such safeguards included in the ICC reform, however, China and Russia both might see reform as a low-risk way to enhance their international images, as it would reduce the soft power costs that they currently suffer, or potentially might suffer in the future, as a result of their perceived obstructionism in the Security Council.

China pays a particularly high price in terms of its international image and soft power when it protects regimes perpetrating gross human rights violations, and obstructs international action to protect victim populations, as it arguably has done in the case of Darfur. As an emerging world power China seeks international acceptance and credibility, even as it pursues rapid economic growth based in part upon expanded energy trade and investment with countries like Sudan. With responsibility for R2P in the Security Council, China has been forced into the role of defender of the Sudanese government, lest it compromise its highly profitable and strategically important relationship with Sudan. This reminds the world repeatedly of China's own poor human rights record, and undermines China's strategy of portraying itself as a non-threatening rising power that seeks global cooperation.[51] Aware of the soft power costs of its obstruction in the Security Council, China has engaged

[50] On China's continued willingness to ruthlessly suppress political opposition, see, for example, Victor D. Cha, 'Beijing's Olympic-Sized Catch 22', *Washington Quarterly*, 31/3: 105-123 (2008).

[51] Zheng Bijian, 'China's Peaceful Rise to Great Power Status', *Foreign Affairs*, 84/5: 18-24 (2005).

other nations diplomatically on a variety of issues,[52] and has even begun to change its position on Sudan: notably, China abstained from voting on UNSC resolution 1593 (which referred the Sudan to ICC) rather than exercising its right to veto. Empowering the ICC to deal with R2P would free China of a responsibility that would appear to carry more costs than benefits for Beijing.

Like the United States, China also has a keen interest in how the Rome Statute review conference defines Crimes of Aggression, and therefore would do well to attend the conference. And a USA decision to join the court could put considerable pressure on the Chinese government to recalibrate its own policy. Mingxuan Gao and Junping Wang have suggested that, 'China cannot remain forever an outsider when the majority of nations have joined the ICC'.[53] Were the Obama administration to join ICC and push reform, the Chinese might well conclude that its best option was to join the process in order to negotiate terms that addressed their concerns.

It should be remembered also that China was actively involved in the drafting of The Rome Statute, albeit it ultimately did not sign the treaty, because of concerns over the court's jurisdiction, its capacity to pursue self-initiated investigations, and the definition of the crimes that fall under ICC jurisdiction.[54] Like the US, China has expressed concern about possible abuse of the Principle of Complimentarity and a fear that the ICC Prosecutor might abuse the power to initiate *proprio motu* investigations. However, the record of the court to date has not born out such fears: as mentioned above, the ICC Prosecutor has shown considerable restraint in his prosecutorial choices. Chinese concerns that linkage between Crimes of Aggression and War Crimes might facilitate ICC prosecution also have not been born out in practice, as the ICC prosecutor has restricted his actions to only the most serious and egregious of mass human rights violations.[55] The history of the ICC to date is that of a court that understands that its own legitimacy and efficacy require that it exercise its functions with restraint and political realism.

Of the UNSC Five, Russia is the most likely to resist both joining the court and supporting juridical R2P. Russia's human rights record is arguably as bad

[52] Stephanie Kleine-Ahlbrandt, Andrew Small, 'China's New Dictatorship Diplomacy', *Foreign Affairs*, 87/1: 38-56 (2008).

[53] Mingxuan Gao, Junping Wang, 'Issues of Concern to China Regarding the International Criminal Court' (2007) http://www.icclr.law.ubc.ca/Publications/Reports/ICC%20Reports/IssueofConcern.pdf, accessed 3 August 2009.

[54] Ibid. pp. 8-11.

[55] For situations and cases currently on the ICC docket, see http://www2.icc-cpi.int/Menus/ICC/Situations+and+Cases/Cases/, accessed 3 August 2009.

as China's, because of the conflict in Chechnya, extra-judicial executions, and the government's refusal to investigate them. In 2007 nearly 22.5% of pending cases in The European Court of Human Rights were directed against the Russian Federation.[56] But whereas China has emphasised its desire for a peaceful rise as a pillar of the international economy, Russia has struck a more nationalistic tone in recent years, as it has re-emerged as an assertive great power possessing substantial energy resources, and willing to show its strength.[57]

Nevertheless, there are limits and high costs to unilateral Russian assertions of power. Russia's leaders know that they pay a price when they assert hard power abroad, as demonstrated by the collapse of Russian stock prices after the August, 2008 incursion into Georgia.[58] Russia's leaders also know that their economy is highly and excessively dependent upon oil and gas, which are likely to be wasting assets as alternative energy sources displace fossil fuels in the years ahead. The current global economic crisis and decline of energy prices have exposed how dependent Russia is upon its economic links to the global economy, demonstrating the importance that Russia not be perceived as an unreliable or threatening economic partner.

Russian legal scholar Bakhtiyar Tuzmukhamedov has observed that serious domestic legal obstacles to Russia joining ICC do not exist.[59] He notes that while there are parts of the Russian constitution that are potentially at odds with the Principle of Complimentarity, several legislative means exist which could overcome these problems.[60] Furthermore, the ICC has created political measures in the past to facilitate membership by individual nations, such as non-retroactivity, and could do so again to accommodate Russia.[61] Tuzmukhamedov also notes that while the Rome Statute has not yet been submitted to the Russian Parliament, an inter-agency Panel has been set up to help draft laws that would allow Russian cooperation with the ICC.

---

[56] ECHR Pending Cases as of 1/6/2007.

[57] In *Petrostate: Putin, Power and the New Russia*, (New York: Oxford University Press, 2008), Marshall Goldman chronicles Russia's rise to energy super power status, and observes how natural resource wealth enables Russia to reassert itself geopolitically.

[58] Charles King, 'The Five-Day War', *Foreign Affairs*, 87/6: 2-11 (2008).

[59] Bakhtiyar Tuzmukhamedov, 'The ICC and Russian Constitutional Problems', *Journal of International Criminal Justice*, 3/3: 621-626 (2005).

[60] Ibid.

[61] The Rome Statute contains a non-retroactivity clause. The ICC cannot prosecute crimes that occurred prior to 1 July 2002. The Rome Statute of the International Criminal Court, A/CONF.183/9, Article 11 (1).

Like China and USA, Russia also has a big stake in how the 2010 Review Conference will address the Crime of Aggression,[62] which will come under ICC jurisdiction after the conference defines the crime and determines how the court will exercise its jurisdiction. Like China and USA, it would be in Russia's interest to participate in the Review Conference, so that the Crime of Aggression and its enforcement are defined in manners consistent with Russia's interests. To do so, it would need to join the court.

Were USA, China and Russia to join ICC, they would be in strong positions to help shape the definition of Crimes of Aggression, and they would be able to get a non-retroactivity clause for the crime included in the text. Just as the ICC does not prosecute crimes that occurred before 1 July 2002, when the review conference defines Crimes of Aggression, it could specify that the ICC will prosecute no Crime of Aggression that occurred before the date of agreement. Of course, joining the court would also allow these governments to participate in the choosing of justices and prosecutors, and in general to participate fully in the court's evolution.

In short, avoiding ICC jurisdiction by not joining the court may not be the best, or even a feasible, long-term strategies for USA, Russia, and China, as the costs of non-membership are likely to grow over time, as more countries join the court. A USA decision to join the court might significantly intensify pressure on Russia and China to reconsider their strategies toward the court as well. And since all three of these countries have engaged in activities that could be considered Crimes of Aggression, and have done so *after* the Statute came into force in 2002, continued rejection of the court would mean not being able to participate in defining this crime and insuring non-retroactivity. Arguably, a more prudent choice would be to join the court, and to participate in its development, including defining the Crime of Aggression.

Conclusion

The coincidence of a Rome Treaty review conference and a new USA administration with a strong Congressional majority and a clearly expressed desire to recast United States foreign policy and the USA international image presents an opportunity for empowerment of the ICC to determine R2P, subject to the safeguards and political constraints which we have outlined in this paper.

---

[62] China's presence in Tibet, Russia's Five Day War with Georgia and The United State's occupation of Iraq are all possible crimes of aggression.

The reforms we propose to the Rome Statute will be politically difficult – perhaps even more difficult than even the original drafting of the Statue was. And surely without USA leadership, it is unlikely that such reforms could happen. But we should not assume that because reform will be difficult that failure is inevitable. The rapidity of the ICC's development to date is an object lesson. No one expected the Rome Treaty to be ratified as quickly as it was: to the surprise of most observers and participants, it took less than 2 years for the required 60 states to ratify the treaty. Clearly, there is strong international support for the International Criminal Court, as well as considerable support for the principle of R2P. The next few years will provide an opportunity for the international community to strengthen its capacity to realise the latter by enhancing the powers of the former.

Conclusion

Alex J. Bellamy, Sara E. Davies and Luke Glanville

Although the chapters in this volume articulate different perspectives on the relationship between the Responsibility to Protect (RtoP) and international law, and focus on different elements of that relationship, several important common themes have emerged that are worth briefly reiterating. These relate in particular to the questions of whether RtoP has legal effect and the nature of that effect, the principle's future trajectory and impact on *opinio juris* and state practice, and whether potential further legalisation of the principle constitutes a normative advance or a problem. Before reiterating some of the key points made in the preceding chapters in relation to these questions, it is worth remembering the important insight offered by Edward Luck in the opening chapter.

Traditionally, as we noted in the introduction, legal and moral debate about how the international community should respond to genocide and mass atrocities has tended to pit sovereignty against human rights, suggesting that the former be overridden when states fail to deliver the latter. This approach proved highly controversial and despite numerous attempts to resolve the contradictions, no such resolution proved possible. The key problem, as Luck points out, is that states of all stripes are committed to the preservation of their sovereignty, though this commitment manifests itself in different ways. Unsurprisingly, postcolonial states are primarily concerned with their territorial sovereignty – that is their freedom to govern within their jurisdiction without undue interference and coercion from powerful external states. They are reluctant to transfer authority to international bodies over which they have little control and view their sovereignty as a critical defence of national self-determination. However, the global north is no less committed to the preservation of sovereignty, though it manifests in different ways. Because of their histories and material strength, these states are less concerned about territorial sovereignty but are nonetheless eager to protect what Luck describes as their 'decision-making sovereignty' – in this case their capacity to decide for themselves how they will respond to specific cases of genocide and mass atrocity.

As Luck points out, it is mistaken to think that the world's most powerful states were also the most significant advocates of RtoP. Many member states with force projection capacities were deeply reluctant to transfer decision-making about how, when and where their forces were deployed – a pattern consistent with the West's general reluctance to place its forces under UN command. As a result of these shared concerns about sovereignty, the consensus that emerged on RtoP in 2005 depended on three key elements: (1) it was a commitment based on sovereignty and aimed at strengthening sovereignty, not on overriding it; (2) it was grounded on the existing legal obligations of states; (3) the Outcome Document was carefully and deliberately worded and therefore represents a definitive accounting of the scope and nature of RtoP as agreed by the international community. This agreement was forged by extensive consultation and negotiation and represents a consensus among the UN membership. Whilst it involved significant compromises on the part of RtoP advocates, it is important to recognise that it also involved compromises from states that are protective of their sovereignty.

Given this, it is perhaps not surprising that in relation to the first question – the legal effect of RtoP – there was broad consensus. Those chapters that examined this question agreed that RtoP does not constitute new law or create new legal obligations. Ekkehard Strauss demonstrates in depth that the UN's commitment to RtoP was not of a legal nature, but was instead a political declaration. RtoP, the chapters agreed, is based on the UN Charter and existing international humanitarian, human rights, and refugee law. As Welsh and Banda point out, it helps establish a political and moral imperative to implement existing law, but it does not create new legal obligations. With that in mind, it is interesting to note that many chapters observed that RtoP's three pillars had different legal qualities. Pillar one – the responsibility of the state to protect its own population from genocide, war crimes, ethnic cleansing and crimes against humanity – is well-documented and precisely codified in international humanitarian and human rights law. Nonetheless, as Gierycz points out, attention to this pillar and its legal quality ought to give rise to ways of using international human rights bodies, such as then UN Human Rights Council and regional bodies, to encourage and assist in the implementation of RtoP. As such, she argues that National Human Rights Institutions be identified as core agents of RtoP, especially in relation to pillar one. There was also broad agreement that the duty to assist states (pillar two) to fulfil their legal obligations is also a well established responsibility, though Bellamy and Reike point out that the precise scope of this duty is less well defined. Less clear still is the legal quality of pillar three. Authors broadly agreed that RtoP did not create any additional legal obligations to protect populations in other countries, which was without doubt a necessary condition for the 2005 consensus. Brunnee and Toope argue the emergence of such obligations is inhibited by inconsistent state practice, whilst Welsh and Banda emphasise that such ambiguities are inherent in this part of the RtoP.

It is worth pausing a moment to consider the problem of indeterminacy raised by Welsh and Banda, which clearly affects RtoP's third pillar and – albeit to a lesser extent – its second pillar too.[1] Whilst norms shape shared understandings and limit the behaviours that can be justified by reference to them, such that actors will be inhibited from acting in ways that cannot be plausibly justified, what a norm prescribes in a certain situation is rarely fixed and absolute.[2] The more precisely a norm indicates the behaviour it expects in a given situation, the stronger its compliance-pull.[3] RtoP's first pillar, for example, is a relatively determinate norm: it expects that states refrain from perpetrating four specific crimes. By comparison, the specific demands imposed by pillar two and especially pillar three are indeterminate. It is seldom—if ever—clear what the RtoP requires in a given situation. This is partly because of the indeterminacy of the norm itself and its place relative to other norms such as non-interference. Indeterminacy is produced by a combination of uncertainty among the norm's authors about what is expected, disagreements about what ought to be expected, and a shared interest in preserving flexibility for the future.[4] When crises erupt, the problem is amplified by the inevitable effects of intervening variables such as competing judgments about the facts of the case (for example, about the cause, existence, and scale of mass atrocities) and different assessments about the most prudential response. As a result, it is plausible to legitimize both sides of debates about forceful intervention in Darfur, no-fly zones in Sudan, the indictment of Omar al-Bashir, the deployment of IGAD, AU or UN peacekeepers in Somalia, heaping criticism and sanctions upon Sri Lanka, criticizing Israel and/or Hamas, the deployment of Western troops to the DRC, Sudan and Somalia, sanctions, engagement or the status-quo in relation to North Korea and Myanmar, and much else besides by reference to the RtoP. The indeterminacy of what RtoP requires

[1] This discussion draws on Alex J. Bellamy, 'Responsibility to Protect – Five Years On', *Ethics and International Affairs,* 24/2 (2010).

[2] This idea, and way of formulating it, is borrowed from Nicholas J. Wheeler, *Saving Strangers: Humanitarian Intervention in World Politics* (Oxford: Oxford University Press, 2000). It is based on Quentin Skinner, 'Analysis of Political Thought and Action', in James Tully (ed.), *Meaning and Context: Quentin Skinner and His Critics* (Cambridge: Polity, 1988), p. 117.

[3] Thomas Franck, *The Power of Legitimacy Among Nations* (New York: Oxford University Press, 1990), p. 52.

[4] Ibid., pp. 52-54.

in these cases weakens its compliance-pull because it is difficult to know with any certainty what is required by RtoP and therefore the extent to which actors are satisfying shared expectations of appropriate behavior. Of course, as Quentin Skinner argued, actors 'cannot hope to stretch the application of the existing principles indefinitely; correspondingly, [the actor] can only hope to legitimate a restricted range of actions'.[5] It is therefore fair to say that active support for *genocidaires* and defense of complete inaction in the face of mass atrocities would be obviously inconsistent with RtoP. But once states agree that *something* ought to be done, RtoP grants international society a free hand to determine *what*. This indeterminacy severely restricts RtoP's compliance-pull, and hence its ability to encourage states to find consensus and make additional contributions.

The best explanation as to why RtoP is used inconsistently relates to this problem of indeterminacy. Given that it is difficult to determine with any degree of certainty what, other than not committing the four crimes or actively aiding their commission, RtoP requires in any given situation, it is unlikely that—without requisite transformation of national interests and institutional reforms that reduce the costs associated with enhanced engagement by improving efficiency and effectiveness—the principle will 'pull' actors towards more consistent and effective commitments to protecting civilians in danger. It is important to recognize that there are different reasons why actors want to legitimize their behaviour by reference to a shared norm. At one end of the spectrum, norm compliance is caused by instrumental decisions: actors obey a norm not because they think it has inherent value (i.e. it is 'internalised'), but because they believe that norm-violation will impose prohibitive costs. Close to this is 'non-instrumental conformism' or 'mimicry', where compliance is generated not by overt calculations of costs in relation to particular actions but by a more generalised concern about social exclusion.[6] When a norm is indeterminate, actors who comply for instrumental or mimicry-related reasons are unlikely to be pulled into changing their behaviour. Instead, they are likely to adopt the norm's language whilst persisting with established patterns of behaviour. They are able to do so precisely because it is so difficult for other members of the society to determine whether or not they are acting

[5] Skinner, 'Analysis of Political Thought and Action', p. 117.

[6] Jonathan Symons, *International Legitimacy: Contesting the Domestic Analogy*, phd thesis, University of Melbourne, 2007, p. 121. The mimicry label is taken from Alistair Iain Johnston, *Social States: China in International Institutions, 1980-2000* (Princeton: Princeton University Press, 2008).

in a manner consistent with the norm. As Brunnee and Toope make clear, more work is needed to build shared understanding of what RtoP means. This involves both thematic dialogue of the sort evidenced in the 2009 General Assembly debate and state practice that uses RtoP and tests its boundaries. Significantly, Rosenberg, Brunnee and Toope, Bellamy and Reike, and Welsh and Banda all point to moral principles and/or nascent legal trends that might establish clearer pillar two and three in the future.

This brings us to the second question, that of the future trajectory of RtoP in international law. Here, three important points emerged from the preceding chapters. First, as Welsh and Banda argued, although the RtoP does not create formal legal obligations it may influence the way in which states understand their duties as members of the international community. In particular, it is worth observing that RtoP makes it harder for members of the UN Security Council to avoid taking a position on crises thought likely to produce mass atrocities. This seems to chime with Luck's argument that RtoP is only likely to affect behaviour once it refashions interests. This will only happen through persistent dialogue and state practice. Second, Contarino and Lucent, and Rosenberg, noted that various strands of international law were already pointing towards the development of legal obligations to 'save strangers'. In particular, in *Bosnia v. Serbia* the ICJ went a long way towards clarifying the content of the duty to prevent genocide and the International Law Commission's work on the responsibilities of states and international institutions create grounds for thinking that legal obligations might emerge in the future. Third, several contributors – including Strauss – argued that if RtoP does influence behaviour and does start to be used more or less consistently, then it might acquire the necessary *opinion juris* and state practice to constitute a principle of customary international law. Whether that is altogether desirable is another – hotly contested – question, to which we now turn.

The final issue we want to emphasise is the question of legalisation. In short, should RtoP be seen as a legal mechanism or as a political commitment? This is such a difficult question that the preceding chapters expressed different views on the question of whether legalization has already occurred – Welsh and Banda arguing that it has, via the General Assembly resolution affirming the World Summit Outcome Document, Strauss insisting that it has not and that there was no intention among member states in that direction. There are also differences on the desirability of legalisation. In arguing for a leap in that direction that would empower the International Criminal Court (ICC) to judge whether RtoP applied to a given situation, Contarino and Lucent would reduce the potential for RtoP to be abused, increase the political will to take timely and decisive action, and strengthen the legitimacy of the UN Security

Council. To this we might add Gierycz's contention that a focus on existing legal protection tools might help close the gap between the UN's security and human rights arms and assist the organisation to protect as one. However, whilst it is important to think innovatively and to challenge conventional wisdom, enthusiasm for legalisation should be tempered with a sober assessment of the politics. Recall Luck's insistence that the 2005 consensus was only possible because two types of sovereignty concerns were addressed. Moves to transfer decision-making from states to legal bodies would resuscitate worries about the protection of territorial and decision-making sovereignty and could potentially undermine that consensus. As Luck, and Brunnee and Toope confirm, resistance to the transfer of decision-making would come not just from the Non-Aligned Movement and other representatives of the global south, but also from powerful states in the global north and especially the permanent members of the Security Council. In the end, there is no substitute for the long-haul of developing RtoP through extended dialogue and consistent state practice. It is a journey that has only just begun.

Index